BRIEF

Issues in Cultural Analysis

ASCA Yearbook

Pharos

Kok Pharos Publishing House
P.O. Box 5016, 8260 GA Kampen - The Netherlands
ISBN 90 390 0242 8 / CIP / NUGI 631

Table of Contents

INTRODUCTION

Cultural Analysis: On Theorizing the Present

Hent de Vries

Brief is the new yearbook of the *Amsterdam School for Cultural Analysis, Theory and Interpretation* (ASCA), a research and graduate school, founded in 1994 and located at the University of Amsterdam. ASCA takes as its aim the bringing together of scholars and graduate students active in literary studies, philosophy, religious studies, anthropology, film and television studies, musicology, and the study of dance. Specialists in their respective fields, they share a commitment to working within an *interdisciplinary* and outspokenly *theoretical* framework. Members of ASCA let themselves be inspired by a host of philosophically challenging, yet historically and empirically informed, questions that have come to define the contemporary debate on such issues as the modern and the postmodern, culture and the multicultural, memory and the present, narrative and the construction of identity, globalization and transnationalism. These questions are not new, to be sure, nor is the common denominator for ASCA, a systematic and structural — or, if you like methodological, macro- and, more often, micrological — mode of "analysis" of these phenomena, by any means unprecedented.

Both thematically and methodologically, these multifarious issues have been introduced by quite a few different schools of thought over the last few decades. They range from Frankfurt School Critical Theory, represented most notably by Western marxists like Adorno and Benjamin — authors whose lasting contribution consists in analyzing the logic of production, not so much within the realm of political economy, but first of all of high and mass culture — through semiotics, structuralism, and poststructuralism all of which have been fused into the curious blend of philosophical, anthropological, and psychoanalytical modes of inquiry whose leading proponents have by now become part of the canon for generations of students and scholars alike (and this more or less independently of their premature and often derogatory association with *la pensée '68*). And this — admittedly eclectic — list could easily be extended. Thus, it could be asserted with equal plausibility that ASCA explores and pursues the intellectual, curricular, and, at times, political agenda of *cultural studies*, while remaining faithful to the theoretical and indeed philosophical credentials that made these most recent transformations inside literary studies (and the humanities broadly defined) possible in the first place. After and beyond "theory," what becomes necessary is more theory still.

For while cultural analysists are increasingly sensitive to the shortcomings of the respective research perspectives cited above, both theoretically and practically or politically speaking, they are nonethless reluctant to share some of the premises that lie at the basis of the present academic turn "back to basics." Far from defining their work in terms of a cultural hermeneutics, and instead of looking back in a merely nostalgic mood to the heydays of "theory," cultural analysts remain faithful to the far-reaching and explicitly addressed philosophical concerns that in so many contemporary studies that pursue a neohumanist, neohistoricist, or postcolonial agenda seem to have moved to the background or have become more and more implicit, to say the least.

Cultural analysts, then, *analyze* culture. What does that mean? Instead of analyzing analysis all too directly, it might be usefull to jump ahead to ASCA's object of inquiry: culture and, more precisely *culture broadly defined*, which in principle encompasses any production and organization of words and gestures, images and sounds, none of which can stand on its own and none which claim any ontological, epistemological or axiological primacy *per se*. In addition, this hospitable denominator called "culture" captures all modes of theoretical reflection, not only the reflection on these words and gestures, images and sounds, but also the reflection on this reflection, the effects that this reflection of the second order produces in the reflected, and this *ad infinitum*. The paradox — some would say the conceptual confusion — of this interpretation of culture is that if indeed singular meanings — the sign and the body, but also the idiomatic and the idiosyncratic — form the "substance" of culture, then so does the whole spectrum of theoretical and meta-theoretical considerations that seeks to situate these singularities in a given or yet to be invented conceptual framework or that, to complicate matters further, raises the question of the logical or metaphysical conditions of the possibility of any conceptual framework in general. Strictly speaking, even the grandest of theories or narratives is "nothing but" a series of words and gestures, images and sounds, that ought to be studied both *en détail* and in terms of its conceptual import and therefore at more than one level of abstraction at once. Conversely, it can be maintained that every single word or gesture, image or sound, should be considered, neither as an atom or monade nor as a microcosm and mirror of the world, but as a world of possible associations and interpretations, of semantic effects and of unexpected appropriations. In that sense, and in contradistinction to the view held by the ancients, *there can only be the study or, for that matter, science of the singular.* Put otherwise: the singular is the true universal. And *vice versa.*

While fully aware of the historical ramifications of their object of inquiry, the interest of cultural analysts is first of all directed towards the field of *contemporary* culture. Yet, if cultural analysis is oriented towards an analysis of the present in terms of its representation (of its forms, effects, and implications), then this does not exclude the fact that the most challenging work in this field consists, precisely, in the critical re-examination of classical and modern interpretations of the value of the present as well as of the concept and the practice of representation in the past and the present. Cultural analysts, then, are also those who study an historical object while taking their point of departure or their frame of reference from contemporary theoretical perspectives. There is no cultural analysis without at least some privileging of the present over the past, nor, for that matter, is cultural analysis possible without a privileging of interpretation over and against the mere gathering and archivization of empirical facts.

Surely, analysis means something different here than that which has come to be known under the name of analytical philosophy, a predominantly Anglo-American and Scandinavian style of philosophizing which is often, and often too hastily, opposed to so-called Continental philosophy. But the lines of demarcation between the different uses of analysis in cultural analysis and analytical philosophy are far from certain. This can already be seen from the fact that some of the most interesting work in contemporary cultural analysis relies heavily on quite a few central notions taken from that most analytical of disciplines, namely speech act theory, such as the "performative" or even "performativity," the logic of "citation" and of "proper names," the "promise," the "contextual frame."

All this has made it clearer than ever before that the concept and the practice of cultural analysis should not be taken literally — or analytically — as meaning the "taking apart" of culture. Rather, cultural analists could be said to interpret the way in which cultures take things, people and themselves "apart." Culture, thus defined, is a polemical and divisive concept and praxis at least as much as it is the quest for a certain commonality and the provisional stabilization of shared ideas, values, and goods. Culture is not necessarily (and not very often) a "pretty" thing. Whether as high-, low- or mass-culture, culture is a culture-war, a war of worlds. This strategic and non-normative use of its concept should not lead one to conflate its meaning with that of the German word *Bildung*, let alone with the French word *culture*. One cannot "have" culture as one can have, say, character or taste. Culture is neither a property nor a disposition even though it can truly be "the story of one's life." What remains of the study of culture and what allows culture to be analyzed for the first time, is far removed from the *idea* (*ideal*, *ideality*, and, indeed *ideology*) that at the end of the 19th century fueled the desire to define the *moral sciences*, the *Geistes-* or *Kulturwissenschaften* in terms both unrelated and related to those of the natural sciences (or the "sciences" strictly speaking). But the resistance of culture, as it is analyzed here, is also directed against the implicit anthropomorphism and -centrism that all too easily comes to dominate the more recent attempts at "defending" the "humanities," in Europe and elsewhere.

Informed or, as it were, haunted by the past — based much more upon a catastrophic rather than a teleological or even progressive view of history as a process, as the development of a preestablished potential — cultural analysts thus direct their interest first of all towards the understanding of contemporary culture. Their focus, again, is on *the present* which is studied in terms of the modes of its (conceptual, narrative, visual) *representation*. This emphasis does not exclude the fact that the most challenging work in this field consists, precisely, in a critical examination of classical and modern, traditional and canonical, interpretations of the value of the present as well as of the very concept and practice of representation. For all its insistence on the present and the representational, cultural analysis is also — and, perhaps, first of all — concerned with the anti-representational stance, in literature and the arts, in criticism and philosophy, in the contemporary postcolonial and multicultural discourses on original hybrity and the negotiation of identities. Although the following texts are single-authored articles and can be roughly divided according to disciplinary backgrounds, this is the common ground of which they each try to cover an aspect or element. This central focus becomes particularly clear in the recent debates on the notion of mimesis, the museum, literary and historical truth, the new media and virtual reality, as well as on the spectral dimensions of politics in the post Cold War era. The first issue of this yearbook collects the lectures devoted to these subjects which were recently presented in Amsterdam.

LECTURES

Reading Life: Literature as understanding and the understanding of literature

Mieke Bal

The contributions by Edit Zsadányi and Jonathan Culler are easy to categorize: they belong to the discipline of literary studies. Culler is a well-known figure within that discipline, and his books, *Structuralist Poetics*, *The Pursuit of Signs*, and *On Deconstruction*, containing discussions of contemporary approaches to literature from the vantage point of philosophy and language theory, are rightly famous. Culler fans will also know his first book, *Flaubert: the Uses of Uncertainty*, an exceptionally fine study of this over-commented author, which in my estimation has not been surpassed in depth, adequacy, and analytical refinement ever since. A sample from his current work on Baudelaire is presented in this volume. Zsadányi, a young Hungarian scholar specializing in modernist literature, won a grant from the Hungarian Academy to spend a year at ASCA after completion of her dissertation on silence and the unsayable. Her study of Djuna Barnes's *Nightwood* shows her bold and sturdy mind at work on one of Western literature's favorite "difficult" masterpieces.

Both of these papers, which are easy to categorize at first sight, complicate the discipline within which they situate themselves nevertheless quite firmly, thus exemplifying ASCA's commitment to interdisciplinarity even within single disciplines. Zsadányi starts from a linguistic and cognitive framework to understand metaphor, and Barnes's central, double metaphor of nightwood. Her simple, yet incisive gesture of taking apart the title's two components, and relating each to a different conceptual framework, thus operating an incision that becomes an ever widening gap, enables her to process a patient, systematic analysis that brings her much farther afield into the contribution of cognitive theory than its major proponents — the Lakoff and Johnson school, including Mark Turner — could foresee. The analysis of the metaphors is astutely carried out so as to comprehensively account for the totality of this incredibly complex novel, while simultaneously providing close readings of two of its core chapters: the conversation with doctor Matthew O'Connor and the concluding chapter. This procedure thus becomes a three-tiered analysis: demonstrating how a renewed close reading is indispensible in any attempt to do justice to the particular in view of the general, and vice versa, as Hent de Vries argued in his presentation of the volume, Zsadányi does justice, in the same move, to the central metaphors as single units, to major junctures in the current of its "streaming" prose, and to the work as a whole. Through this analysis, then, she gives the best possible demonstration of the component "analysis" in the ASCA project.

But there is more to it; interdisciplinarity, even within a single discipline calling upon others for methodological enrichment, runs the risk of a self-fulfilling projection: you assume a text has philosophical relevance, you take some philosophical concepts that you deem "applicable", and hence, the job is done. This is a major danger, and the one, I presume, that makes many a "monodisciplinary" scholar wary of the current interest, or "fashion", of interdisciplinarity. Zsadányi puts to rest these doubts, however justified they are in view of the many publications that claim interdisciplinarity while infuriating proponents of the "other" discipline who feel abused as picturesque background or documentation. Stating explicitly what her working hypothesis is, she allows the text to contradict her, thus assigning to the literary work philosophical status in a way that goes beyond the usual thematic analysis. The decisive moment, the moment where the analysis turns the table on its methodological premises, comes when she writes that she was wrong. The implication, that the text is (always) right, is no submissive nod to high culture, but, instead, an enabling of the text to "speak back", to keep its complexity, even it enigmatic mystery, while forcing it to show its hand. For contradiction, unlike negativity as in binary opposition, is not logically vague; to prove the critic wrong is a task of specification from which the text cannot escape simply because of its mysterious beauty. But the important move is to make the novel a discussion partner, thus extending the interdisciplinary debate by including the object as subject, not in the old humanistic sense in which art is by definition superior to the discourse about it, but in a newer sense, inspired by deconstruction and the new psychoanalysis, where even the traditionally muted object is made to achieve subjective status without its messages being by definition "better" than what the critics have to say.

Something of a similar order happens in Culler's innovative discussion of what appears to be a thematic analysis. The title of this essay, "Prostitution and *Les Fleurs du Mal*," already complicates the deceptive simplicity of its subject through its reference to prostitution instead of prostitutes, and through its use of "and" instead of "in" with regards to *Les Fleurs du Mal*. Culler sets out to demonstrate the problematic relations between a number of issues and concepts current in literary studies: history and literary analysis, social history and literary history, social criticism and literary criticism, theme and structure, character and institution, words and meanings. Like Zsadányi, in the end he allows the poet to say something new to the critics, something about the critical endeavor itself. His implicit plea is for a reconsideration, not a rejection, of the historical in literary history, a reconsideration that takes place in the (his) present. From the vantage point of an academic contending with the notions that serve as guiding concepts, Baudelaire becomes an emblem of a theorist challenging preconceptions. This is a highly innovative approach to, and view of, Baudelaire, whose images of women, as long as we see them as images — stable, still, invested with values projected from present-day feminism — are primarily conceived of as deeply misogynist. Without detracting from the negativity of those images, which are negative indeed qua images, Culler moves beyond such thematics to question the very method by which such insight is achieved, at the cost of the literariness of this word-art. Words are the stuff of poetry, and Culler's patient endorsement of the multiplicity of the word *vers* — worms, and verses, corruption and poetry, hence, prostitution and art, and the undermining of boundaries that comes with corruption — is but one example of the subtle way in which Culler undermines thematics as a reassuringly stabilizing method.

Both Zsadányi and Culler, albeit in different ways, conduct analyses that demonstrate the specificity of ASCA's project including what this project has in common with other approaches. Standing firmly in the present and being explicit about it, they analyze literature closely, avoiding sweeping generalizations as much as minute but ultimately futile formalism. Both Culler, situating the initial problem in the tradition of his discipline and overcoming it while maintaining the tension, and Zsadányi, proving herself wrong in the too-affirmative premises of her "borrowed" discipline, take as a starting point and reach as an outcome a self-reflection that used to be considered liberating from disciplinary dogma, yet became another trap of self-indulgence. Here, however, in both of these cases it becomes one strand of thought among others, pointless if not accompanied and challenged by the critics' "other halves" or "other selves", engaging with the text they espouse, value, but do not blindly obey.

Both papers also share a position in and on history that complicates easy periodizations which oppose contemporary postmodernity to a modernity surpassed by it while also situating itself within both. Modernity as discussed by Culler problematizes the notion that the present has moved beyond the modern, precisely in its tenacious collocation of misogyny and selfreflective collusion in the lethal threat assigned to women, a collusion that, he states, "seems positively energizing, producing a radical otherness of feminine sexuality which is threatening to men." While resonant with contemporary feminism — perhaps the most significant position of presentness for an innovative cultural history — this view emerges from an inquiry that is not locked up within that movement. The disproportionate figures of prostitution Culler discerns throughout Baudelaire's poems, both figures of the feminine and of the poetic, are truly *lyrical.* Through these insights, then, the critic shrewdly and, for the most part, implicitly re-focuses literary history toward a literariness that entails self-reflexivity as a powerful weapon against misogyny. Thus he shows, in the face of *paronto-centric* arrogance (the self-centeredness of a present that considers itself as the outcome of evolutionary liberation from a barbaric past), that the past of early modernity is still with us, in its more simplistic forms. And he shows that poetry from an age in which poetry was still unproblematically lyrical is more expressive of our contemporary selves than we seem to be able to be, thus giving a new sense to lyricism. Similarly, Zsadányi enables Barnes to hold up a mirror to our contemporary clichés as embodied in conceptual metaphors about life as a journey through the forest of its counterpart: the night of death.

From within one of the humanities' most unquestioned traditional disciplines, then, these two papers make that discipline rub against its other, as represented by the papers presented by Hent de Vries, of a more directly philosophical orientation, and that by Žižek, presented by Thomas Elsaesser, in which psychoanalysis and the Marx Brothers enable insight into great thinking. This rubbing together leaves a trace in each partner, and whereas it causes the tradition to wear off where it ought to, it also reassures those who fear its loss while daring them to venture into the realm of its boundary territory: history from the present, theory as a partner, close analysis that turns objects into co-subjects. Literary studies, clearly has a future within the new developments that ASCA promotes.

Prostitution and *Les Fleurs du Mal*

Jonathan Culler

I have for some time now been struggling with the problem of the relation between history and literary and cultural texts, while working on a book on Baudelaire. I have tended to think of this problem as simply the problem of literary history. Most simply posed, it is this: am I investigating an object with its own history — Literature, or French literature, or the French lyric — or does the notion of "literary history" enjoin me, rather, to treat Baudelaire's lyrics as above all part of the history of nineteenth century France? There is no doubt that I must do both, but this is not very helpful — certainly not a solution — for even when I try to go in both directions, I always have to make choices, both about the overall strategy for a book and at each moment: in which direction — toward the literary tradition or toward contemporaneous discourses and events — should a particular image lead me? My title, "Prostitution and *Les Fleurs du Mal*," captures an especially charged instance of the larger problem, because prostitution is both an important social practice in mid-nineteenth-century France and a literary topos with a rich history. In thinking about images of prostitution in *Les Fleurs du Mal*, should I concentrate on contemporary prostitution, the real women whose voices, shall we say, are silenced in *Les Fleurs du Mal*, or should I look to the literary tradition in which these these images are inscribed? It is my aim to explore this uneasy confluence.

Walter Benjamin writes that, faced with the limited success of his own work, Baudelaire "threw himself into the bargain"and thus to the end proved in his own person what he considered the unavoidable necessity of prostitution for the poet. [*Er hat sich zuletzt ... mit in der Kauf gegeben... Er hat sich seinem Werk nachgeworfen und damit für seine Person bis ans Ende bewahrheitet, was er von der unumgänglichichen Notwendigkeiten der Prostitution für den Dichter dachte.*] It is one of the decisive questions for the understanding of Baudelaire's poetry: in which ways had the face of prostitution altered with the growth of the great cities. For this much is certain: Baudelaire gives expression to this change, it is one of the chief objects of his poetry.

As so often happens in Benjamin, what he says about Baudelaire applies much better — more literally and concretely — to Balzac, for whom the changing face of prostitution is indeed a chief object of his art, in a way that it isn't for Baudelaire, whose verse has little to say about it. But note that, as usual, Benjamin's remark is rather puzzling and demands exegesis (a major reason for his popularity among critics: his formulations give them interesting exegetical assignments). In speaking of the "unavoidable necessity of prostitution for the poet," Benjamin seems to claim not, as Baudelaire suggests, that a prostitute is the right sort of mistress for a poet, who can find stimulation and inspiration, as well as sexual gratification in prostitutes, but that Baudelaire prostituted himself, commodified himself, and that this is connected to the changing face of prostitution in the modern city and said to be one of the chief objects of his poetry.[1]

Now there is a sense in which Baudelaire made a spectacle or commodity of himself, in publishing a collection entitled *Les Fleurs du Mal*, which was designed to shock and which was prosecuted for outrage to public morals, but he seems much less prostituted in this sense than many of his contemporaries, from Béranger to Balzac, who sold themselves effectively. If Baudelaire prostituted himself, he made no money doing so. Indeed, Benjamin's remark seems above all a symptom of the widely felt connection between Baudelaire's modernity and prostitution.

When Baudelaire writes that "la vie parisienne est féconde en sujets poétiques et merveilleux," he singles out "le spectacle...des milliers d'existences flottantes qui circulent dans les souterrains d'une grande ville — criminels et filles entretenues" (II, 495-6).[2] But the figure of the prostitute has, since Baudelaire, been taken as exemplary of a dawning modernity in a way the criminal has not. It is striking, when you consider that prostitution is often called the oldest profession, just how far in mid nineteenth-century France prostitutes were taken to represent modernity. T.J. Clark writes in *The Painter of Modern Life,* "That the courtesan was thought to be a main representative of modernity in the 1860s is hardly in need of demonstration: every second book of gossip or sociology has the same story to tell."[3]

And books of poetry too. For example, in a slim volume entitled *Modernités* by Jean Lorrain, the title poem about Parisian life has the following chorus or refrain:

> Modernité, Modernité!
> A travers les cris, les huées,
> L'impudeur des prostituées
> Resplendit dans l'éternité.[4]

Their shamelessness synecdochically defines modernity for eternity. This poetic attempt to define modernity takes as its refrain the capacity of prostitution to pass from the audible (*les cris*) to the visible (*resplendit*) and to represent synecdochically the instant in relation to the eternal. Prostitution is not just one institution or activity among others but what fixes the present for externity.[5]

Why are prostitutes taken to exemplify modernity? Let me quickly sketch a few reasons before coming to what seems to me the special case of Baudelaire. First, one might argue that the image of the prostitute is a way of bringing into visible, accessible experience the effects of modern capitalism, the emergence of a proletariat on the edge of misery. Analysts of the time linked prostitution to the insufficiency of factory wages for women on the one hand, and on the other to the growth of railways and the proliferation of new fortunes, which were thought to create a demand for prostitution. Prostitutes also conveniently embody threats of social disorder, from political insurgency to infanticide and alcoholism, as Jann Matlock has argued in a very rich recent book, *Scenes of Seduction: Prostitution, Hysteria, and Reading Difference in Nineteenth-Century France.*

Second, the prostitute fascinates writers, novelists especially, as a source of plots.[6] A lurid embodiment of the instability of the modern world, the courtisan can rise from humble beginnings to wealth and power (Baudelaire 's friend Nadar speaks of the courtesans as the true "classe dirigeante"[7]). But this power is extraordinarily unstable, ruined in a moment by age or disease or, when the need arises, an unknown poison, as in the case of Balzac's Valérie Marneffe in *La Cousine Bette.* In the novels of the period prostitutes represent the mobility, instability, reversibility of the new social and economic order, where position can be bought and is subject to surprising reversals.

Third, the prostitute embodies dangerous artifice in an age acutely aware of the falsity of appearance. In the new anonymity of modern cities anxieties about appearance seem to have become focused on the prostitute, in contradictory ways. In arguments about prostitution that date from Alexandre Parent-Duchatelet's influential book of 1837, *De la Prostitution dans la ville de Paris,* writers are scandalized simultaneously by the gaudy display of prostitutes and by the danger that prostitutes might be indistinguishable from respectable women. Parent-Duchatelet wrote

> Prostitutes are as inevitable in an agglomeration of men as sewers, cesspits, and garbage dumps; civil authority should conduct itself in the same manner in regard to the one as to the other: its duty is to keep a close eye on them, to attenuate by every possible means the disadvantages inherent to them, and for that purpose to conceal them, to relegate them to the most obscure corners, in a word to render their presence as unnoticed as possible."[8]

This formulation is outrageous in its determined pursuit of the analogy between women and sewers, but the attempt to make social problems as *unapparent* as possible remains basic public policy today, at least in the United States.

The point is that the *appearance* of prostitutes is seen as dangerous, whether it is easily distingished from or easily confused with that of other women. They exemplify the power of appearance as such: "Ne suffit-il pas que tu sois l'apparence?" asks Baudelaire's "l'Amour du mensonge." Prostitutes become the most concrete embodiment of dangers and attractions of the newly anonymous modern city.

Fourth, in the fantasmatic image of the prostitute, the erotic power of feminine sexuality becomes a commodity, a lurid metonymy of a world in which everything is for sale, but, more than that, an object valued in a fantasmatically driven process of exchange, a process thought distinctive of the modern world. Available to any purchaser, the commodity marks a world of arbitrary signs and anonymous social relations, a general condition of alienation, yet takes the form of alluring objects inviting the beholder to possess them. Benjamin writes, "The commodity celebrates its becoming human in the whore" [*Ihre Menschwerdung feiert sich in der Hüre*].[9] In this sense, the prostitute embodies a signifying process felt to be particularly modern, connected with advertising and other modes of sign production.

Fifth, the figure of the prostitute offers writers and artists an intimation of their own condition in the modern world — though the connection betweeen prostitution and authorship has a venerable history. Baudelaire's early poem "Je n'ai pas pour maîtresse une lionne illustre," (My mistress isn't an elegant courtesan) reflects that though his mistress sells herself — "pour avoir des souliers elle a vendu son âme" — he can scarcely feel superior, "Moi qui vends ma pensée et veut être auteur" (I, 203). Both of them are failing to hold back what should be private and inward but are putting it forth, in an operation of formalizing that makes the private accessible to anyone, to *le premier venu.* And later reflections develop the link, making prostitution a syndrome that the poem cannot escape: "Qu'est-ce que l'art?" Baudelaire asks, and he replies: "Prostitution" (I, 649). Art is prostitution not so much because the artist sells himself — though Baudelaire spent his life offering himself for sale without finding a buyer — but because, according to Baudelaire's conception, the artist, like the prostitute, "se donne au premier venu" — to a ragpicker, a beggar, a little old woman — in what Baudelaire calls "cette sainte prostitution de l'âme qui se donne tout entière, poésie et charité, à l'imprevu qui se montre, à l'inconnu qui passe" (I, 291). This male fantasy of a prostitution or submission to the other which would also be a source of power and artistic authority — "cet incomparable privilège, qu'il peut à sa guise être lui-même et autrui" (I, 291) — has as its counterpart, as we shall see, the imagination of the universal erotic power of the prostitute who sells or gives herself.

These last two rubrics — the prostitute as the becoming human of the commodity and prostitution as the fate of the modern writer — make prostitution a syndrome or literary figure rather than acts of particular women (or men), but in speaking of "Prostitution and *Les Fleurs du Mal*" I want to distinguish this poetry from a literature centered on the literary figure of the prostitute. In the work of Victor Hugo, Eugène Sue, and Alexandre Dumas, fils, for example, attention to the prostitute as personnage leads to an analysis of character and, often, to the theme of the prostitute as victim — whether of society or of her own weakness; a victim who may be redeemed by her "heart of gold" and reintegrated into the moral order by her love for a man. Baudelaire — and herein lies a good part of his "modernity" — avoids this kind of sentimentality and this theme. He does not concern himself with the individuality of the prostitute nor with her redemption — certainly not through love. In *Les Fleurs du Mal* the emphasis falls not on the prostitute as character but on prostitution as a figurative structure. To sketch what I think is involved, I begin with "Le Crépuscule du Soir," where Baudelaire offers a rather bizarre description of the urban time and space that subtends his poetry. After asserting that evening brings comfort or relief to tired workers, to

Les esprits que dévore une douleur sauvage,
Le savant obstiné dont le front s'alourdit,
Et l'ouvrier courbé qui regagne son lit.

the poem continues:

Cependant les démons malsains dans l'atmosphère
S'éveillent lourdement, comme des gens d'affaire,

Et cognent en volant les volets et l'auvent.
A travers les lueurs que tourmente le vent,
La Prostitution s'allume dans les rues;
Comme une fourmilière elle ouvre ses issues;
Partout elle se fraye un occulte chemin,
Ainsi que l'ennemi qui tente un coup de main;
Elle remue au sein de la cité de fange
Comme un ver qui dérobe à l'Homme ce qu'il mange. (I, 94-5)

In this poem we are dealing not with the prostitute (the figure of the prostitute) nor with the anecdote of a flaneur noticing a prostitute, as the speaker of "Le Cygne" recalls noticing a swan. One way of measuring the distinctiveness of this poem is to compare it with some lines by Baudelaire's friend Alphonse Esquiros, which appeared in a book of his about prostitutes, *Les Vierges folles* — a book which, incidentally, mentions that houses of prostitution are recognizable in some quarters by "quelques fleurs placées dans des pots ou des caisses devant la fenêtre d'un balcon d'entresol...ces fleurs announcent des femmes à vendre" — a notable connection.[10] Here are the verses. The scene is much the same as in Baudelaire's poem:

Le jour a fui: le gaz dans ses tuyaux d'airain
Rallume pour la nuit son soleil souterrain;
C'est l'heure où sous nos yeux, chauves-souris de la vice,
Les filles de Paris commencent leur service:
Les voyez-vous courir pour vendre à chaque pas
Leur jeunesse aux chalands, l'amour qu'elles n'ont pas?

What sets Baudelaire's lines apart is the move away from prostitutes on the streets to an allegorical proposition. His poem is not about individual prostitutes, prostitutes in general, or even, really, prostitution as a readily definable social practice involving real women. No, here prostitution is something else. We might say that prostitution is what articulates this space, structures it, gives it its power and danger. On the one hand, prostitution "s'allume dans les rues," lights up, creating the visible space of night, like the gas lamps which are so often linked to the representation of prostitutes and prostitution. Discourse concerned with regulating prostitution was particularly concerned to limit external *signs* of houses of prostitution, forbidding prostitutes to appear in windows, and generally preventing, as Parent-Duchatelet put it, "que la prostitution frappe des regards"[11]; in this poem prostitution is not just eminently visible but provides the light of what we call "night-life."

On the other hand, prostitution is like an anthill, a structure that contains a whole world in its labyrinthine interior. It thus stands for the city itself, with its narrow passages: in "Les Petites Vieilles," Baudelaire speaks of "les plis sinueux des vieilles capitales," and the "fourmillant tableau" of Paris — ants once again (I, 89-

90). In "Les Sept Vieillards," the famous apostrophe to Paris is:

Fourmillante cité, cité pleine de rêves,
Où le spectre en plein jour raccroche le passant!
Les mystères partout coulent comme des sèves
Dans les canaux étroits du colosse puissant. (I, 87)

To compare prostitution to an anthill is to make it the "fourmillante cité" itself, the space in which anonymous, multiple urban encounters take place. There is perhaps a hint here of "la grande prostituée" of the Apocalypse in the Bible, who has written on her forehead "Babylone la grande," but the tone and imagery here seem quite different. There the great prostitute sits on the waters. Here the poem speaks not of city as prostitute but of "la prostitution":

Partout elle se fraye un occulte chemin,
Ainsi que l'ennemi qui tente un coup de main;
Elle remue au sein de la cité de fange
Comme un ver qui dérobe à l'Homme ce qu'il mange.

Not only does prostitution, androgynously, both open itself ("ouvre ses issues") and thrust forward ("se fraye un chemin"); it is at once the container (fourmilière) and the contained (what seethes in the heart of the city). It comes across here both as an active threat, the parasitical force that threatens to deprive man of what sustains him, and the labryinthine structure of the city which, opening itself, offers itself, with all its hidden dangers. The final line on prostitution gives us a pun dear to Baudelaire: *vers* are never just worms for the poet of "Une Charogne," and the challenge for readers is to work out how the link might function here: how is *verse*, like prostitution, the worm that steals away man's substance? For example, *verse*, the gaudy external display of the poet, as prostitution is the gaudy external display of sexuality, threatens to empty out the inside of its substance, making the poet, like the whore, the purveyor of apperances, a mere versifier. Going further, one might note that the formal elements of sign making have the power to empty out meaning — just as the flaunting of iterable signs of sexuality in prostitution is taken, finally, as empty, as a dead letter (the skeleton is never far away, as we shall see later). Whatever interpretive possibilities we pursue, the allegorical narrative, encouraging us to concentrate on the labyrinthine structure threatened by the enemy which seems a version of itself, gives us a complex intersection. Interior and exterior, container and contained, both the threat of death and what is threatened, prostitution is hard to pin down because it is the force that hyperbolically structures this space and this time, linking debauchery and dying (a link the subsequent lines of the poem reinforce) as the destruction or transcendence of boundaries, such as those of the self.

A remarkable letter of Gustave Flaubert's will help to spell out some of the relations at work in this idea of prostitution — which Flaubert calls "so complex a point of intersection that looking into it makes you dizzy." This letter, written to his mistress Louise Colet in 1853, calls Leconte de Lisle "un peu bourgeois" for saying he could never make love to a whore, and takes off from there. "C'est peut-être un goût pervers, mais j'aime la prostitution et pour elle-même," Flaubert begins, "indépendamment de ce qu'il y a en-dessous."[12] [*It may be a perverse taste, but I love prostitution for itself, independently of what is beneath.*] I'm not sure what is beneath prostitution, but Flaubert's reflection makes explicit the process whereby a generalized prostitution detaches itself from the prostitute or the sexual act which is sold or purchased and becomes a structure through which a number of elements of modernity can be situated. Flaubert continues:

> I've never been able to see one of those décolleté women pass by under the gaslights, in the rain, without my heart beating faster, just as monks' robes with their knotted cords excite my soul in I know not what deep and ascetic corners. This idea of prostitution offers a point of intersection so complex — lust, bitterness, the void of human relations, the frenzy of muscles, and the ring of gold — that looking deeply into it makes one dizzy; and one learns so many things! And one is so sad! And one dreams so well of love! Ah, writers of elegies, it is not on ruins that you should go lean your elbows, but on the breasts of these gay women.
>
> [*Je n'ai jamais pu voir passer aux feux de gaz une de ces femmes décolletées, sous la pluie, sans un battement de coeur, de même que les robes de moines avec leur cordelière à noeuds me chatouillent l'âme en je ne sais quels coins ascétiques et profonds. Il se trouve, en cette idée de la prostitution, un point d'intersection si complexe, luxure, amertume, néant des rapports humains, frénésie du muscle et sonnement d'or, qu'en y regardant au fond le vertige vient, et on apprend là tant de choses! Et on est si triste! Et on rêve si bien d'amour! Ah! faiseurs d'élégies, ce n'est pas sur des ruines qu'il faut aller appuyer votre coude, mais sur le sein de ces femmes gaies.*]

Prostitutes are to modernity what ruins are to antiquity — an analogy not so surprising, given the theme of the disfigurements of age and disease in the literary discourse of prostitution. Flaubert continues:

> Yes, that man has missed something who has never awoken in an anonymous bed [*un lit sans nom*], who has never seen sleeping on his pillow a head that he will never see again, and who, leaving at sunrise, hasn't crossed the bridges with a desire to throw himself into the water — so much do you feel like belching life up from the depths of your heart. Even it it is only the shameless costumes, the temptation of the chimera, the unknown, the aura of the *maudit*, the old poetry of corruption and venality. [*Et quand ce ne serait que le costume impudent, le tentation de la chimère, l'inconnu, le caractère maudit, la vieille poésie de la corruption et de la vénalité!*] During my first years in Paris I used to sit in front of Tortoni's on hot summer evenings and,

> watching the sun set, I would watch the streetwalkers stroll by. At such moments I consumed myself with Biblical poetry [*Je me devorais là de poésie biblique*]. I thought of Isaiah, of fornication in high places, and I walked back along the rue de la Harpe repeating to myself the verse, "And her throat is smoother than oil" [*"Et son gosier est plus doux que de l'huile."*] The Devil take me if I have ever been more chaste!

(Here, interestingly, it's a *vers* of the Bible rather than a tapeworm that is involved, when "je me dévorais"). In this passage, prostitution detaches itself from the sexual act to become the point of intersection of a whole series of topoi of a thought and a poetry at once nostalgic and cynical (veering romanticism to the modern). I'm particularly interested in the link between prostitutes, poetry, and self-consumption — "je me dévorais là de poésie biblique." But note also in this letter the emphasis on the anonymity of the prostitute — the woman herself counts for nothing: she is just "une tête qu'on ne reverra plus — not even "une femme sans nom," who might provoke curiosity (who is this mystery woman?). Flaubert speaks, rather, of "un lit sans nom," a nameless bed (perhaps also, given the intersection with Biblical poetry, a nameless "read"?).

The prostitute here is a gaudy screen for projection, "une tentation de la chimère," where value is provided by the male imagination, which can draw upon an ancient store of poetic imagery, stretching back to the Bible, and on modern "amertume." Loving prostitution for itself, independently of what lies beneath, seems to mean, in Flaubert, engaging in a structure where desire and imagination grow dizzy reflecting on themselves through literary images, in a condition of chastity.[13]

Now there are moments in Baudelaire that would fit this model, where emphasis falls on operations of the speaker's consciousness that supply all value and interest, but Flaubert's account omits what is a crucial element of the prostitutional relation in *Les Fleurs du Mal.* Recall "Le Crépuscule du Soir," where prostitution is the enemy that threatens man as well as the city that it represents. Invariably, Baudelaire's prostitutional figures are invested with a radical otherness, a sexual power that is heightened or compounded by indifference to man. Should we say that for "l'homme moderne," whom Baudelaire is said to have represented so skillfully, the most threatening form of the imagined indifference of the world is the indifference of women, who refuse to return to him a flattering image of himself? Is this, perhaps, "le ver qui dérobe à l'Homme ce qu'il mange" — which threatens what sustains him in his quality as man — or is this interpretation a psychologization inadequate to Baudelaire's strange, hyperbolic constructions? Certainly, prostitution, in *Les Fleurs du Mal,* involves imagined feminine figures who are redoubtable in their indifference; they may sell themelves, they may be impassively available or unavailable, but they are never satisfied in their relations with men. Think, for example of the poem whose title is its first line, "You'd entertain the universe in bed,"

Tu mettrais l'univers entier dans ta ruelle,
Femme impure! L'ennui rend ton âme cruelle.
Pour exercer tes dents à ce jeu singulier,
Il te faut chaque jour un coeur au râtelier. (I, 27)

The prostitute, as a human commodity available to anyone, embodies for Baudelaire a lack of relation between man and woman. The very impersonality of the prostitute's relation to men, her lack of satisfaction, is imagined to give her a power of disdain and indifference — though again, this interpretive language of mine seems to tone down, to reduce to a psychological scenario, a hyperbolic narrative that claims to get at something other than the motives and feelings of individuals. The poem "Allégorie," often interpreted as allegorizing the prostitute, is a case in point. Monumentally remote from any actual prostitute, this figure cannot be reduced to the human manifestation of the qualities she displays.

C'est une femme belle et de riche encolure,
Qui laisse dans son vin trainer sa chevelure.
Les griffes de l'amour, les poisons du tripot,
Tout glisse et tout s'émousse au granit de sa peau.
Elle rit à la Mort et nargue la Débauche,
Ces monstres dont la main, qui toujours gratte et fauche,
Dans ses jeux destructeurs a pourtant respecté
De ce corps ferme et droit la rude majesté.
Elle marche en déesse et repose en sultane;
Elle a dans le plaisir la foi mahométane,
Et dans ses bras ouverts, que remplissent ses seins,
Elle appelle des yeux la race des humains. (I, 116)

(Can she belong to the race she is calling?) Whatever we call this feminine figure, she embodies in monumental, non-human form, qualities that figure in the representation of prostitution, such as an imagined indifference of feminine sexuality to male love-making — the combination of an idolatrous or Mohammedan commitment to pleasure and an impermeability to the "griffes de l'amour." Her skin of granite — she is *la donna petrosa* — is a generalised insensibility which is part of the prostitute's availability: she welcomes all humanity. "Cette vierge inféconde," as she is called in the next line, as opposed to the Virgin Mary, who stands for the supposed purity of motherhood, is sterile, preserves a certain virginity through her very availability and indifference, remaining untouched, unmarked by the men she takes on. Inviting possession — "elle appelle des yeux la race des humains" — she resists it, in a process the poem calls "nécessaire à la marche du monde."

Elle croit, elle sait, cette vierge inféconde
Et pourtant nécessaire à la marche du monde,
Que la beauté du corps est un sublime don
Qui de tout infamie arrache le pardon.
Elle ignore l'Enfer comme le Purgatoire,
Et quand l'heure viendra d'entrer dans la Nuit noire,
Elle regardera la face de la Mort,
Ainsi qu'un nouveau-né, — sans haine et sans remords. (I, 116)

Her very lack of interiority steals, seizes "pardon for every infamy." Already inhuman, she can look death in the face, as one identifies with it who knows neither fear nor regret.

This unusual thematic nexus of eroticism, virginity and barrenness in a monumental female figure is reinforced by a neighboring poem, "Les Deux Bonnes Soeurs," which treats death and debauchery as "deux aimables filles," kindred prostitutes in their shared virginity and barrenness; they remain unaffected by the numerous men who pass through their arms; they are never impregnated.

La Débauche et la Mort sont deux aimables filles,
Prodigues de baisers et riches de santé,
Dont le flanc toujours vierge et drapé de guenilles
Sous l'éternel labeur n'a jamais enfanté. (I, 114)

They are brought together, as deux aimables filles, even potential rivals, by the attentions of the poet: the man who finds himself in the clutches of literary production, a man cast indifferently as satanic poet or badly payed courtesan, is like a man who finds terrible pleasures, tasted without remorse, in the beds of these two prostitutional figures.

Au poète sinistre, ennemi des familles,
Favori de l'enfer, courtisan mal renté,
Tombeaux et lupanars montrent sous leurs charmilles
Un lit que le remords n'a jamais fréquenté.

Et la bière et l'alcove en blasphèmes fécondes
Nous offrent tour à tour, comme deux bonnes soeurs,
De terribles plaisirs et d'affreuses douceurs. (I, 114-15)

But strikingly here, despite the claim to frequent the beds of these two women, the poet cannot define himself through a relation with them, except proleptically, by asking them to bury him, or rather, seeking to enforce the presupposition that

Debauchery will bury him, with the help of Death's graft, by asking *when* they will do so.

> Quand veux-tu m'enterrer, Débauche aux bras immondes?
> O Mort, quand viendras-tu, sa rivale en attraits,
> Sur ses myrtes infectes entre tes noirs cyprès?

This is a poem on the necessarily disproportionate relation between these prostitute figures and the male speaker.

This strange poem evokes the connection Georges Bataille makes in *La Part maudite* in calling the prostitute "the figure of death under the mask of life," since eroticism which she signifies "is itself the locus where life and death become confused with one another."[14] I shall pursue that connection further in concluding, but first I will sketch what I take to be the discursive processes in which these two poems, with their unusual thematic nexus of eroticism, virginity, and barrenness, participate, and thus attempt in some part, to locate them historically.

The notion evoked here and in "Allégorie" that prostitutes are barren is a curiously persistent one in nineteenth-century France. Parent-Duchatelet goes out of his way to note that his investigations showed that prostitutes were not sterile, as was generally believed, though they did have a very low rate of pregnancy and of successful birth. But he does initiate an elaborate effort, with his statistical studies and classifications of prostitutes, to subject the prostitute to a socio/medical discourse of control, transforming social and moral issues into administrative procedures: registration, medical inspection, and isolation within *maisons closes*, themselves restricted to certain districts. This is part of the bourgeois recapture of the city from the proletariat, and as in the earlier remarks I quoted from Parent-Duchatelet comparing prostitutes to sewers and refuse dumps, it involves an attempt to de-eroticize prostitution. In addition to banning erotic materials from houses of prostitution, for example, Parent-Duchatelet insists that prostitutes be transported in closed carriages so as not to be seen, congratulates the morals of the police on reducing licentious displays and praises the sense of *pudeur* retained by modern prostitutes. The greatest danger is that prostitutes may become lesbians, "the lowest form of vice which a human creature can attain."[15] Reglementarianism, as it is called, seeks to discipline, medicalize, and deeroticize prostitution.[16]

The other major discursive practice here is that of Mariolatry and its seculiar extensions. In December 1854, less than three years before the publication of *Les Fleurs du Mal*, the Catholic Church proclaimed the doctrine of the Immaculate Conception, the official climax of a movement of Mariolatry that in France had helped revitalize a Church that had been weakened by the Revolution and provided a powerful image to replace the Marianne of revolutionary fervor. Louis Veuillot, an acquaintance of Baudelaire, declared at the time that "L'époque qui suit le siècle de Voltaire pourra s'appeler le siècle de Marie."[17] The virgin provided a way of focusing diffuse religious dogma and emotion on a single figure, who is a commodification of otherness: the Virgin Mary is the one person in the universe to have been born free of the taint of original sin, absolutely other, therefore, but whose otherness is the essence of femininity and motherhood. 19th century Mariolatry is a religion of the virgin and the mother — virgin as mother — celebrated even by those who are not good catholics, such as Auguste Comte whose *Système de politique positive* of 1854 evokes "l'utopie de la Vierge-Mère," or the socialist Pierre-Joseph Proudhon, who writes that "Si le christianisme s'est trompé, c'est en faisant de la règle l'exception, c'est en restreignant au Christ et à la Vierge ce qui doit être le privilège de toute naissance légitime" [If Christianity erred it is in making an exception what should be the rule and in restricting to Christ and the Virgin what should be the priviledge of every legitimate birth][18]; or the historian Jules Michelet, whose book *La Femme* of 1859, urges that "La femme est une religion. Sa destinée est telle que, plus elle restera haute comme poésie religieuse, plus elle sera efficace dans la vie commune et pratique" [Woman is a religion; her destiny is such that the higher she remains as religious poetry the more efficacious she will be in ordinary and practical life.][19]

In putting together eroticism, virginity and barreness, Baudelaire engages these two discursive practices at unexpected points: investing his powerful feminine figures with a threatening sexuality he counters both the religion of the virginal mother and the reglementarian discourse devoted to making the prostitute a public health functionary, but in keeping the two most implausible qualities of the central figures in these discourses — the virginity of the virginal mother and the barreness of the prostitute — he retains a transformative reference to those discourses, redirecting them toward a different result. In the context of and in contrast with these two discursive practices, Baudelaire's lyrics, for all their misogyny, seem positively energizing, producing a radical otherness of feminine sexuality which is threatening to men in its indifference and link with death.

Let me conclude with a look at one of the strangest and most powerful poems of the collection. It is one of the six poems that was banned by the court when *Les Fleurs du Mal* was prosecuted for offense to public morals. This is Baudelaire's "Interview with a Vampire," "Les Métamorphoses du vampire." If other poems of the collection stress the impassibility, the indifference of a powerful feminine sexuality that refuses to reflect back for male lovers a flattering image of themselves, here we encounter a feminine figure flaunting her seductiveness and her power. Though clearly something more and other than a prostitute, she is a professional in love. She speaks — something unusual in itself:

— "Moi, j'ai la lèvre humide, et je sais la science
De perdre au fond d'un lit l'antique conscience.

Je sèche tous les pleurs sur mes seins triomphants,
Et fais rire les vieux du rire des enfants.
Je remplace, pour qui me voit nue et sans voiles,
La lune, le soleil, le ciel, et les étoiles!
Je suis, mon cher savant, si docte aux voluptés,
Lorsque j'étouffe un homme en mes bras redoutés,
Ou lorsque j'abandonne aux morsures mon buste,
Timide et libertine, et fragile et robuste,
Que sur ses matelas qui se pâment d'émoi,
Les anges impuissants se damneraient pour moi!" (I, 159)

The speaker of "Les Deux Bonnes Soeurs" beseeches "Débauche aux bras immonde" to bury him, but here the female speaker's claim to "suffocate a man in her redoubtable arms" seems more threatening, even diabolical. Debauchery's link to death is so close, though, that the threat to male mastery and narcissism posed here can be overcome in the wink of an eye.

In the next stanza, when she has sucked all the marrow out of his bones, and he turns back to kiss her, he finds, first, a putrefying corpse and then, as if this were still too threatening, the debris of a skeleton. This vampire seems to have been not just poisoned by her victim — poison works too slowly for this tale — but metamorphosed by a poetic operation which, like personification itself, can produce instantaneous changes.

Quand elle eut de mes os sucé toute la moelle,
Et que languissamment je me tournai vers elle,
Pour lui rendre un baiser d'amour, je ne vis plus
Q'une outre aux flancs gluants, toute pleine de pus!
Je fermais les deux yeux, dans ma froide épouvante,
Et quand je les rouvris à la clarté vivante,
A mes côtés, au lieu du mannequin puissant
Qui semblait avoir fait provision de sang,
Tremblaient confusément des débris de squelette,
Qui d'eux-mêmes rendaient le cri d'une girouette
Ou d'une enseigne, au bout d'une tringle de fer,
Que balance le vent pendant les nuits d'hiver. (I, 159)

Prostitutional figures can be invested with a threatening, even diabolical sexual power because there are always ways for the male poetic imagination to neutralize the threat, by perceiving the skeleton beneath the flesh and producing metamorphoses, but the final scene here is not one of male triumph. The ending of this poem presents us with a strange space, where the "débris" of the skeleton makes the noise of a weathervane or of a sign buffeted by the wind. This noise created by the wind recalls the very striking simile from another of the six poems condemned by the court for outrage to public morals, "Femmes damnées: Delphine et Hippolyte," where "le vent furibond de la concupiscence/ Fait claquer votre chair ainsi qu'un vieux drapeau" (I, 155). The wind seems linked to the force of desire and the reduction of the body to skeleton, weathervane, sign, or flag. But to elucidate the odd scene of "Les Métamorphoses du vampire," we might juxtapose it with the space sketched by the lines of "Le Crépuscule du soir" where the wind is also blowing:

> A travers les lueurs que tourmente le vent,
> La Prostitution s'allume dans les rues.

There prostitution lights up like a sign in the streets which are eerily empty of the crowds that make the city the prostitutional anthill. In the subsequent poem, the prostitute/vampire, who doesn't light up but *replaces* light — "Je remplace, pour qui me voit nue et sans voiles,/ La lune, le soleil, le ciel, et les étoiles" — becomes a skeleton hanging in the wind, a weathervane producing sounds like an aeolian harp, or creaking like a sign — the prostitutional skeleton as sign. In both cases what is striking is the movement of eerie abstraction, toward a space charged with a certain mystery, but emptied out, by the link of sex with death, as skeleton displaces flesh or as the enemy worm eats away at its host, in what one might be tempted to see as the melancholic movement of history itself, if "Le Voyage" is to be believed.

I have emphasized operations by which Baudelaire takes up themes and images associated with a prostitution said to represent modernity and uses them to produce *disproportionate* female figures endowed with a radical otherness. Against the movement of the century to exalt a purified woman or to discipline and control the signs and practices of commodified sexuality, Baudelaire reestablishes the link between sexuality and death, flesh and corpse, through evocations of a sexual power that is often diabolical and that finds no fulfillment in relations with men. But above all, he creates hyperbolic figures, wagering that it is at this level of personified forces, Eros and Thanatos, the personified sign, that the world and its history must be described and confronted.

NOTES

1. Walter Benjamin, *Gesammelte Schriften*, vol. I, part 2, p. 687.
2. All quotations from Baudelaire are taken from the Pléiade *Oeuvres complètes*, ed. Claude Pichois, 2 vols. (Paris: Gallimard, 1975-6). References to this volume are given in parentheses in the text.
3. T.J. Clark, *The Painter of Modern Life* (Princeton: Princeton University Press, 1984), p. 103.
4. Jean Lorrain, *Modernités* (Paris: Giraud, 1885), pp. 9-12. To take another example, in 1868 when Alexandre Dumas writes a new preface to his earlier play, *La Dame aux Camelias*, he asks where is the

world going and answers, "Je vous le dirai: Nous allons à la prostitution universelle." A generalized prostitution becomes the mark of modernity.
5. Compare Baudelaire's definition in *Le Peintre de la vie moderne* of the quest for "la modernité" as the attempt to "dégager de la mode ce qu'elle peut contenir de poétique dans l'historique, de tirer l'éternel du transitoire" (II, 694).
6. See Charles Bernheimer, *Figures of Ill Repute* (Cambridge: Harvard University Press 1989).
7. Quoted in T.J. Clark, *op. cit.*, p.110.
8. Alexandre Parent-Duchâtelet, *De la prostitution dans la ville de Paris* (Paris, Bailliere: 1837), 203.
9. Walter Benjamin, *Gesammelte Schriften*, vol. I, part 2, 671.
10. Alphonse Esquiros, *Les vierges folles* (Paris: Delavigne, 1842), 148.
11. Alexandre Parent-Duchâtelet, *De la prostitution dans la ville de Paris*, 148.
12. Gustave Flaubert, *Correspondance*, ed. Jean Bruneau (Paris: Gallimard, 1989), II, 340. Letter of 1 June 1853.
13. What are the relations which structure this prostitutional space defined by Flaubert? In Baudelaire's "Amour du mensonge," the woman whom one is tempted to identify as a prostitute because she stands in the gaslight, is an anonymous surface onto which desires and phantasms of the speaker are projected.

Quand je contemple, aux feux du gaz, qui le colore,
Ton front pâle, embelli par un morbide attrait,

the speaker asks why she attracts him:

Es-tu le fruit d'automne aux saveurs souveraines?
Es-tu vase funèbre attendant quelque pleurs,
Parfum qui fait rêver aux oasis lointaines,
Oreiller caressant, ou corbeille de fleurs? (I, 98-9)

The answer comes: "Mais ne suffit-il pas que tu sois l'apparence?" She is pure appearance. What might lie behind that appearance does not matter: "Qu'importe ta bêtise ou ton indifférence?" Her own qualities are of no importance in the anonymous and phantasmatic relationship. This prostitutional space, which seems that sketched in Flaubert's letter, is a space of arbitrary signs, signifiers which can take on whatever significations the desires and phantasms of the male speaker dramatized in these poems projects onto them. But in Baudelaire's poetry there are other important factors at work, as we shall see.
14. George Bataille, *The Accursed Share* (New York: Zone Books,1988), vol II, 142-3.
15. Alexandre Parent-Duchâtelet, *De la prostitution dans la ville de Paris*, 96-97, 100, 113-119, 144-145.
16. Le reglementarisme is "an unceasing effort to discipline the prostitute; the ideal being the creation of a category of *prostituées-moniales* [enclosed prostitute-nuns], *bonnes 'travailleuses', mais automates et surtout mauvaises jouisseuses*" [good workers, but automatons and above all who take no pleasure]. Alain Corbin, *Les Filles de Noce* (Paris), 25.
17. Quoted by Stéphane Michaud, *Muse et Madone* (Paris, xx, 1985), 20. Michaud writes, "the Virgin Mary becomes an object of commerce. She feeds in these years the flourishing market of industrial art, labelled Saint-Sulpice, gives her name to drapery and fancy goods stores which wish to deserve the reputation of reliable firms. 1830 sees the inauguration of one of the first department stores of Paris: La Belle Jardinière. The establishment promotes itself on the prestige of one of Raphael's most famous madonnas. The Virgin Mary's efficacious patronage of more than one beauty, toiletry, or health product shows clearly what has occured: the Virgin is bait" [la Vierge constitue un appât].
18. Quoted in Michaud, 68.
19. Jules Michelet, *La Femme* (1859) (Paris, 10/18, 1981), 119.

Reframing the Frame: Analysis of "Night-Metaphors" in Djuna Barnes' *Nightwood*

Edit Zsadányi

Djuna Barnes' *Nightwood* has often been characterized as a strange and esoteric novel of the thirties (Minter, 164). Interpretations mostly attempt to explain the strange character of the novel. In my analysis, which concentrates on the metaphorical language of the work, I would also like to give an explanation of its "strangeness," arguing that the novel undermines some of the basic conceptual metaphors of the western tradition. In the first part of the paper my purpose is to confront the metaphorical conceptions of life challenged by the novel, which we usually take for granted. In the second part, reversing the direction of investigation, I would like to give an interpretation of the novel on the basis of the reevaluated conceptions.

I.

The atmosphere of disillusion of intellectual life after World War I is clearly present in the novel and offers an appropriate background to the characters' hopeless search for a way out of their desperate situation. *Nightwood* is set mainly in Paris, although it also shows scenes in Berlin and the final chapter takes place in America. The story of *Nightwood* centers on the desperate relations between five people. Robin Vote is the focus for all significant actions and speeches. Though all the main characters are strongly attracted to her, Robin's character is difficult to define. Robin marries

Felix Volkbein and soon after the birth of their child, she becomes Nora Flood's lover. Some years later she leaves Nora for Jenny Petherbridge and they move to the United States, where in the end, she returns to Nora. According to Mihaly Szegedy-Maszak the novel challenges the traditional roles of the two genders. He refers to several reversed patterns relating to gender. For example, "The story of Hedwig and Guido" is the caricature of traditional femininity and masculinity. The next generation reproduces the same pattern: Felix plays the reversed role of the fairy Prince while Robin plays that of the Sleeping Beauty. Robin is always dressed like a man. Matthew O'Connor compares her to the Prince on the white horse that — according to the doctor — we have always been seeking (Szegedy-Maszak, 161).

Dr. Matthew O'Connor is an outside observer of the characters' passionate relations. His long-lasting monologues and discussions with Felix and Nora provide interpretations of the novel's action. The most important story of the novel and of the dialogues between Nora and the Doctor, is the love-relation between Nora and Robin. That story is the profound and impossible love of a woman who contemplates and understands a woman, who rages and destroys (Field, 147).

The references for intertextual relations and literary influences are wide-ranging, from medieval morality plays (Frank, 49) through Elizabethan prose and fin de siècle literary Decadence to classic modernist literature. Joyce and T. S. Eliot had special influence on Djuna Barnes' writings. For instance, Tiresias of *The Waste Land* resembles the figure of the doctor. He is the foreteller who knows most about the bodies and minds of men and women (Scott, 102). The structural principles of *Nightwood* are similar to that of *Ulysses* in terms of the technique of fragmentation. Fitting narrative fragments of *Ulysses* together, the reader can gain an instinctive knowledge of Dublin life. Fitting together the eight chapters of *Nightwood* as eight fragments, the reader can have an instinctive knowledge of the human spirit. On the other hand, there are remarkable differences between the structural principles of these two novels. "These chapters are knit together, not by the progress of any action — either narrative action, or as in the stream-of-consciousness novel, the flow of experience — but by the continual reference and cross-reference of images and symbols that must be referred to each other spatially throughout the time-act of reading" (Frank, 32).

Accepting the above claim that images are important as the structural principle of the novel, I will analyze the linguistic metaphors relating to the "night" images.

It is now a widely held belief that a metaphor is not simply a linguistic entity, but rather a conceptual phenomenon that plays a major role in human cognition. To explain metaphor as a cognitive process one must assume culturally based thinking patterns of the human mind. Viewed internally, as MacCormac summarizes, metaphors operate as cognitive processes that produce new insights and new hypothesis. Viewed externally, metaphors operate as mediators between the human mind and culture (MacCormac, 2). Lakoff and Turner also suggest that metaphors are grounded on cultural experience, and to study metaphor is therefore to be confronted with one's own mind and one's own culture.

> Poetic metaphor far from being ornamentation, deals with central and indispensable aspects of our conceptual systems. Through the masterful use of metaphoric process on which our conceptual system is based, poets address the most vital issues in our lives and help us illuminate those issues, through the extension, composition, and criticism of the basic metaphoric tools through which we comprehend reality (Lakoff and Turner, 215).

Following the claim of cognitive studies that poetic metaphors can teach us to recognize our conceptual metaphors, I would like to explore the way this novel reevaluates a thinking pattern of life which has always been conceived in western tradition as the negative side of "normalcy." While examening conceptual metaphors, I will apply the methods of cognitive theory which clearly distinguishes linguistic (poetic) metaphors from conceptual (basic) metaphors (generally indicated by the use of all "upper-case letters") (Lakoff and Johnson, 6). While analyzing poetic metaphors, I apply Richards's category of *tenor* and *vehicle* (Richards, 52), because these terms designate the pictorial dimension and the figurative character of the metaphor (Ricoeur, 147).

Nightwood as a metaphor holds much information about the cultural frame in which it functions. One of the important claims of Lakoff and Johnson which I use in my analysis is that linguistic metaphors ought to be derived from conceptual metaphors. This claim implies that a conceptual metaphor may manifest itself in a single linguistic metaphor. Lakoff and Johnson's theory of conceptual metaphors has been challenged from a psychological viewpoint by cognitive scientists who question whether conceptual metaphors really exist in the minds of the individual speakers (Steen, 16-18). On the other hand, the theory of conceptual metaphors has been acknowledged as social or cultural patterns that function as "conceptual repository of our cultural knowledge" (Steen, 101). My approach intends to exploit this cultural aspect of conceptual metaphors.

Nightwood, as a poetic metaphor evokes two basic metaphorical concepts of life in western tradition. *Night* recalls and challenges the LIFETIME IS A DAY concept, where night corresponds to death; *wood* recalls the LIFE IS A JOURNEY metaphorical concept, in which *wood* can be seen as being lost, being out of the road of life-journey. In the following, I would like to explore how this novel reevaluates these two conceptual metaphors.

1. Analyzing the LIFE IS A JOURNEY metaphor

Lakoff and Johnson refer to the first lines from Dante's *Divine Comedy*:

> In the middle life's road,
> I found myself in a dark wood.

We understand, by virtue of the LIFE IS A JOURNEY metaphor, that somewhere during maturity, the speaker found himself in a condition of being "lost," that is, without clear purpose in life. In this metaphor the traveler corresponds to the living person, the path of journey to the events of life, the destination of the journey to the purpose of life and impediments to difficulties in life. When the traveler finds himself at a dead end, he wants to find a new way out of the dead end (Lakoff and Turner, 3). Correspondingly, when somebody is in a critical situation, he or she wants to change his or her life. Because of these qualities, LIFE IS A JOURNEY is "one of our most powerful tools we have for making sense of our lives" (Lakoff and Turner, 65).

The novel recalls the LIFE IS A JOURNEY metaphor in the story of all three characters who fall in love with Robin. Each introduction of a character invites the reader to expect a life-story, a story of a life as a journey. The life-stories begin with the introductions of the figures and their personal histories, which intertextually relates the realist and the romantic traditions of the novel in which the whole life, or an important part of the life of a character, is followed by the narrator. All such novels rely on the conception of LIFE IS A JOURNEY. *Nightwood* evokes this tradition and through it this concept of life. The introductions of Felix, Nora and Jenny Petherbridge are given in very detailed and accurate forms as if whole life-stories would follow their introductions.

> Jenny Petherbridge was a widow, a middle-aged woman who had been married four times. Each husband had wasted away and died: she had been like a squirrel racing a wheel day and night in an endeavour to make them historical.
>
> She had a beaked head and the body, small, feeble, and ferocious, that somehow made one associate her with Judy; they did not go together. Only severed could any part of her have been called right. There was a trembling ardour in her wrists and fingers as if she were suffering from some elaborate denial. (Barnes, 65)

The novel starts with the birth of Felix and a detailed description of his parents: Guido and Hedvig Volkbein. After the detailed presentation of his family background, the reader would expect that the novel would be the story of his life. However, it recounts his life until his marriage to Robin. Then the story switches to Nora's lifestory. After a detailed description of her character and cultural background, the reader is interested in continuing Nora's story, but this line of life stops at the point when Robin returns to her and they meet in the woods.

Similarly, Jenny Petherbridge's lengthy introduction is not followed by her whole story. The story-telling stops at the point of her love affair with Robin. All further information on the characters in the second part of the novel relates their love-relations to Robin. In other words, they do not continue their life journeys. They are all left by Robin, suffer from their loneliness yet do not want to continue their lives without their feelings for her. They choose to suffer rather than continue their lives without the memory of Robin. They see their lives differently from the conception: LIFE IS A JOURNEY. In the conceptual metaphor, when the traveler is at a dead end, he wants to get out of it, and find another way to continue the journey. Similarly, when one is in a difficult situation, one wants to overcome the difficulties. These characters do not behave according to this metaphoric concept. They want to stay in their dead ends even at the price of suffering. They recall their love-stories again and again, which evokes the pleasure they each had with Robin, but also prolongs their suffering. This pattern is repeated in the novel in each case. Nora and Felix consult with the doctor about their love-experience, while Jenny turns to Felix to share her despair with another. As a consequence, *Nightwood* suggests a different conception of life. Life is seen as a journey to the point at which one wants to step out of the journey, when one wants to get rid of the concept and the power of the LIFE IS A JOURNEY metaphor. On a more abstract level, the purpose of life is to reframe a preexisting frame of life. This conception of life does not provide a completely independent view of life, but rather extends it, thus making the concept more compound.

2. Analyzing the LIFE IS A DAY metaphor

In this section, I will examine the poetic metaphors relating to night in the chapter "Watchman, what of the night," focusing on the conceptual metaphors upon which they are based.

The storytelling is suspended in this chapter and the narrator-narratee dialogue (Prince, 9) is replaced by a dialogue between Nora and the Doctor. The narratee is led to this part of the story but is then left alone without the guidance of the storyteller. Nora's interest here is to understand what is night. This is, of course, not only a theoretical question — as the doctor would say — "even the greatest generality has a little particular." In actuality, Nora wants to understand Robin's way of life. Moreover, she wants to find a solution for her own identity crisis. She asks literal questions and receives metaphorical answers. She has to reformulate her question which remains unanswered or inscrutable.

> Nora turned away. "What am I to do?"
> "Ah, mighty uncertainty!" said the doctor. "Have you thought of all the doors that

> have shut at night and opened again? Of women who have looked about with lamps, like you, and who have scurried on fast feet? (93)

The pattern of restructuring the frame can be observed in the time-space structure of this chapter. In the beginning, the location is described in detail by the narrator. The situation is very clear: it is three o'clock at night, and Nora and Matthew O'Connor are having a conversation in the doctor's poorly furnished room. As the discussion continues, the initial situation steadily disappears: the storytelling-situation turns into a dramatic situation, a dialogue which ends with the doctor's monologue. There is no closure of the initial story-telling situation. We do not know when and in what circumstances Nora leaves the doctor's room. The location which was the background, or the frame of the conversation, simply disappears. The narrator does not finish her story, and instead remains silent and lets the doctor speak. This narratorial omission in the end allows the possibility that the conversation on night rewrites its locational frame. During this dialogue, metaphor as a linguistic phenomenon, and as a means of conveying knowledge, is also becoming problematic. The only way to understanding night, the only way to knowledge, is through metaphoric language. We do not know whether Nora understands the night or not. Similarly, we can never be sure whether metaphorical language can lead to understanding or not. This is an open structure again on the level of a metadiscourse on knowledge and metaphor.

Now let us turn to a close analysis of the doctor's metaphorical speech of night. I have collected one-by-one all of the "night-metaphors" in this chapter. (By night-metaphors, I mean any metaphorical statement including *night.*) My working hypothesis is that some of these poetic metaphors will recall the LIFE IS A DAYTIME conceptual metaphor, and that others, that do not fit into this concept, may recall a different metaphorical concept of life. My main scholarly interest is to illustrate this different concept of life as a cultural phenomenon.

I have made two groups of these metaphors: one which is *in* accordance with the LIFETIME IS A DAY conceptual metaphor or related metaphorical concepts such as DEATH IS NIGHT. I have also listed here the metaphors that rely on the oppositional relation of day/night, light/dark, and good/bad, such as BAD IS BLACK and GOOD IS LIGHT. These conceptual metaphors (Lakoff and Turner, 185) are likewise related to the LIFE IS A DAY concept. I will call this group the *in*-group. Those metaphors that do not fit into these concepts compose the second, or *out*-group.

Analysis of the in-group

I take for granted that LIFE IS A DAY is one of the basic metaphorical concepts of life in the western tradition. I also accept the metaphorical opposition of light and dark, day and night, and good and bad as basic figures, as basic thinking patterns of Christian culture. In the metaphor LIFE IS A DAY, we see stages of life, claimed by Lakoff and Turner, as corresponding to the stages of the day. Birth is dawn, morning corresponds to youth, maturity is noon, old age is twilight, the moment of death is sunset, and the state of death is night (Lakoff and Turner, 6).

The only metaphorical chain of the *in*-group I intend to examine here is the following:

> Our bones ache only while the flesh is on them. Stretch it as thin as the temple flesh of an ailing woman and still it serves to ache the bone and to move the bone about; and in like manner the night is a skin pulled over the head of the day that the day may be in a torment. We will find no comfort until the night melts away; until the fury of night rots out its fire. (85)

There is a complete two component metaphor embedded in the simile: *the night is a skin pulled over the head of day*, which recalls and challenges at the same time the traditional night-day, good-bad opposition. This metaphor claims the dominance of night over day and questions the periodical changes of day into night. "Skin" stands as a metonymy for sensitiveness, and "head" stands as a metonymy for rationality. The metaphor recalls the duality of rational mind and instinctive body but questions their oppositional relation. It claims the predominance of instincts over rationality. There is no cure for feelings; it feels what it feels, just like the skin is the mean of the "senses." Day and night, rationality and feelings are two sides of one continuous development governed by the latter term. Christian mentality distinguishes these two sides of human personality as two different parts and creates an oppositional relation between them, whereby one is the negative side of the other. This metaphor claims the existence of the two but argues against their oppositional relation.

The doctor repeatedly objects to this opposition and advocates the French way of life that sees the day and night as a whole.

> "I'm telling you of French nights at the moment," the doctor went on, "and why we all go into them. The night and the day are two travels, and the French — gut-greedy and fist-tight though they often are — alone leave testimony of the two in the dawn; we tear up the one for the sake of the other; not so the French." (82)

Ernst van Alphen has emphasized the importance of characterizing the French and the American way of life in the doctor's talk.

> The doctor distinguishes between the attitudes of French and Americans towards the night. We should keep in mind in this respect that Nora, Jenny and the doctor are Americans. The American keeps the day and night carefully separated out of fear of losing his dignity. The French, in contrast, see day and night as a continuous

> whole. The Parisian nights are the nights which pass over into days by means of the drunkenness caused by the wine drunk during the day.... Robin with her French way of life in the Parisian nights is opposed in this respect to her American lovers." (Van Alphen, 17)

The above metaphors, and all others distinguishing French and American conceptions of life, argue against the opposition of night/day and good/bad. The reader is continually forced to reconsider his or her automatic oppositional thinking pattern. Robin cannot be understood through the oppositional categories of the others. Getting closer to Robin, which is at the same time understanding herself, forces Nora to rethink her own attitude towards Robin. The pattern of reframing the cognitive frame is again observable here. During the course of understanding the other, the one reframes her cognitive categories. The character of Robin is accessible only when Nora reevaluates her own means of understanding, when she reformulates the oppositional structure of her own mentality.

In sum, there is an inherent subversion going on. The metaphors of the *in*-group basically rely on our general metaphorical conception of night and day, but at the same time they undermine their oppositional relation. The night-metaphors of the *in*-group elaborate and criticize at the same time that the GOOD IS LIGHT, BAD IS BLACK conceptual metaphors, and the day/night, good/bad oppositions, figures. The LIFE IS A DAY is a secondary concept while the DEATH IS NIGHT metaphor is more conceivable, since death and night are both the recurring subjects of the conversations. Because of the appearance of the DEATH IS NIGHT concept, the conversation on night, which is at the same time a conversation on love, is affected by a likeness to experiencing death.

Getting to know the other side is a sort of death experience. "But what of our own death — permit us to reproach the night, wherein we die manifold alone" (97).

Analysis of the out-group

I have listed those night-metaphors which fit neither the former metaphorical concepts, nor the night/day opposition. I will examine them as poetic metaphors following the linguistic approach of metaphor which emphasizes the study of the sentence (Black, 73) and, within the sentence, the distinction between tenor and vehicle (Richards, 52).

My working hypothesis here is that in analyzing the linguistic metaphors, I will find an underlying metaphorical concept: that NIGHT IS SOMETHING. I have numbered the metaphors of the *out*-group from 1 to 13, and have made a chart on the basis of the tenor-vehicle structure of the metaphors.

Out-group

1. — The night, Beware of that dark door! (80)
2. — "Doctor, I have come to ask you, to tell me everything you know about the *night*" (79)
3. — "have you ever thought of the *night*?" (80)
4. — "I can see, you have not! You should, for *the night has been going on for a long time*" (82)
5. — "I've never known *it* before — I thought I did, but it was not knowing at all." (82)
6. — "But," Nora said, "I never thought of the *nights as a life* at all — I never lived it — why did she?" (82)
7. — To think of the acorn it is necessary to become the tree. And the *tree of night* is the hardest tree to mount, the dourest tree to scale, the most difficult of branch, the most febrile to the touch, and sweats a resin and drips a pitch against the palm that computation has not gambled (83-84)
8. — "For the lover, it is the night into which his beloved goes," he said, "that destroys his heart; he wakes her suddenly, only to look the hyena in the face that is her smile, as she leaves that company" (87)
9. — Wait! I'm coming to the *nights of nights* — the nights you want to know about the most of all — for even the greatest generality has a little particular (89)
10. — the face is for fools! If you fish by the face you fish out trouble, but there's always other fish when you deal with the sea. The face is what anglers catch in the daylight, but the *sea is the night*" (93)
11. — Have you thought of all the doors that have shut at night and opened again? Of women who have looked about with lamps, like you, and who have scurried on fast feet?... and all the windows, great and small, from which love and fear have peered, shining and in tears. Put those windows end to end and it would be a casement that would reach around the world; and put those thousand eyes into one eye and *you would have the night combed with the searchlight of the heart* (93)
12. — Have I not shut my eyes with the added *shutter of the night* and put my hand out? (94)
13. — I'm an angel on all fours, with a child's feet behind me, seeking my people that have never been made, going down face foremost, drinking the *waters of night* at the water hole of the damned, and I go into the waters, up to my heart, the *terrible waters.* What do you know of me? May you pass from me, damned girl! Damned and betraying! (95)

	VEHICLE	TENOR
1.	dark door	night
2.	night	X
3.	night	X
4.	[sg.] has been going on for a long time	night
5.	[sg.] I've never known before	it [night]
6.	life	night
7.	tree of dourest tree hardest tree	night
8.	into which his beloved goes	night
9.	night of nights	Jenny Petherbridge metonymy
10.	sea	night
11.	thousand eyes into one eye	night
12.	added shutter	night
13.	waters of terrible waters	night

Summarizing the result of the chart, the following metaphorical statements can be made on night.

X is night — is dark door
— has been going on for a long time
— Nora has never known before
— life
— tree
— into which his beloved goes
— sea
— added shutter
— waters

In the second and third sentence, *night* is the vehicle and the tenor is missing (X). This missing tenor is the subject of the conversation on night. In the other cases, *night* is the tenor which has to be understood in the pictorial term of the vehicle. Since the constituents of the metaphor are not exchangeable (*Achilles is a lion* is different from *The lion is an Achilles*), the vehicles referring to night, as a tenor, will not directly refer to the missing tenor (X) of the *night* as a vehicle. Because of the irreversible character of metaphors, and the switch between *night* as a tenor and *night* as a vehicle, the X (which is the main core of the conversation) can never be entirely comprehensible.

The vehicles of the tenor *night* raise obstacles creating a new metaphorical conception of night. My working hypothesis was not correct. It is not possible to find an underlying metaphorical concept, a conceptual metaphor that embraces all these poetic metaphors. It seems that these metaphors try to avoid the description. They refuse to give an answer, even a metaphorical answer to the question *what is night like?* What can be understood as night? Now, we are faced with metaphors that refuse the attempt to find a common ground, though they all refer to the same tenor. They do not create an independent metaphoric life-conception, a NIGHT IS SOMETHING conceptual metaphor. The characteristics that can be attributed to all of them can only be of a negative character; they are the metaphors that do not belong to the day/night opposition. Therefore, while escaping from the oppositional structure, they create another opposition. We are again in the trap of dichotomy,the figure of opposition was repeated.

On the other hand, we cannot deny the existence of these powerful linguistic metaphors that contribute significantly to the imagistic structure of *Nightwood*. Vehicles such as sea, tree, water, door are very familiar everyday images. They are not at all alien to the reader. In front of us, we have very familiar metaphors which refuse to answer the what-is-night question. We are aware of the existence of something and we do not know what it is. To understand these metaphors, the interpreter may have to change the approach and reformulate the question. The way of understanding must be to change the frame of comprehension. The pattern of reframing the frame is repeated and observable here, again, on the level of interpretation. The reader has to reframe the question, "What is night?"

In the following paragraphs, I examine the metaphors in a different way. I will analyze them separately and then try to find a common principle amongst them.

> To think of the acorn it is necessary to become the tree. And the tree of night is the hardest tree to mount, the dourest tree to scale, the most difficult of branch, the most febrile to the touch, and sweats a resin and drips a pitch against the palm that computation has not gambled. (83)

While reading this metaphoric chain I have to face the difficulty that its interpretation needs a wider context. The passages before and after this text seem relevant to understanding the metaphors. But these texts also create their contexts. The doctor's stream of speech is constructed in a way that it refuses meaning as concentrated in words and sentences.

Moreover, it refuses the readers' attempt to delineate the subject. When one tries to analyze a certain passage, it turns out that the passage is growing. It is not possible to distinguish one part of the text from the other. The whole text — just like a poem — with its network of references creates a certain meaning. The above metaphor (to think of the acorn...) has to be situated in a wider context:

> We swoon with the thickness of our own tongue when we say, I love you, as in the eye of a child lost a long while will be found the contraction of that distance—a child going small in the claws of a beast, coming furiously up the furlongs of the iris. We are but skin about a wind, with muscles clenched against mortality. We sleep in a long reproachful dust against ourselves. We are full to gorge with our names for misery. Life, the pastures in which the night feeds and prunes the cud that nourishes us to despair. Life, the permission to know death. We were created that the earth might be made sensible of her inhuman taste; and love that the body might be so dear that even the earth should roar with it. Yes, we who are full to the gorge with misery should look well around, doubting everything seen, done, spoken, precisely because we have a word for it, and not its alchemy.
>
> To think of the acorn it is necessary to become the tree. And the tree of night is the hardest tree to mount, the dourest tree to scale, the most difficult of branch, the most febrile to the touch, and sweats a resin and drips a pitch against the palm that computation has not gambled. Gurus, who, I trust you know, are Indian teachers, expect you to contemplate on the acorn ten years at a stretch, and if, in that time, you are not wiser about the nut, you are not very bright, and that may be the only certainty with which you will come away, which is a post-graduate melancholy—for no man can find a greater truth than his kidney will allow. (83-84)

Reading these metaphors in a wider context the *night* could be interpreted as the long process of human existence, lives after lives, generations after generations. Whenever the individual has the chance to experience this everlasting long process of being itself, he or she experiences very special, elevating moments, which are at the same time miserable, since they recall the feeling of mortality, of being excluded from the everlasting process. The bodily experience of love is life and death experienced at the same time, the experience of belonging to the course of being and experience of its temporality. "We were created that the earth might be made sensible of her inhuman taste; and love that the body might be so dear that even the earth should roar with it." This experience of the totality of being as suffering cannot be put into words, since this is partly beyond human scale, human categories are not appropriate to them, thus giving a name to this complex bodily experience is nothing else than misunderstanding. "Yes we who are full to gorge with misery should look well around, doubting everything seen, done, spoken, precisely because we have a word for it, and not its alchemy." If I take the acorn as a metaphor of individual life, the way to understand it is to experience it being itself. To understand Robin's behavior, first Nora has to have some idea of it being itself, which is a very difficult and painful process. The way to acquire this knowledge goes through suffering that is the experience of the hopeless love towards Robin.

The next metaphor, night as a sea again argues for a contextual understanding.

> "But," said one fellow, "it's the face that you tell by. Faces is it! I screamed, the face is for fools. If you fish by the face you fish out trouble, but there's always other fish

> when you deal with the sea. The face is what anglers catch in the daylight, but the sea is the night!" (93)

In my interpretation, the sea is again the metaphor of being, the metaphor of the living environment of all the different kinds of fish. Night also stands for a different way of understanding which takes into consideration as many aspects as possible. There are many fish, there are many aspects to account for. If someone thinks in terms of complexity instead of concentrating on a delineated subject, he or she will understand the most of his subject, will find many fish that are situated in the sea.

In metaphor number eleven, instead of saying *what* is the night, the glance which looks to the nights is described. The direction is given instead of the thing. Women who are looking for love when the day is over experience this feeling. Instead of naming the feeling itself, the metaphor refers to the experience by telling in a wider context who feels this and in what circumstances they feel it. In this way the metaphor could verbalize a complex life-experience that is unsayable in the sense that it rejects the direct question, "what is night like?"

The last *metaphors* of the *out*-group I examine are the following:

> Have I not shut my eyes with the *added shutter of the night* and put my hand out? "And it is the same with girls" he said "those who *turn the day into night*, the young, the drug addict, the profligate, the drunken and the most miserable, the lover who watches all *night* long in fear and anguish. These can never again live the life of the day. When one meets them at high noon they give off, as if it were a protective emanation, something dark and muted. The *light* does not become them any longer." (94)

The clause *put my hand out* refers to a blind man who is able to keep direction by putting his hand out. The adjective *added* relates to an additional feature of night that the day may not have. *Shut my hand* is a deliberate action of the doctor as if he would change his perception from seeing into another field of sensation. Night in this sense is the metaphor of an inside seeing, the way the blind perceive the world. Giving up seeing is to have another insight of the world. Night in this metaphor is to see that which cannot be seen, to understand the inner feature of things. There is a conceptual analogy of understanding without seeing between the doctor in the above sentence and Gloucester's words in King Lear.

Cornwall, Regan's husband, gouges out Gloucester's eyes. Then he informs Gloucester that it was Edmund who betrayed him. At that moment, when Gloucester loses his sight, he sees what happened in the past. He mistreated his son, Edgar.

> Old Man: You cannot see your way
> Gloucester: I have no way and therefore want no eyes;
> I stumbled when I saw. Full of this seen,

Our means secure us and our mere defects
Prove our commodities. Ah! dear son Edgar
The food of thy abused father's wrath;
Might I but live to see thee in my touch,
I'd say I had eyes again. (IV,1, 18-24)

Later on, King Lear and Gloucester meet, they recognize each other, despite the madness of the one and the blindness of the other.

Lear: Read.
Glou: What! with the case of eyes?
Lear: O, ho! are you there with me? No eyes in your head, nor no money in your purse? Your eyes are in a heavy case, your purse in a light: yet you see how this world goes.
Glou: I see it feelingly.
Lear: What! art mad? A man may see how this world goes with no eyes. (IV, 4, 147-155)

When the doctor purposely shuts his eyes and puts his hand out, he wants to "see feelingly" how the blinds see. The further metaphors *turn the day into night*, and can never again *live the life of the day*, return again to the day/night, good/bad opposition, but already together with this additional meaning, "night" is not only the negative side of lightness, but also a different way of perception. The lover who watches all night long, who sees feelingly, is not only the one who suffers, who is on the negative side of normalcy, but also the one who has a different conceptualization of life which can be seen from her unique perspective.

After analyzing separately the metaphors of the *out*-group, it is possible to say something on *night* as an independent concept of the oppositional views of life. *Night* is a complex notion which cannot be described by characteristics, cannot be understood in terms of another notion. In my interpretation *night* is the metaphor of being, as well as the individual experience of being. Also, *night* is the metaphor of the perspective of the individual who views his or her life from the aspect of being.

This "night" perspective provides a different kind of knowledge: other than defining and describing, other than metaphorical understanding. This understanding is an intuitive comprehension, "seeing feelingly," as well as a contextual comprehension. This is understanding the part in relation to the whole, in the same way the acorn belongs to the tree, and the fish to the sea. This belonging is a necessary component of their characteristics. The night-metaphors of the *out*-group resist the search for a common semantic field because what is common to them is exactly the refusal of the delineation and description of the object as a cognitive approach. Night is not a concept, but a meta-concept, not a certain idea to which the linguistic metaphor provides the approach, but it is the approach, a complex epistemological notion: understanding intuitively and feelingly the part in the context while reframing that context. *Night* continually recurs in a new context. During this repetitive process the reader acquires a certain understanding of night, just like one acquires language, while in the meantime his or her notion of understanding is reformulated by the "night-metaphors."

II.

In this section I would like to give an interpretation of the novel from the perspective of the reevaluated conceptions of life examined in the first part. Considering the problematic aspects of metaphoric language and comprehension suggested by *Nightwood*, we can have a closer understanding of the strangest part of the novel: the final chapter.

The doctor's metaphoric way of speaking is very difficult to follow. There is always a disturbance in communication which makes visible the problems of metaphor itself. The shocking repetition of metaphors, and with it, the constant repetition of disturbance in communication makes metaphors, as a cognitive means of language, problematic. Paul de Man refers to a similar phenomenon in Rilke's poem "Am Rande der Nacht." In his interpretation, the poem which is "the example of the most classical metaphors" at the same time makes questionable the figural potential of language (de Man, 37).

Many philosophers have argued that there is a close relation between metaphor and the metaphysical philosophical tradition. Nietzsche claimed that tropes are not only linguistic modes, among others, but they characterize language as such. Therefore we experience reality metaphorically. The "truth" of our culture is nothing other than metaphorical understanding (Nietzsche, 180). Paul de Man emphasizes the tight relation between metaphysics, language and rhetoric in Nietzsche's case, claiming that the "key to Nietzsche's critique of metaphysics [...] lies in the rhetorical model of trope or, if one prefers to call it that way, in literature as the language most explicitly grounded in rhetoric" (de Man, 109). Heidegger's metaphoric categories remind us to take into consideration the way metaphors shape philosophical discourse (Harries, 83). Moreover, metaphysics itself — claims Derrida — has been constructed on metaphors.

> [...] This whole philosophical delimitation of metaphor is already constructed and worked upon by metaphors. How could a piece of knowledge or language be clear or obscure *properly speaking*? Now all the concepts which have played a part in the definition of metaphor always have an origin and a force which are themselves metaphorical." (Derrida, 54)

Paul de Man argues for the recognition of the power of figural language in philosophical discourse. After analyzing Locke's and Condillac's Essays he concludes : "All philosophy is condemned, to the extent that it is dependent upon figuration, to be literary and, as the depository of this very problem, all literature is to some extent philosophical." (de Man, 28)

Frank Ankersmit claims that there is a close connection between metaphorical perception and Kantian transcendentalism. He points out two basic similarities between the structure of metaphor and that of transcendentalism.

> First, cognitively speaking, the two function in a similar way. For both enable us to organize (our knowledge of) (the chaotic manifold of) the world, and both the metaphorical point of view and the transcendental subject do this organizing by withdrawing from the world or from the knowledge of the world that is organized by either of them. [...] But there is still another, less formal but perhaps because of that even more important similarity between transcendentalism and metaphor. [...] This striving to familiarize the unfamiliar, to make us feel "at home" in this world, to effect a kind of Stoic "oikeioosis," can also be attributed to both transcendentalism and metaphor. [...] metaphor always invites us to see a less familiar system in terms of a more familiar system. "Familiarization" truly is at the heart of metaphor. (Ankersmit, 158-159).

Accepting the above argumentation about the relation between metaphor and metaphysics, it follows that a novel which challenges metaphors, challenges the transcendentalist tradition as well.

Some of the night-metaphors of the *out*-group explicitly challenge familiarization when they undermine the tenor-vehicle relation within their own structure since the traditional function of the vehicle is to make familiar the unfamiliar notion of the tenor. The vehicles of the sixth and tenth cases (*life* is night, and *sea* is night) have extremely wide connotations, so they cannot function to make an unfamiliar idea accessible. The notions of life and sea have so many aspects that they cannot provide a specific view of night. Secondly, the notions of *door* and *shutter* in the first and twelfth metaphor refer to a certain relation, but they do not say anything about the thing itself. Therefore, as vehicles, they do not complete the function of familiarization. Thirdly, in the seventh and thirteenth sentences, the metaphors following the night-metaphor (tree of night and water of night) are referring back to the vehicle (*tree* and *water*) instead of the tenor, night: "And the *tree of night* is the hardest *tree* to mount, the dourest tree to scale, the most difficult of branch...". Thus, while a long metaphoric elaboration is going on about night, the emphasis is subtly shifted from the tenor to the vehicle, from night to tree. Similarly, the metaphors after *waters of night* refer to water, the vehicle, but not *night*, the tenor.

The subversion of metaphorical understanding points at its own imperfection and opens up another way of comprehension, in exactly the way that the metaphorical process is lacking. The incompleteness of metaphorical discourse by virtue of what it lacks suggests another kind of comprehension: experience. It is the bodily experience of love that does not fit the familiarization logic of metaphor. This is what the metaphor, by definition, always lacks. Experience cannot be domesticated, cannot be understood in terms of another thing. Experience can only be understood by itself. The textual problem of expressing something which refuses expression, saying the unsayable is also solved in this way. The unsayable experience is involved in the text as the lack of metaphorical speech.

Night calls upon the association of "deficiency" as well. The repetition of the image of "night as deficient" provides the continuous presence of the unsayable entity and experience. In this way the unsayable sexual attraction which is the main motivation in the character's relation is always present though never addressed explicitly. This presence/absence play in the text corresponds to Nora's and the others' situations: Robin is always present and never present in their lives.

The self-destructing metaphorical speech of the Doctor suggests experience as an alternative comprehension versus the transformative logic of metaphor. Ankersmit's argument on the notion of experience is in accordance with this poetic thought suggested by the novel. Ankersmit claims that Aristotle's notion of experience may enable us to overcome the transcendentalist tradition. Whereas the transcendentalist subject appropriates or domesticates the world, in the sense that it transforms the world after its own image, perception as conceived by Aristotle shows precisely the opposite tendency since it is the senses or the mind that take on the form of the objects of the outside world (Ankersmit, 196).

The night-metaphors of the *out*-group follow the logic of experiential perception since the metaphorical process actually goes from tenor to vehicle, and not from vehicle to tenor. This subverts further the traditional structure of metaphor and metaphoric comprehension. When Nora asks Doctor, "I have come to ask you to tell me everything you know about the night," she has already known the night, since she has already experienced it — and so has the Doctor. Both have to know the night before they can begin to talk about it. Earlier I pointed out that in the tenor/vehicle structure of the *out*-group, an incomprehensible X value is necessarily present. This X is outside of the metaphorical language system because it comes from the characters' previous experience. The metaphorical conversation on night is an experiment to transform the always escaping experience into the domesticating pattern of language and metaphor.

By considering the inseparable togetherness of the problems of metaphoricity, language and metaphysics, we may have a better understanding of the last chapter of *Nightwood.* Nora does not have the right approach to Robin. The domestication is not successful in her case. She cannot make contact with her even when she follows her into the Parisian nights. The only thing that she can do is to wait until she comes back. She cannot keep her, she can not make Robin return to her. The metaphorical and linguistic logic of appropriation cannot help. The long discussions with the doctor do not relieve her either, since these are basically interpretation, or in other words, familiarization of what has happened. The only possibility for their reunion to occur is if Robin returns. Her return can be interpreted as the metaphor of an anti-metaphor, the metaphor of the experiential knowledge when the direction of comprehension is reversed: the mind takes on the form of the perceived objects. Nora gets Robin back after years of torment, during which she has learned that there is no direct route from Robin to her, no way of domestication.

The barking scene can be seen as a ritual homecoming to the always repressed but always present undomesticated part of human personality and human culture. Robin's return is a pathetic moment. Her presence makes the woods silent, as if a goddess has arrived.

> Sometimes she slept in the woods; *the silence that she had caused by her coming* was broken again by insect and bird flowing back over her intrusion... As *she had frightened the woods into silence by her breathing*, the barking of the dog brought her up, rigid and still. (169)

The figure of Robin (her boyish appearance and the dog motifs) recalls the figure of Artemis and the story of Acteon (Scott, 104). Robin is the one upon whom no one should look; she cannot be domesticated. Whoever tries to impose on her has to be punished. The last scene of barking recalls the ancient myth. The experience of Robin's return cannot be expressed with words. Nora is silent when Robin and her dog are barking at each other.

> Then she [Robin] began to bark also, crawling after him - barking in a fit of laughter, obscene and touching. The dog began to cry then, running with her, head-on with her head, as if to circumvent her; soft and slow his feet went padding. He ran this way and that, low down in his throat crying, and she grinning and crying with him; crying in shorter and shorter spaces, moving head to head, until she gave up, lying out, her hands beside her, her face turned and weeping; and the dog too gave up then, and lay down, his eyes bloodshot, his head flat along her knees. (170)

The elementary experience of the return of the lover has no verbal referents. The familiarizing logic of language is inappropriate in this case. Robin's desperate barking does not fit in the "symbolic order" of language; however, it is an elementary emotion that movingly presents itself and cries for getting accepted into human communication. The final scene closes the whole novel and at the same time presents a final metaphor that illustrates the artistic effort occurring throughout the novel. *Nightwood*, always at the border of language, desperately argues for the recognition of a suppressed but existing component of western culture. A component that is out of language and out of domestication but exists as a non-category in the heart of human nature.

Accordingly, Robin's fight with the dog can be read as a certain kind of homecoming to the undomesticated life. Robin returns to her lover at night in the woods. This is at the same time a metaphorical return to the undomesticated world, the wilderness of nature and the wilderness of human nature. The metaphors *night* and *wood* meet each other in the final chapter.

The narrative structure of the novel supports the idea of a "homecoming." The first four chapters contain the narratives of five people. The next three chapters are basically dialogical interpretations of their stories without the help of the narrator, during which, the characters, especially Nora, learn a different conception of life and knowledge. The last bizarre scene, when the narrator returns again, can be understood from the perspective formulated by the dialogues. It is as if the narrator would lead the reader "to the other side" from which the final scene is becoming comprehensible. The narratee has to go through a long detour until she finds herself home again, in the familiar storytelling situation. Looking at the scene from the new perspective, the reader can interpret it. The "homecoming" scene is at the same time a "homecoming" in the reading experience.

The last chapter, "The Possessed," elaborates further on the possible denotations of the metaphor *nightwood.* There is a play between the literal and metaphorical meaning, since the lovers actually meet at night in the woods. On the other hand, *nightwood* is a compound word, both of its elements involve numerous meanings, as I illustrated in section I. Their encounter makes these meanings even richer. When the *night,* as a certain comprehension, is connected with *wood* as wilderness, it suggests the interpretation that the *night*-way of life and way of comprehension has led to a recogniton and return to the wild side of our personality and culture. When *wood* is read as being lost and linked to *night* as the perception of reframing the frame, the difference between the two metaphoric concepts disappears, since reframing the frame is always a kind of being lost. These two different readings are covered by the same metaphor. This allows for an interpretation in which the two alternatives complete each other: being lost in space and mind is at the same time a homecoming, a cultural experience and a return to the forgotten side of life.

Conclusion

After analyzing the night-metaphors in *Nightwood,* I concluded that the metaphors, based on the LIFETIME IS A DAY and the related oppositional concepts, undermine the opposition while keeping the duality of day/night, good/bad and light/dark. Metaphors that did not fit in the above concepts did not create new conceptual metaphors of life, and thus created an oppositional relation to the others. In this way the opposition which was undermined as a basic thinking pattern of western culture, was repeated again.

On the other hand, night-metaphors of the *out*-group offered a conception of life which is at the same time a conception of knowledge. Life can be viewed as a participation in the chain of being which, at the same time, gives a certain perspective of the individual life. This perspective provides a new way of comprehension. The continuous repetition of night-metaphors helps the reader to experience this new way of comprehension.[1]

Pleasure and suffering are not distinguishable in the novel. Love as well as suffering are important means of knowledge just like rationality, therefore they undermine the basic Western oppositions of body and mind. The novel puts into the foreground a lesbian love which is itself considered alternative within western culture.

Taking everything into consideration, the concept provided by the night-metaphors and the modified version of LIFE IS A JOURNEY metaphor suggest a wider and more complex notion of life than the traditionally accepted ones. They argue for the acceptance of an alternative conceptualization of life and knowledge within Western culture. Nora's literal questions and the doctor's metaphorical answers, their understandings and misunderstandings, make visible the problems of literal speech as well as metaphorical speech. The metaphor as a linguistic and conceptual phenomenon, built on duality and familiarization, is also challenged by the novel.

On the other hand, we should not overlook the fact that the subversion of the familiarizing logic of metaphor occured within metaphoric language. It follows that metaphoricity has other potentials than familiarization. While deconstructing the familiarizing aspect of metaphoric languge, *Nightwood* created a new insight on knowledge. The novel supports the argument of Ankersmit to a certain extent, but it extends it as well. Familiarization is, indeed, very important in the metaphoric language of *Nightwood.* If it were not, its deconstruction would not be possible. At the same time, the metaphoric discussion on night creates a new concept on knowledge. This supports the views that claim that metaphor creates new insights.

The ongoing discourse on knowledge in *Nightwood* is simultaneously a discourse *on* metaphor. This inseparable togetherness of knowledge and metaphor in the novel is in accordance with the recent studies on metaphor that suggest that metaphoric process is an omnipresent principle of cognition.

1. The novel has a very contradictory relation to western values and thinking patterns. The denial of LIFE IS A JOURNEY concerns at the same time a very biblical figure: finding the point in life when one steps out of LIFE IS A JOURNEY can be interpreted as a kind of revelation — as Hent de Vries called to my attention. Also, the reasoning pattern that the way to understanding is to reframe our own frame of understanding, is a basic pattern of thought of biblical tradition.

References

Alphen, Ernst van, *Affective Reading: Loss of Self in Djuna Barnes's* Nightwood. Unpublished manuscript. University of Leiden, Department of Comparative Literature 1992.

Ankersmit, F.R. "Kantian narrativism and beyond" *The Point of Theory: Practices of Cultural Analysis.* ed. Mieke Bal and Inge E. Boer. New York: Continuum/Amsterdam: Amsterdam University Press 1994, 155-197.

Barnes, Djuna, *Nightwood.* New York: New Direction Publishing Company 1961.

Black, Max, *Metaphor In Philosophical Perspectives on Metaphor.* ed. Mark Johnson. Minneapolis: University of Minnesota Press 1981, 63-82.

Derrida, Jacques, "White Mythology" *New Literary History* 6, 1974, 5-74..

Field, Andrew, *Djuna: The Life and Times of Djuna Barnes.* New York: G.P. Putnams Sons.1983

Frank, Joseph, *The Widening Gyre: Crisis and Mastery in Modern Literature.* Bloomington: Indiana University Press 1968.

Harries, Karsten "Metaphor and Transcendence" in *On Metaphor.* ed. Sheldon Sacks. Chicago and London: The University of Chicago Press 1979, 71-88.

Lakoff, G. and Johnson, M., *Metaphors We Live By.* Chicago: University of Chicago Press 1980.

Lakoff, G. and Turner, M., *More Than Cool Reason: A Field Guide to Poetic Metaphor.* Chicago: Chicago University Press 1989.

MacCormac, Earl R. *A Cognitive Theory of Metaphor.* Cambridge and Massachusetts: The MIT Press 1985.

Man, Paul de, *Allegories of Reading: Figural Language in Rousseau, Nietzsche, Rilke and Proust.* New Haven and London: Yale University Press 1979;

Man, Paul de, "The Epistemology of Metaphor" in *On Metaphor.* Ed. Sheldon Sacks. Chicago and London: The University of Chicago Press 1978, 11-28.

Minter, David, *A Cultural History of the American Novel: Henry James to William Faulkner.* New York: Cambridge University Press 1994 .

Nietzsche, Frederick "On Truth and Falsity in Their Ultramoral Sense" (1873) in *The Completed Works of Frederick Nietzsche.* Ed.Oscar Levy., Trans. Maximilian A. Magge. New York: Gordon Press 1974.

Prince, Gerald "Introduction to the Study of Narratee" in: *Reader-Response Criticism.*ed. Jane P. Tompkins. Baltimore: Johns Hopkins University Press 1980, 7-25.

Richards, I.A. "The Philosophy of Rhetoric" (1936) in *Philosophical Perspective on Metaphor.* ed. Mark Johnson. Minneapolis: University of Minnesota Press 1981, 48-62.

Ricoeur, Paul *The Rule of Metaphor: Multi-Disciplinary Studies of the Creation of Meaning in Language.* London: Routlege and Kegan Paul 1979.

Scott, James B. *Djuna Barnes.* Boston: Twayne 1976.

Steen, Gerald *Metaphor in Literary Reception: A Theoretical and Empirical Study of Understanding Metaphor in Literary Discourse.* Amsterdam: Free University of Amsterdam Press 1992;

Steen, Gerald, *Understanding Metaphor in Literature.* London and New York: Longman House 1994.

Szegedy-Maszak, Mihly, "The Unsolvable Mystery", Afterword for the Hungarian translation of *Nightwood.* Trans. Janos Szeky. Pozsony: Kalligram Press 1994 , 157-165.

Introduction: Slavoj Žižek

Thomas Elsaesser

In May 1995, ASCA welcomed Slavoj Žižek, philosopher, roving ambassador and Lacanian cultural analyst from the Republic of Slovenia. Žižek is the noted author of such intriguing titles as *The Sublime Object of Ideology* (1989), *Looking Awry* (1991), *Tarrying with the Negative* (1993), *The Metastases of Enjoyment* (1994), not forgetting his *Everything You Always Wanted to Know About Lacan But Were Afraid to Ask Hitchcock* and *Enjoy Your Symptom!* (both 1992).

Such a prolific publication output and Žižek's presence on the international conference circuit has been a double-edged introduction to his work. He has put his native city on the map, and the first time I met Žižek was indeed in Ljubljana, at the end of a conference in which he participated by virtue of the fact that his imminent arrival was both constantly announced and constantly deferred. On the last day, we were having our farewell dinner at a restaurant, when the hum of conversation audibly hushed and a burly figure entered, making a certain few of the guests rise from their chairs as if pulled up by a tornado's awesome sweep. Žižek immediately settled down to an animated exchange with one of them, seemingly oblivious to the rest. Minutes later he stood up to move to another table. This was repeated another four or five times, with — let me call these well-known personalities "Vienna," "Los Angeles," "Paris" and "New York" — each waiting for a turn. When he came to our table, he immediately involved us in an intricate debate, about the open mouth of Bernini's St Theresa in Rome, before dashing off and returning to "Paris" and "Vienna," no doubt picking up his controversial contention about the war in Bosnia being a 21st century war and not a 19th century leftover, or taking John Rawls' concept of "distributive justice" to task for having no viable concept of the state.

Like the Grand Master at a chess tournament, Žižek clearly relished playing several sets of opponents simultaneously, and while we were mulling over his last move, we could hear further down the table a burst of laughter or a stifled groan at yet another outrageous suggestion or fiendish paradox that Žižek was tossing to his partners. This flamboyance and improvisatory brilliance has no doubt contributed to Žižek's reputation as "a one-person culture mulcher," or "the best intellectual High since Anti-Oedipus," which in turn is probably the greatest barrier to a more sustained engagement with his thought. Now that the first flush of international excitement has died down over this exotic phenomenon — an intellectual from the "East" (from former Yugoslavia, no less) who seems to know the "West" better than the West knows itself — it would certainly be worthwhile to give both his style of thought, and the overlapping fields he has mapped out for himself, a moment of reflection.

For if ASCA's task is to promote interdisciplinary research without pretending to recover some lost golden age of the unity of human knowledge, and instead develop the boundary areas between disciplines, at the points where insights can be generated and new energies be set free, then Žižek's agenda is clearly germane to ASCA's aims and aspirations. Each of his books sets up a number of sites of struggle, of battle-zones in the fields of politics and the arts, high culture and the movies, airport novels and Wagnerian opera, and each site — rather like the tables at the restaurant in Ljubljana — gets revisited in turn, in book after book. Often, one is not quite sure whether Žižek revisits them, like a firefighter dousing the flames with Kant and Kierkegaard, or like an arsonist kindling dying embers back to life with some inflammatory material from Stephen King or Wilhelm Worringer.

Yet it is especially at the methodological cutting edge of ASCA, where the contending paradigms of "analysis" and "interpretation" are rubbing against each other like tectonic plates, that Žižek's contribution might be seen as most stimulating. For here is someone who, in the full knowledge of all the philosophical critiques mounted against it, and all the political caveats many times expressed, vigorously wants to reinstate psychoanalysis as the most pertinent hermeneutics in our present situation. Noting how the doubts about the adequacy, and dissent over the direction of Freudian "politics of the subject" have constituted the intellectual energies of very diverse currents, from post-structuralism to schizo-politics, from feminism to the new historicism, Žižek nonetheless claims that a fundamental "misunderstanding" is at work.

This misunderstanding might be said to hinge on the widespread assumption that psychoanalysis is, in Paul Ricoeur's terms, a "hermeneutics of suspicion," an interpretation machine that not only works with, but is driven by binary thinking, in which surface and depth, the hidden and the manifest, the inside and the outside render any effort at "analysis" a vain game of mirrors, reinstating "full subjects." Into this conceptual architecture, Žižek never fails to re-introduce what he considers to be the self-evident force of which psychoanalysis is the trace, namely an a-symmetry and incommensurability at work at all levels, which both holds together what we call culture, and makes it the ultimately tragic endeavor it must remain in the face of both life and death.

This is perhaps why the notion of the "symptom" occupies such a key place in Žižek's thinking. It would lead too far to go into the aetiology of this term in either Jacques Lacan's or Žižek's thinking, but let us retain that the symptom, that originary mark on the (female, hysterical) body with which psychoanalysis began to initiate its "dialogue," is, precisely, not a manifestation to which a hidden depth corresponds, but something that has always, like ornament, engaged the surface, seducing the observer into imagining the hidden, the veiled, the yet-to-be-revealed. And when Žižek calls upon his readers to "enjoy your symptom," he is above all inviting the sideways glance, the anamorphotic relationship, operating not as a geometry or an order of representation, but as an intermittence, an unassimilable something, a remainder which is at once a resistance and an excess. Interpretation, conducted as cultural analysis, must, like the "sexual relationship" Žižek discusses in his lecture, remember the a-symmetry built into it, which alone dignifies it with the name of love. Similarly, Žižek's reprise of the Lacanian concern with desire and the Other not only applies to these filmic texts he unfolds and enfolds before our eyes, but offers a meditation precisely on what ASCA has made its very raison d'etre: to be vigilant of boundaries being drawn where none exist, and of distinctions not being made where they have to be introduced.

When the venerable Dutch literary journal *De Gids* devoted an issue to Žižek, the Amsterdam newspaper *de Volkskrant* ran a review spiked with sarcastic remarks, to the effect that readers of literary magazines must be heavily into S/M to allow the editors "to spank them regularly with leathery bits of psychoanalysis." As a comment on enlightened liberalism "enjoyment of its symptoms," this is not so far off the Žižekian mark, contrary to what the reviewer might have intended. But in reply to the *Volkskrant*, let me borrow an old Marx Brothers joke: Žižek may be announced as an important thinker; he may even be hyped as an important thinker, but make no mistake, he is an important thinker. Engaged in profanations, perhaps along the lines of Kierkegaard's paradoxes of faith, where the sacred is only to be invoked by virtue of its obverse, or in the sense that graffiti-like defacements have been known to tear down walls, not least because irreverence is sometimes the highest form of tribute, Žižek's fondness for the "grimaces of the real" have brought some much needed *gravitas* to the business of living "between two deaths," as our fin-de-siecle struggles with the "new world order."

SEXUAL RELATIONSHIP IN THE AGE OF VIRTUAL REALITY

Slavoj Žižek

A recent English publicity spot for a beer renders perfectly the asymmetry in the relationship between the sexes. Its first part stages the well-known fairy-tale anecdote: a girl walks along a stream, sees a frog, takes it gently into her lap, kisses it, and, of course, the ugly frog miraculously turns into a beautiful young man. However, the story isn't over yet: the young man casts a covetous glance at the girl, draws her towards himself, kisses her — and she turns into a bottle of beer the man triumphantly holds in his hand. For the woman, the point is that her love and affection (signalled by the kiss) turn a frog into a beautiful man, a full phallic presence (in Lacan's mathems, the big Phi); for the man, it is to reduce the woman to a partial object, the cause of his desire (in Lacan's mathems, the object small a). On account of this asymmetry, "there is no sexual relationship": we have either a woman with a frog or a man with a bottle of beer — what we can never obtain is the "natural" couple of the beautiful woman and man.

Two recent films, Kieslowski's *A Short Film on Love* and Sautet's *A Heart in Winter*, both endeavour to render this asymmetry by means of the male gesture of rejection, of refusal to engage in sexual commerce; however, as we shall see, the scope of the two gestures is almost exactly opposed.

There is an unexpected formal homology between the two central instalments (5 and 6) of Kieslowski's Decalogue, *A Short Film on Killing* and *A Short Film on Love*: in both cases, we are dealing with a failed metaphoric reversal-substitution. The second act, instead of accomplishing a successful "sublation / *Aufhebung*" of the first act (by way of compensating for its damage and reestablishing the lost balance), actually makes things worse by ending up as a repetition of the first act. In *A Short Film on Killing*, a young unemployed man commits the brutal and meaningless murder of a taxi-driver; the second part then renders in painful detail the trial and the execution of the murderer. This rendering of the machinery of law at work is so disturbing because it registers the failure of the "metaphor of Law," i.e. of the metaphoric substitution of the punishment for the crime: the punishment is not experienced as just retribution that undoes the harm brought about by the crime, but rather as its uncanny repetition — the act of punishment is somehow tainted by an additional obscenity that makes it a travesty, an obscene repetition of the original crime in the guise of Law. *A Short Film on Love* is also a film about a failed metaphoric substitution, the substitution (of the beloved for the loving one) that, according to Lacan, defines love. From his bedroom in a large dreary concrete apartment block, Tomek, a young postal clerk, each evening and night spies on Maria Magdalena [*sic*], a mature, sexually attractive and promiscuous woman who lives in the same block, opposite Tomek's backyard. His activity is not limited to passively observing her sexual prowess in dealing with her numerous lovers; step by step, he intervenes in her life, sending her false notices of money-orders so that she will come to his window in the post office, calling plumbers to her apartment in the middle of her love-making, etc. When, finally, he gathers courage, contacts her and discloses that he is the source of her recent nuisances, her curiosity is aroused. She entices him into a humiliating sexual game which ends in his attempted suicide. After his return from the hospital, their respective roles are reversed: stirred by her guilt, she "stretches out her hand," constantly observes his window from her apartment, frantically endeavours to attract his attention in order to make him come to her again and so as to offer him her apologies, whereas he now ignores her. In short, the metaphor of love fails, when the beloved object turns into the loving one, she is no longer loved.

A closer analysis renders visible a fundamental ambiguity that pertains to this film, an ambiguity that becomes fully visible in the crucial difference between the two versions of *A Short Film on Love*, the original 60 minutes TV version and the 90 minutes version for the theatrical release. The longer version ends up in a kind of Catholic reconciliation and compassion (with Maria sitting by Tomek's bed, silently holding his hand, the implication of it being that a kind of spiritual contact took place between the two beyond the self-destructive dialectic of sexuality), whereas in the TV version, their encounter remains failed, non-synchronized. In this precise sense, *A Short Film on Love* is the stage of a "class struggle" in art, the battleground of the two lines, the irreconciled "materialist" and the spiritualist "idealist," in dealing with the fundamental deadlock of love. When, upon their becoming acquainted, Maria asks Tomek what he effectively wants from her, a mere kiss, a little tenderness, or a full sexual act, his resolute answer is "nothing." This "nothing," of course, is the unmistakeable index of true love: Tomek is not to be satisfied with any positive content or act (going to bed with him, for example) by means of which Maria could reciprocate his love. What he wants her to offer in return is the very "nothingness" in her, what is "in her more than herself" - not something that she possesses but precisely what she does not have, the return of love itself. In response to his unconditional demand of love, Maria arouses him by offering her sexual services to him, so that, inexperienced as he is, he reaches orgasm before intercourse proper takes place, and then, triumphantly, tells him: "Now you see, this is all love is really about! Go and wash yourself in the bathroom!" This gesture of offering herself, her body, to him, effectively amounts to an act of utter rejection and/or humiliation: what she accomplished therewith is radical desublimation, i.e. she renders palpable the gap that separates the void of the Thing from the physiological functioning of sexual intercourse. In order to exemplify this gap, one is tempted to evoke the scene from Terry Gillian's *Brazil* in which, in a high-class restaurant, the waiter recommends to his customers the best offers from the daily menu ("Today, our tournedos is really special!", etc.), but what the customers get upon making their choice is a dazzling colour photo of the meal on a stand above the plate, and on the plate itself a loathsome, excremental, paste-like lump. This humiliation, this experience of the gap between the "nothingness" of the true object of love and the desublimated bodily sexual mechanism, is more than he can stand: utterly ashamed, he runs out of her apartment and cuts his veins. What follows thereupon is a shift of perspective from his to her point of view, so that, in a sense, his suicide does succeed, i.e. he totally obliterates himself as the narrative point of view. And, as we already hinted, at this point, the two versions differ: the longer one takes a Catholic turn and suggests the possibility of a compassionate solidarity beyond carnal passions, of a spiritual communion that can fill out the void of the inherent impossibility of a sexual relationship, whereas in the shorter version, the deadlock remains unresolved.

On a second look, one is compelled to state that the crucial metaphoric substitution in *A Short Film on Love* actually runs contrary to the standard substitution by means of which the loved one changes into the loving one, i.e. solves the impasse of not knowing what the other (the loving one) sees in him by returning love: the true enigma of the film is Tomek's change from the loving one into the object of Maria's love. So how does he succeed in substituting his position of the loving one with the position of the beloved? How does he capture Maria's desire? The answer, of course, resides in the very purity and absolute intensity of his love: he acts as the pure $, the subject whose desire is so burning that it cannot be translated into any concrete demand — this very intensity, because of which his desire can only express itself in the guise of a refusal of any demand ("I want nothing from you"), is what makes him irresistible. This second metaphoric substitution is not simply symmetrical to the first one: their difference hinges on the opposition of "to have" and "to be." In the first case, we are in the dimension of having (the loved one doesn't know what he has in himself that makes him worthy of the other's love, so, in order to escape this deadlock, he returns love), whereas in the second case, the loving is (becomes) the beloved object on account of the sheer intensity of his love.

What one has to reject here is the notion that Tomek's love for Maria is authentic and pure, spiritual, elevated above vulgar sensuality, whereas Maria, disturbed by this purity, intends to humiliate him and later changes her attitude out of a feeling of guilt. It is, on the contrary, Tomek's love which is fundamentally false, a narcissistic attitude of idealization whose necessary obverse is a barely concealed lethal dimension. That is to say, *A Short Film on Love* should be read against the background of slasher-films, in which a man observes and harasses a woman who traumatizes him, finally attacking her with a knife: it is a kind of introverted slasher in which the man, instead of striking at the woman, deals a blow to himself. The reason his love for Maria is not genuine does not reside in its "impure" character: the murderous burst of self-inflicted violence is the inherent obverse of its very "purity." This inauthenticity of his love is corroborated by his inability to undergo the experience of desublimation, of the splitting between the woman qua impossible-idealized Thing and the flesh-and-blood woman who offers herself to him, i.e. by the way this experience sets in motion the murderous *passage à l'acte*: the measure of true love is precisely the capacity to withstand such a splitting. Maria's love for him, in contrast, is fully authentic: from the moment Tomek tells her he wants nothing from her, true love — which, as Lacan points out, is always a love returned — is here, and her humiliation of Tomek is merely a desperate attempt to disavow this fact.

Our second example, Claude Sautet's *A Heart in Winter* (*Un coeur en hiver*), a film on the deadlocks of love from the same period, tells the story of a love triangle between two high-class violin makers and Camille, a young, beautiful and charismatic violin-player. When Camille starts to live with one of them, she thereby perturbs the well-established routine of their professional relationship. Gradually, by the help of his ambiguous, active-passive, cooperation, she falls in love with the other partner, Stephan; however, when, in a passionate outburst, she declares her love and offers herself to him, Stephan calmly explains to her that it's all a misunderstanding — maybe he was flirting a little with her, but he definitely does not love her. Stephan's character is rather enigmatic: the point is not that Camille isn't his true love, but rather that he simply feels no need for love — there is no place for love in his psychological universe. This incapacity to love accounts for the kind of inner peace and completion irradiated by his personality: unperturbed by any emotional turmoils, profoundly apathetic, he is able to devote himself fully to his craft. In other words, far from being a person whose mask of normal social functioning conceals madness, Stephan is a person who, although to an outside view he may appear "abnormal," possesses an inherent norm, measure, completeness. We are dealing here with a variation on the Lacanian motif of "non-all": what, in a way, makes him more "complete" and harmonious than "normal" people, i.e. what makes him a person who, in a way, lacks nothing, is the very aspect that appears from the outside as his deficiency or even psychic mutilation. In other words, the trap one has to avoid in analyzing Sautet's film is the search for any kind of "psychological" background or foundation that would account for Stephan's incapacity to love: there is no need here for any "psychoanalytical" reference to sexual frustrations, childhood traumas, etc. When, in the course of the film, Stephan himself evokes the possibility of such an explanation, he obviously indulges in an irony homologous to that of a neo-Nazi skinhead who is always quick to provide a socio-psychological explanation of his violence against foreigners. Stephan is an empty subject: beneath the surface of his acts there is no plenitude of "pathological" content, no secret desires and anxieties. One is tempted to draw a comparison between Stephan and Wagner's Parsifal: when, alone with Camille in his car, Stephan utters his final "Je ne vous aime pas," is he not a contemporary Parsifal who, by not giving way to the woman's advances, redeems her (enables her to pursue her artistic career)?[1] Is his subjective position, like that of Parsifal, not also marked by a radical indifference, namely indifference towards the desire of the Other? Stephan is a subject who is simply not "gnawed" by the desire of the Other, by the enigma of "Che vuoi?", of what the Other wants from me — and since (Lacan *dixit*) desire as such is the desire of the Other, one is compelled to draw the inevitable conclusion that Stephan strictly speaking is not a desiring subject, that he simply does not dwell in the dimension of desire. Therein resides the uncanny "coldness" of his character, its "flatness", the absence of any enigmatic depth. On that account, Stephan is incapable not only of love but even of common friendship, which always involves a minimum of empathy: he is able, without any hesitation, to deliver a lethal injection to his elder friend-teacher, a kind of paternal surrogate, thereby putting an end to the meaningless agony of his mortal illness. Is not this indifference towards the Other's desire strictly equivalent to what Lacan designates as "subjective destitution"?

It is against this background that one should approach the complex problem of the necessity of renunciation in an erotic relationship. Let us take as our point of reference Kierkegaard who provided the hitherto most elaborated account of this necessity. In all three Kierkegaardian "stages," aesthetic, ethical and religious, the same sacrificial gesture is at work, each time in a different "power/potential" (in Schelling's sense of the term). The religious sacrifice is a matter of course (suffice it to recall Abraham's readiness to sacrifice Isaac, Kierkegaard's supreme example), so we should concentrate on the renunciation that pertains to the "ethical" and the "aesthetic":

— The ethical stage is defined by the sacrifice of the immediate consumption of life, of our yielding to the fleeting moment, in the name of some higher universal norm. In the domain of erotics, one of the most refined examples of this renunciation is provided by Mozart's *Cosi fan tutte.* If his *Don Giovanni* embodies the Aesthetic (as was developed by Kierkegaard himself in his detailed analysis of the opera in *Either/Or*), the lesson of *Cosi fan tutte* is ethical — why? The point of *Cosi fan tutte* is that the love that unites the two couples at the beginning of the opera is no less "artificial," mechanically brought about, than the second falling in love of the sisters with the exchanged partners, dressed up as Albanian officers that results from the manipulations of the philosopher Alfonso — in both cases, we are dealing with a mechanism which the subjects follow in a blind, puppet-like way. Therein consists the Hegelian "negation of negation": first, we perceive the "artificial" love, the product of Alfonso's manipulations, as opposed to the initial "authentic" love; then, all of a sudden, we become aware that there is actually no difference between the two — the original love is no less "artificial" than the second. So, since one love counts as much as the other, the couples can return to their initial marital arrangement. Ethical is in this sense the domain of repetition qua symbolic: if, in the Aesthetic, one endeavours to capture the moment in its uniqueness, in the Ethical, a thing only becomes what it is through its repetition.[2]

— In the aesthetic stage, the seducer works on an innocent girl whom he considers worthy of his efforts, but at a crucial moment, just prior to his triumph, i.e. when for all practical purposes her surrender is already won, and the fruits of his labor have only to be reaped, he has not only to renounce the realization of the sexual act but, over and above, to induce her to drop him (by putting on the mask of a despicable person and thus arousing her disgust).[3] Why this renunciation? The realization of the process of seduction in the sexual act renders visible the goal the seducer was striving at in all its transience and vulgarity, so the only way to avoid this horror of radical "desublimation" is to stop short of it, thereby keeping awake the dream of what might have happened — by losing his love in time, the seducer gains her for eternity.[4] One must be careful here not to miss the point: the "desublimation" one tries to avoid by renouncing the act does not reside in the experience of how realization always falls short of the Ideal we were striving for, i.e. of the gap that forever separates the Ideal from its realization; in it, it is rather the Ideal itself that loses its power, that changes into repugnant slime — the Ideal is, as it were, undermined "from within." When we approach it too closely, it changes into its opposite.

The ending of Michael Curtiz' *Casablanca* (Humphrey Bogart staying in Casablanca and letting Ingrid Bergman go with her heroic husband) is so deeply satisfactory because it condenses, in one and the same gesture, these three attitudes. The first, "aesthetic" way to read Bogart's gesture is to discern in it an awareness that, although they are passionately in love, the fulfilment of their relationship (the two of them staying together) would necessarily turn sour — so it's better to maintain the dream of possible happiness. The second reading is "ethical": Bogart gives preference to the universal political Cause over the idiosyncrasy of private pleasure (and thereby proves worthy of Bergman's love). There is, however, a third possible reading which renders visible Bogart's final renunciation as a cruel narcissistic act of vengeance on Bergman, i.e. as a punishment for her letting him down in Paris: after making her confess that she truly loves him, it's now his turn to reject her in a gesture whose cynical message is "You wanted your husband — now you're stuck with him, even if you prefer me!" This very logic of vengeful, humiliating and cruel "settling of accounts" makes Bogart's final gesture "religious," and not merely "aesthetic." It is therefore wrong to ask the question "Which of these three readings is true?" — the impact of Bogart's final gesture relies precisely on the fact that it serves as a kind of neutral "container" for all three libidinal attitudes, so that one and the same gesture satisfies a multitude of inconsistent, even contradictory desires (to avoid the disappointment of realizing one's desire; to fascinate the woman by assuming a moral stance of self-sacrifice; to take revenge for a narcissistic wound).

In all three "stages," the same gesture of sacrifice is thus at work in a different "power/potential": what shifts from one to the other is the locus of impossibility. That is to say, one is tempted to claim that the triad Aesthetic-Ethical-Religious provides the matrix for the three versions of the impossibility of sexual relationship. What one would expect here is that, with the "progression" (or rather leap) from one to the next stage, the pressure of prohibition and/or impossibility gets stronger: in the Aesthetic, one is free to "seize the day," to yield to enjoyment without any restraints; in the Ethical, enjoyment is admitted, but on condition that it remains within the confines of the Law (marriage), i.e. in an aseptic, "gentrified" form that suspends its fatal charm; in the Religious, finally, there is no enjoyment, just the most radical, "irrational" renunciation, for which we get nothing in return (Abraham's readiness to sacrifice Isaac). However, this clear picture of progressive renunciation immediately gets blurred by the uncanny resemblance, noticed by many a sagacious commentator, between Abraham's sacrifice of Isaac (which, of course, belongs to the Religious) and Kierkegaard's own renunciation to Regina (which belongs to the aesthetic dialectics of seduction). On reflection, one can thus ascertain that, contrary to our expectations, the prohibition (or rather inhibition) loosens with the leap from one to the next stage: in the Aesthetic, the object is completely lost, beyond our reach, due to the inherent instability of this level: in the very gesture of our trying to lay our hands on the fleeting moment of pleasure, it slips between our fingers; in the Ethical, enjoyment is already rendered possible in a stable, regular form via the mediation of the Law; and, finally, in the Religious — what is the religious mode of the erotic, if its aesthetical mode is seduction and its ethical mode marriage? Is it at all meaningful to speak of a religious mode of erotics in the precise Kierkegaardian sense of the term? The point of Lacan is that this, precisely, is the role of courtly love: the Lady in courtly love suspends the ethical level of universal symbolic obligations and bombards us with totally arbitrary ordeals in a way which is homologous to the religious suspension of the Ethical; her ordeals are on a par with God's ordering Abraham to slaughter his son Issac. And, contrary to the first appearance that sacrifice reaches here its apogee, it is only here that, finally, we confront the Other qua Thing that gives body to the excess of enjoyment over mere pleasure. If the aesthetical endeavours to seize the full moment ends in fiasco and utter loss, paradoxically, the religious renunciation, the elevation of the Lady into an untouchable and unattainable object, leads to the trance of enjoyment that transgresses the limits of Law.

Back to Kieslowski and Sautet. These Kierkegaardian paradoxes provide the conceptual apparatus that enables us to account for the difference between *A Short Film on Love* and *A Heart in Winter.* In both films, we encounter a man's "I want nothing" which puts an obstacle in the way of sexual intercourse, i.e. both Tomek and Stephan turn down the woman's proposal, but this rejection has a totally different meaning in each case. In *A Short Film on Love,* we are dealing with "I want nothing" of the desire which aims at "the objet a" in the other: the true meaning of this "I want nothing" is "I want you absolutely, in the very kernel of your being, in the void that constitutes the elusive vortex of your subjectivity, and I am not ready to exchange it for any substitute in the guise of some positive (sexual) service." With regard to Kierkegaard, this means that Kieslowski remains within the Religious: at a level more fundamental than the Catholic communion of souls in the longer version of the film, Tomek's attitude is religious, his "I want nothing" is a desperate attempt to counteract the "debasement in the sphere of love" by way of elevating the woman to the dignity of a Thing. Sautet's Stephan, in contrast, confronts us with something incomparably more uncanny: what we have here is a man who "wants nothing" because he simply lacks nothing: he is not "gnawed" by the enigma of the Other's desire, he is fundamentally indifferent towards "objet a," the object-cause of desire, his subjectivity is not organized around a traumatic excess of the surplus-enjoyment. Why not? There is only one answer possible: because he himself occupies the place of this object. In short, the opposition between Tomek and Stephan is the opposition between $ and a, between the pure subject of desire and the "saint," somebody who has undergone "subjective destitution" and thereby turned into a pure being of drive beyond desire. What lurks in the background of this necessity of renunciation common to Tomek and Stephan is the impasse of the late-capitalist liberal-democratic permissiveness: how we are to propel again the desire to copulate today, in an age when, due to its direct accessibility, i.e. due to the lack of obstacles that would heighten its value, the sexual object is more and more depreciated — or, to quote Freud's classic formulation:

> ... the psychical value of erotic needs is reduced as soon as their satisfaction becomes easy. An obstacle is required in order to heighten libido; and where natural resistances to satisfaction have not been sufficient men have at all times erected conventional ones so as to be able to enjoy love.[5]

The point is not simply that we set up additional conventional hindrances in order to heighten the value of the object: external hindrances that thwart our access to the object are there precisely to create the illusion that without them, the object would be directly accessible — what such hindrances thereby conceal is the inherent impossibility of attaining the object. In order to render palpable this deadlock, let us for a moment turn to an example from another domain, that of the so-called "information superhighways." If, in the near future, all data, movies, etc., were to become instantly available, if the delay were to become minimal so that the very notion of "searching for" (a book, a film, etc.) were to lose meaning, would this instant availability not suffocate desire? That is to say, what sets in motion human desire is a short-circuit between the primordially lost Thing and an empirical, positive object, i.e. the elevation of this object to the dignity of the Thing — this object thus fills out the "transcendental" void of the Thing, it becomes prohibited and thereby starts to function as the cause of desire. When, however, every empirical object becomes available, this absence of the prohibition necessarily gives rise to anxiety: what becomes visible via this saturation is that the ultimate point of prohibition was simply to mask the inherent impossibility of the Thing, i.e. the structural deadlock of desire.[6]

One thing is therefore sure: the advent of cyberspace will shatter and transform beyond recognition the very basic structure of our capacity to desire, since it will lay bare the paradox of desire by way of cutting the ground from under the feet of the creative sublimation that enables us to escape this paradox of desire (the fact that desire is sustained by lack and therefore shuns its satisfaction, i.e. the very thing for which it "officially" strives): we elevate an empirical, ordinary object to the "dignity of the Thing," i.e. we posit it as unattainable/prohibited, and this inaccessibility keeps alive the flame of our desire. However, on account of its logic of instant gratification, the universe of "virtual reality" signals the very opposite of what its name announces: the end of the virtual space of symbolization, or, as Winnicott put it, of the space of transitive objects - everything is instantly here, but bereft of its substance and thus instantly devalued.[7] "Virtual reality" is then a kind of Orwellian misnomer: it stands for the very opposite of virtuality, for the saturation of the virtual space of symbolic fiction. So the big enigma is: how, through what kind of limitation of access, will capitalism succeed in re-introducing lack and scarcity into this saturation?

This predicament allows us to throw some new, perhaps unexpected light on the changed status of subjectivity in our post-modern late-capitalist society, i.e. of the shift towards a "pathological Narcissus," to whom the Other (the desiring subject) as such appears as a violent intruder. Whatever s/he does (if s/he smokes, laughs too loudly or not loudly enough, casts a covetous glance at me, etc.) amounts to a disturbance of my precarious imaginary balance. Threatened by every encounter of the Other's desire, this "pathological Narcissus" endeavours to dwell in the virtual space (in the precise sense this term acquires in the computer universe): in the space of virtual communities in which one is free to change one's identity, in which no link is effectively binding since I can at any moment withdraw from any "relationship." Here, the underlying fantasy of Robert Heinlein's *The Puppetmasters* can be of some help. Today, the motif of parasitic aliens which invade our planet, stick to our backs, penetrate our spinal cord with their prolonged stings and thus dominate us "from within" tastes like stale soup; the film shot in 1994 visually affects us as a rather mismatched combination of *Alien* and *Invasion of the Body Snatchers*. Its fantasmatic background is nonetheless more interesting than it may seem: it resides in the opposition between the human universe of sexual reproduction and the aliens' universe of cloning. In our universe, reproduction occurs by means of copulation, under the auspices of the symbolic agency of the Name-of-the-Father, whereas the alien invaders reproduce themselves asexually, via direct self-copying duplication, and therefore possess no "individuality;" they present a case of radical "immixing of subjects," i.e. they can communicate directly, bypassing the medium of language, since they all form one large organism, One. Why, then, do these aliens pose such a threat? The immediate answer, of course, is that they bring about the loss of human individuality - under their domination, we become "puppets," the Other (or, rather, the One) directly speaks through us. However, there is a deeper motif at work here: we can experience ourselves as autonomous and free individuals only insofar as we are marked by an irreducible, constitutive loss, by division, splitting, only insofar as our very being involves a certain "out-of-jointness," only insofar as the other (human being) ultimately remains for us an unfathomable, impenetrable enigma. The "aliens," on the other hand, function precisely as the complement that restores the lost plenitude of a human subject: they are what Lacan, in his Seminar XI, calls "lamella," the indestructible asexual organ without body, the mythical part that was lost when human beings became sexualized. In contrast to a "normal" sexual relationship, which is always mediated by a lack and as such "impossible," doomed to fail, the relationship with "aliens" is therefore fully satisfying: when a human subject merges with an alien, it is as if the round plenitude of a complete being, prior to sexual divisions, about which Plato speaks in his *Symposion* is reconstituted — a man no longer needs a woman (or vice versa) since he is already complete in himself. We can see now why, in Heinlein's novel, after a human being gets rid of the grip of the parasitic alien, he is completely bewildered and acts as if he has lost his footing, like a drug addict deprived of the drug. At the novel's end, the "normal" sexual couple is reconstituted by means of a (literal) parricide: the threat to sexuality is dealt with.

My point, however, is that what this novel stages in the guise of a paranoiac fantasy is something that is slowly becoming part of our everyday life. Is not the personal computer increasingly evolving into a parasitic complement to our being? Perhaps the choice between sexuality and compulsive playing with a computer (the proverbial "nerd" who is so immersed in a computer that he forgets about his date) is more than a media invention: perhaps it is an index of how, via new technologies, a complementary relationship to an "inhuman partner" is slowly emerging which is, in an uncanny way, more fulfilling than the relationship to a sexual partner? Perhaps Foucault was right (although not for the right reasons), perhaps the end of sexuality is looming on the horizon, and, perhaps the PC is in the service of this end.[8] Any relationship to the intersubjective Other is therefore preceded by the relationship to an object onto which the subject is "hooked" and which serves as a direct complement, a stand-in for the a-sexual primordially lost object. In pop-psychoanalytical terms, one could say that the subject who, via computer qua object-supplement, participates in a virtual community, "regresses" to the poly-morphous perversity of "primordial Narcissism." What should, however, not escape our notice is the radically "prothetic" nature of this (and every) Narcissism: it relies on a mechanical foreign body that forever decenters the subject.

The outstanding feature of computerized "interactive media" is the way they are giving birth to a renewed "drive-to-community" as a substitute for the progressive disintegration of our "actual" community life: what fascinates people far more than the unprecedented access to information, the new ways of learning, shopping, etc., is the possibility of constituting "virtual communities" in which I am free to assume an arbitrary sexual, ethnic, religious, etc. identity. Or, as some journalist put it: "Forget race, gender, class. In cyberspace, you are what you care about." A gay male, for example, can enter a closed sexual community and, via the exchange of messages, participate in a fictionalized group sexual activity as a heterosexual woman. These virtual communities, far from signalling the "end of Cartesian subjectivity," present the hitherto closest attempt to actualize the notion of the Cartesian subject in the social space itself: when all my features, including the most intimate ones, become contingent and interchangeable, only then is the void that "I myself am" beyond all my assumed features the *cogito*, the empty Cartesian subject ($).

However, one must be careful to avoid the trap that lurketh here: the notion that, prior to the computer-generated virtualization of reality, we were dealing with direct, "real" reality: the experience of virtual reality should rather render us sensitive to how the "reality" with which we were dealing always-already was virtualized. The most elementary procedure of symbolic identification, identification with an Ego-Ideal, involves, as Lacan had already put it in the 1950s, apropos of his famous scheme of the "inverted vase," an identification with a "virtual image/ *l'image virtuelle*": the place in the big Other from which I see myself in the form in which I find myself likeable (the definition of Ego-Ideal) is by definition virtual. Is therefore virtuality not the trademark of every, even the most elementary, ideological identification? When I see myself as a "democrat," "Communist," "American," "Christian," etc., what I see is not directly "me:" I identify with a virtual place in the discourse. And insofar as such an identification is constitutive of a community, every community is also stricto sensu always-already virtual. This logic of virtuality can be further exemplified by Oswald Ducrot's analysis of different discursive positions a speaker can assume within the same speech act: assertive, ironic, sympathetic, etc. When I speak, I always constitute a virtual place of enunciation from which I speak, yet which is never directly "me". Today, one likes to point out how the universe of virtual community, with its arbitrarily exchangeable identities, opens up new ethical dilemmas: suppose I, a gay male, assume in a virtual community the identity of a heterosexual woman — what if, within the virtual sexual play constituted by the interchange of descriptions on the screen, somebody brutally rapes me? Is this a case of "true" harassment or not? (Things will get even more complex with the prospect of more persons encountering each other and interacting in the same virtual reality: what, precisely, will be the status of violence when somebody attacks me in virtual reality?) Our point is, however, that these dilemmas are not really so different from those we encounter in "ordinary" reality, in which my gender identity is also not an immediate fact but "virtual," symbolically constructed, so that a gap separates it forever from the Real: here, also, every harassment is primarily an attack on my "virtual," symbolic identity.

This, however, in no way implies that nothing really important is taking place with today's technological virtualization of reality: what takes place is, in Hegelese, the very formal inversion from In-itself to For-itself, i.e. the virtualization which was previously "in-itself," a mechanism which operated implicitly, as the hidden foundation of our lives, now becomes explicit, is posited as such, with crucial consequences for "reality" itself. What we have here is an exemplary case of Hegel's Minerva's owl which "takes off in the evening": a spiritual principle effectively reigns as long as it is not acknowledged as such; the moment people become directly aware of it, its time is over and the "silent weaving of the spirit" is already laying the groundwork for a new principle. In short, the properly dialectical paradox resides in the fact that the very "empirical," explicit realization of a principle undermines its reign. Or, to put it in a different way: what takes place in this passage from In-itself to For-itself is a kind of conflation of the two dimensions which remain apart in the "normal" or "standard" functioning of the symbolic order, that of symbolic fiction and that of fantasy. On the one hand, virtual space is the space of symbolic fictions par excellence: the Other Scene. Purely virtual entities which, although they are to be found nowhere in "reality," are nonetheless effective and regulate our lives. In "reality," there are only individuals and the screens at which they stare, but nonetheless, to quote the now classic words of William Gibson, the individuals hooked onto the screen "develop a belief that there's some kind of actual space behind the screen, some place that you can't see but you know is there." On the other hand, however, the screen of a PC is the window of fantasy at its barest: an empty frame onto which fantasmatic scenarios are projected. Cyberspace is thus both at the same time: the space for the transmitting of messages, for communication, and the imagery of virtual reality. The result of this conflation is a kind of psychotic short-circuit in which the symbol, insofar as it overlaps with (or, rather, falls into) fantasmatic reality, loses its performative power, i.e. no longer effectively "engages" the subject. The problem of the communication in virtual communities is not simply that I can lie (that an ugly old male can present himself as a young beautiful woman, etc.), but, more fundamentally, that I'm never truly engaged, since, at every moment, I can pull back, un-hook myself.

NOTES

1. What our reading of the film did not take into account is, of course, the fact that the woman (Camille) is an object of exchange between the two men: is it not that the two man fight their own battle through her, the one betraying his partnership with the other by entering into a relationship with her, the other taking his revenge for this betrayal by seducing her in his turn. For that reason, he can reject her the moment his seduction succeeds and she offers herself to him - she has no inherent "use-value" for Stephan, the only point of seducing her was to deliver a message to his (male) partner. Such a reading, which introduces the motif of latent homosexuality and male bonding, adequate as it is at its own level, nonetheless fails to provide a satisfactory account of Stephan's gesture of rejection.
2. The closest Hollywood got to the properly ethical notion of repetition was in the series of so-called "comedies of remarriage" from the late thirties and early forties: their point is that it is only the second marriage among the same partners that brings forth an authentic, mature intersubjective link (see Stanley Cavell's study of the American screwball comedy, *Pursuits of Happiness*). Incidentally, the interest of Mike Nichols' *Heartburn* (with Meryl Streep and Jack Nicholson) is that it provides, as it were, the negative of the comedies of remarriage: it is literally a "comedy of re-divorce," i.e. the first divorce of the couple remains within the confines of a Narcissistic love-game, it is only with the second divorce that the symbolic bond that united the consorts is effectively dissolved.
3. A homologous self-sacrificing gesture of dirtying one's image in the eyes of the beloved in order to save him for morality is found in Michael Curtiz' *Angels with Dirty Faces* (1938) in which James

Cagney plays a charismatic Brooklyn gangster admired by a group of slum boys. When he is finally caught and sentenced to the electric chair, he is, of course, not afraid to die and intends to turn his execution into a display of his heroic defiance of death. However, on the eve of the execution, a priest who is aware of the redeeming qualities beneath Cagney's tough act, visits him in his cell and begs him to pretend next morning that he is dying in fear — in this way, he will render a last service to society, i.e. instead of remaining an idol in the eyes of the kids, he will serve them as an example of how crime doesn't pay and will thus promote their reintegration into society. On his way to the electric chair, Cagney casts a quick glance towards the journalists who witness the execution and, when he is sure of being observed, he starts to feign panic, to cry and shout that he doesn't want to die. Next day, when the boys read in a newspaper the report of Cagney's cowardly death, their world falls apart, they are deeply shattered and depressed: they have lost their hero, their ideal ego, the point of identification — and are thereby saved for the morality. Here we have the Lacanian distinction between morals and ethics: Cagney's final act is moral, yet definitely unethical.

4. This paradox can also be explained against the background of the dialectical short-circuit between possibility and actuality: the moment the conquest (of a woman by her seducer) becomes effectively possible, he has to withdraw, i.e. the possibility as such already counts as success. Therein resides a common feature of the psychic economy: often, deep satisfaction is provided by the mere awareness that we could have done something that we desired (slept with a passionately desired sexual partner, taken revenge on a long-time enemy, etc.) — as if the realization of this possibility would somehow spoil the purity of our success.

5. Sigmund Freud, "On the Universal Tendency to Debasement in the Sphere of Love" (1912), *The Standard Edition*, Vol. XI, London: Hogarth 1986, p. 187.

6. Therein resides one of the antinomies of late capitalism: on the one hand, this saturation, this instant gratification that suffocates desire; on the other hand, the growing number of the "excluded," of those who lack the basic necessities of life (proper food, shelter, medical care, etc.) — excess and lack, suffocation and deprivation, are here structurally codependent, so that it is no longer possible to measure the "progress" by an unambiguous standard. That is to say, it is inappropriate to claim that, since some people live in abundance, while other live in deprivation, we must strive for universal abundance: the "universalization" of the form of abundance which characterizes late capitalism is impossible for structural reasons, since, as it was pointed out already by Hegel in his *Philosophy of Right*, in capitalism, abundance itself produces deprivation.

7. As an indicator of this coming crisis, suffice it to recall the "negation of negation" which marks the use of computer technology in the domain of publishing: first, one puts computers to use in order to produce printed newspapers or journals (desktop-publishing, etc.) more efficiently; sooner or later, however, the fatal question is raised: why should we continue to print newspapers at all? Why shouldn't we consider the "virtual" text on the screen as the finished product and distribute it directly via internet? In other words, the new technology is first adopted as a means to realize more efficiently old needs; then, all of a sudden (when it's already too late), one becomes aware that these old needs are no longer functional, that they are rendered obsolete by the new technology.

8. Incidentally, the recently fashionable notion of "interactive media" is also an Orwellian misnomer which conceals its exact opposite, namely the tendency to promote the subject as an isolated individual who no longer properly interacts with others: the "interactive" computer network enables the subject to do his buying (instead of going out to stores), to order food by home delivery (instead of going to a restaurant), to pay the bills (instead of going to a bank), to work (on a computer connected via a modem with the company the subject works for, instead of going to work), to engage in political activities (by participating in "interactive" TV-debates), etc. up to his/her sex life (masturbating in front of the screen or "virtual sex" instead of an encounter with a "real" person). What is slowly emerging here is the true "post-Oedipal" subject, no longer attached to the paternal metaphor.

Cross-Culture: Mimesis, Truth, Politics

Hent de Vries

Both Martin Jay and Werner Hamacher address the issues raised by an anti-representational stance directly by highlightning the complexities involved in the notion of *mimesis* and of *museal exposition* respectively. Jay, the author of seminal works on the intellectual history of Western Marxism, notably of the Frankfurt School (cf. *The Dialectical Imagination* (1973), *Marxism and Totality* (1984), *Adorno* (1984), and *Fin-de-Siècle Socialism* (1989), has focused in his more recent research on some of the central figures in contemporary intellectual debate. Thus his magnum opus *Downcast Eyes. The Denigration of Vision in Twentieth-Century Thought*, published as a Centennial Book by the University of California Press, retraces the preoccupation with a purported ocularcentrism that, according to many so-called post-structuralist authors, has been the organizing principle of the philosophy and the aesthetics of the West. The article which is published below reestablishes a link between this inquiry into the primacy of the visual and the anti-representationalist stances that have recently been voiced against it, on the one hand, and Jay's earlier concerns with the thinkers of that "competing intellectual tradition" of Western neo-Marxism, notably Theodor W. Adorno, on the other. In "Mimesis and Mimetology," Jay turns to the more generic concept that structures the debate on vision, from Plato's great dialogues up to Derrida's *La dissémination*. Here, the concept of mimesis is rethought by letting it pass through the writings of Adorno and by confronting his rearticulation of the concept with that of Philippe Lacoue-Labarthe's *Typographies*. While at first sight Adorno seems to have less reservations against this notion in which some have been tempted to see the very organizing principle of his philosophy, Jay demonstrates that, in the final analysis, this neo-dialectician is as hostile to the "ideology of the genuine or authentic," which, according to a common and historically dominant interpretation, mimesis is said to simply "duplicate." Jay cites an interesting passage from Adorno's *Minima Moralia* in which Adorno as it were anticipates some of the concerns that a decidedly "post-structuralist" author like Lacoue-Labarthe has addressed in his deconstruction of the aestheticization of the political (e.g. in his *La fiction du politique*): in the very concept of "genuinness as such," Adorno writes, "dwells the notion of the supremacy of the original over the deprived. This notion, however, is always linked with social legitimation. All ruling strata claim to be the oldest settlers, autochtonous." All this, however, should not make us forget, Jay argues, that the concept of mimesis receives a different treatment in Critical Theory and post-structuralism. More than any other concept, it resists the all too easy categorizations or adaptations of either school of thought, and therefore allows us to better locate what is at stake in their virtual debate or in the *dialogue de sourds* of their respective proponents.

Werner Hamacher's work, a sample of which will be published this year by Harvard University Press under the title *Premises. Essays on Philosophy and Literature from Kant to Celan*, consists in a radical line of questioning which is impossible to classify. It stands out by its diligent attempts to strike the right balance between reading and politics, unreadability and existential decisiveness, philosophical rigor and bold, indeed wild ideas. In his writings, sustained and repeated discussions of Marx, Freud, Heidegger, Benjamin and Derrida abound as much as detailed analyses of speech act theory, of syllables, omissions, questions marks and such interjections as "but," *Aber*, the theme of more than one essay and the title of a future book.

In his contribution to the present volume, "Expositions of the Mother. A Quick Stroll through Various Museums," Hamacher shows that the discourse on the museum has often been dominated by a sense, sometimes even an ideology, of "loss." This would be clear, *mutatis mutandis*, in the writings of theorists and novelists such as Benjamin, Pomian, Hawthorne, James, Joyce, Nabokov, Borges, Leiris and Proust. The list, it seems, could easily be extended and allows for few exceptions. In Hamacher's account the one exception is that of Valéry.

The very emergence and inner constitution of the museum would be characterized by a "process of desacralization and detechnicization" which would have stripped and alienated its publicly displayed objects from their purportedly original "context" that had once provided them with their "liturgical," "ceremonial," "decorative" or merely "utilitarian" role or function. It is the repeated public exposition of things in the age of reproducibility which is deemed to disperse their original site, their world, their value. Hamacher writes: "After it has been shown through its profanation that art can no longer be experienced, the only experience that still remains is just this experience of the no-longer of art, the experience of God-, of man-, and of artforsakenness, of the abandonment of art. What remains after the end of art — and that means after the end of religion — is the museum." Hamacher's *tour de force* consists in a close reading of a certain Christian figure —

and not just any figure, namely that of the Madonna — in a lesser known essay by Heidegger that laments the transportation of her image (the Sistine Madonna) into the museum. The Madonna, Hamacher shows, is much more here than a figure that comes to illustrates the advent of Being. In a sense, Heidegger's lament reveals the ontic conditionality of his ontology or, put otherwise, the strong — and, "idiosyncratic" — interpretation of a well-determined historical figure (the Mother of Christ) as the privileged mode of presentation of the happening of Being as such. The figure in question is not taken to be the mimesis, the "imitation" or "depiction" of "something that had already previously been at hand." What is described — and, indeed, analyzed — is, on the contrary, "the event of figuration itself," in Heidegger but not in Heidegger alone. At issue, therefore, is not an intellectual history of that invention called the museum or the art of collecting, but an analysis and, indeed, a strong interpretation of the ideology of the exposition — the "ostentatious display of symbolic capital" — in terms of the conditions of its possibility, its idealization, its nostalgia, and its structural limitations. Interestingly, the "transposition" of the "sacral" objects into the realm of the "profane" result at least as much in a reverse movement, as if profanation and sacralization were but two side of the same coin. And it is here, precisely, that Hamacher's considerations touch upon the relation between the "politics of the museum" and a theory of the political in general. It is as if the museum in its infinite quest for the substitution and restitution of "the mother" resembles a politics of "endless democratization" which is at the same time a politics of "distanciation" of the mother. This psychoanalytic turn prepares a final detour, this time through the oeuvre of Proust and Valéry which might promise yet a different perspective on the museum — and an affirmation of the museum in its very departure from the origin — and thereby a possible departure from the (in origin Christian) figure around which all the discourses on the museum exposed here continue to circle in vain. It may even promise a "step out of the museum." It may or it may not. Hamacher's text is as open-ended as is Jay's discussion of the fate of mimesis. Only indirectly, their analyses provide the fundamentally undecidable parameters within whose shifting limits a decision can be taken by the reader alone.

By contrast, the contribution of Simon Critchley addresses the question of the ethico-political injunction of cultural analysis in somewhat more direct terms. Rather than focusing on a specific, historically and philosophically overdetermined concept or figure (mimesis, the museum) by paying attention to the respective processes of conceptualization and figuration, this author presents us with a reading of the evaporation of the common interpretations of the political, in the post Cold War era and, more precisely, in the age of the techno-mediatization of reality, public and private.

Thus Critchley, the author of *The Ethics of Deconstruction*, a comparative study of the work of Jacques Derrida and Emmanuel Levinas, draws our attention to the "call for a re-politicization of deconstruction in terms of a Marxist *hantologie*" (rather than ontology) that seems to be central affirmation of Derrida's recent *Spectres de Marx.* This book had been the subject of a roundtable with Jacques Derrida during the international conference on *Violence, Identity, and Self-Determination* that was organized by ASCA and UCLA's Paris Program in Critical Theory in the summer of 1994 (and whose proceedings will be published by Stanford University Press). One of the most interesting and challenging aspects of Critchley's essay is his critical assessment of the transformation and displacement of the — in origin Marxist, more precisely, Gramscian — concept of hegemony as it takes place in the dialogue between Derrida and authors such Ernesto Laclau and Chantal Mouffe. According to Laclau and Mouffe, the political and modern culture can no longer be understood in terms of the effects that an historical, objective economic infrastructure produces in the ideological superstructure, but only in light of contingent and always provisional "hegemonic articulations." This would hold true for advanced capitalism no less than for its possible "socialist" or radically democratic transformations. The latter would precisely consist in a "progresssive fragmentation of the social and a proliferation of social actors" which, in turn, forms a condition of the possibility of "freedom." Here, again, the emergence of "democracy" is viewed against the background of a "dislocation" which is a chance as much as a risk and whose advent should neither be romanticized nor be lamented in a nostalgic turn toward some myth of original or future (archaic or, for that matter, communist) "social transparency." Against this backdrop, Derrida's reinterpretation of the messianic, notably in *Spectres de Marx*, could be understood as a pertinent rearticulation of the theory of hegemony in light of a logics of the specter. Critchley cites Derrida: "Haunting belongs to the structure of every hegemony." And it is certainly no coincidence that the privileged examples of this enigmatic structure of "haunting" that are formalized and analyzed by Derrida are taken from "literature" (Shakespeare's *Hamlet*) and the history of religion. Not only does this circumstance explain the need (and the task) to "translate" and to "negotiate" at any given instance and in each concrete situation (a translation and negotation that Derrida, as Critchley points out, refuses to determine *a priori*). Furthermore, the fact is that Derrida's insistence on the messianic — on an "openness toward the future" that is described in terms of messianicity — reminds us of a certain ethico-theological overdetermination of the political. Again, it would seem that the contemporary analysis of the political and, no less, of culture at large demands that one pay minute attention to the "fictionality" and the "religiosity" discernible at the very heart of what presents itself as the most modern, as the radically secular, and as resolutely profane.

Mimesis and Mimetology: Adorno and Lacoue-Labarthe

Martin Jay

Mimesis, Roland Barthes insisted in *S/Z*, produced a sickening feeling in his stomach, a kind of nausea that came from its conservative reproduction of already existing signs.[1] For the resolutely anti-representational Barthes, any straightforward imitation of the external world, any aesthetic practice based on reference and repetition rather than the free play of signs, was inherently inadequate. A semiotic approach, he argued, must attend to the semantic play in the system, which undoes the closed economy of mimetic imitation. Likewise, in "The Double Session," Jacques Derrida disapprovingly asked if traditional literary criticism, with its search for univocal hidden meanings and the thematic kernels of texts, was not "a part of what we have called the *ontological* interpretation of mimesis or of metaphysical mimetologism?"[2] For Gilles Deleuze and Félix Guattari, mimesis was "radically false," a part of the paranoid order of spatial stasis they called "the copy" as opposed to the liberated, nomadic space of the "map."[3] Jean-François Lyotard identified mimesis with the "master's law" and praised Diogenes's "cynical body" for defying it.[4] And Paul de Man dismissed mimesis as merely one literary trope among others, a trope, moreover, whose alleged naturalness needed to be deconstructed, for "what we call ideology is precisely the confusion of linguistic with natural reality, of reference with phenomenalism."[5]

For these theorists, and for many others normally labeled, for better or worse, post-structuralist, a conventional aesthetic privileging of mimesis or what is taken to be its synonym, imitation, is an ideologically suspect recirculation of the ready-made, a false belief in the fixity of meaning and the possibility of achieving full presence, a language game that fails to see itself as such. Lacan's warnings against the misrecognitions of the mirror stage would be yet another instance of this critique. Whereas in the much older Platonic critique of mimesis, its danger was understood to be the undermining of a stable notion of truth, which is threatened by duplicitous copies of mere appearances, here it is precisely the opposite worry that is at work: the anxiety that mimesis means privileging an allegedly "true" original over its infinite duplications.[6] Or rather, at least in the case of Derrida, it involves that worry *and* its apparent contrary: that the mimetic "double" may itself be taken as self-sufficient, needing no external referent at all. For that assumption, which underlays certain modernist aesthetic practices, implied a no less dubious belief in the full ontological presence of the simulacrum itself.

In apparent contrast, the competing intellectual tradition known as the Frankfurt School found much — albeit not all — in mimesis to praise. Although no less suspicious than post-structuralism of the naive referentialism of naturalist and realist aesthetics, Critical Theory valued mimesis as a valuable resource in its struggle to counter the reigning power of instrumental rationality in the modern world. Drawing on Walter Benjamin's suggestive ruminations of 1933, "On the Mimetic Faculty" and "The Doctrine of the Similar,"[7] and Roger Caillois's 1938 book *Le mythe et l'homme*,[8] Max Horkheimer and Theodor W. Adorno mourned the loss or withering of a primal and inherently benign human capacity to imitate nature as the dialectic of enlightenment followed its fateful course.[9] Although they recognized the sinister potential of mimetic behavior when combined with the instrumental rationality it generally opposed — a potential realized precisely in the mocking Nazi mimicry of the Jews and duplicated in the Culture Industry at its most repressive — by and large, mimesis served as an honorific term in their vocabulary.[10] In his *Aesthetic Theory*, Adorno could thus call the mimetic behavior that is precariously preserved in art "a receptacle for all that has been violently lopped off from and repressed in man by centuries of civilization, during which human beings were forcibly subjected to suffering" and "the endeavor to recover the bliss of a world that is gone."[11]

Not surprisingly, a significant secondary literature has arisen around the enigmatic concept of mimesis in Critical Theory, especially in the thought of Adorno, which one commentator has gone so far as to call the "obscure operator" of his entire system and another "a foundational concept never defined nor argued, but always alluded to, by name, as though it had preexisted all the texts."[12] Commentators have carefully unravelled its over-determined origins in anthropological theories of shamanism and sympathetic magic, zoological analyses of animal mimicry, psychological theories of compulsive repetition, and aesthetic ideas of representation. However, no one, to my knowledge, has attempted the formidable task of thinking about Adorno's positive evocation of mimesis in the light of more recent post-structuralist commentary on the same theme.[13]

Such a task becomes all the more intriguing when it is realized that several thinkers in the post-structuralist camp are less unequivocally hostile to mimesis than the picture painted above would suggest. That is, despite the animadversions against naive referentiality in the work of theorists like de Man, Lyotard and Barthes, mimesis in a more complicated sense has played a positive role in certain post-structuralist theory. A case can be made, in fact, for the Derrida of "The Double Session,"[14] but it is in the work of Philippe Lacoue-Labarthe in particular that the most profound post-structuralist meditation on the implications of the concept can be found. After a brief sketch of Adorno's complicated use of the term, I want to pass on to the ways in which mimesis figures in Lacoue-Labarthe's work, most notably the texts recently collected in *Typography*.[15] By then comparing the two, I hope to provide a new perspective on the significance of this extraordinarily vexed term.

A first approximation of Adorno's use of mimesis, whether in aesthetic, philosophical, anthropological or psychological contexts, would necessarily stress its relational character, its way of bridging the gap between, but not collapsing differences. These differences were not, however, simply between a representation and what is represented, as the dominant tradition of thought about mimesis assumed, nor between one producing subject and another (the genius, say, imitating divine creation), as a subordinate tradition assumed.[16] It is rather between what is traditionally called subjects and objects (or at least the "other" of subjects) in the world. Conceptual thought can be understood as an act of aggression perpetrated by a dominating subject on a world assumed to be external to it; it subsumes particulars under universals, violently reducing their uniqueness to typifications or exemplars of a general or essential principle. Mimesis, in contrast, involves a more sympathetic, compassionate and non-coercive relationship of affinity between non-identical particulars, which do not then become reified into two poles of a subject/object dualism. Rather than producing hierarchical subsumption under a subjectively generated category, it preserves the rough equality of the object and subject involved.

More precisely, it assimilates the latter to the former in such a way that the unposited, unintended object implicitly predominates, thwarting the imperialist gesture of subjective control and constitution that is the hallmark of philosophical idealism. "Mimetic behavior," Adorno insisted, "does not imitate something but assimilates itself to that something."[17] The word "imitation" (*Nachahmung*), he implied, suggests too active a role for the subject, whose making alone cannot be the source of the meaning it finds in the mimetic relation with the other.[18] Instead, Adorno prefered the verb *anschmiegen* (to snuggle up or mold to) to stress a relationship of contiguity.[19] In a way, he was returning to the original Greek use of the term, for example in the Delian hymns or Pindar, when mimesis meant the expression of an inner state through cultic rituals rather than the reproduction of external reality, rituals that included music, dance, and mime.[20] Although in these instances, mimesis meant an outward expression of something inward rather than a relation between subject and external object, in both cases, the mode was more like benign assimilation than domination.

In more passively assimilating itself to the other, the subject of mimesis also preserves the sensuous, somatic element that the abstractions of idealist reason factor out of cognition or sublate into a higher rationality. Precisely which senses are most involved we will examine shortly, but for now suffice it to say that mimesis necessarily entails a crucial role for the body in the interaction between self and world. And what is equally important, it is both the body as the source of pleasure and the locus of pain.

And yet, mimesis, as Adorno develops it, is not to be understood as the simple opposite of reason, as it sometimes has been.[21] It is closer to what Habermas once called a "placeholder" for a "primordial reason," which, however, cannot be satisfactorily theorized without betraying its pre-conceptual status.[22] "The continued existence of mimesis, understood as the non-conceptual affinity of a subjective creation with its objective and unposited other," Adorno explained in *Aesthetic Theory*, "defines art as a form of cognition and to that extent as 'rational'.... What the stubborn persistence of aesthetic mimesis proves is not that there is an innate play instinct, as some ideologues would have it, but that to this day rationality has never been fully realized, rationality understood in the sense of an agency in the service of mankind and of human potentials, perhaps even of 'humanized nature' (Marx)."[23]

Although initially manifest in the context of what Sir James Fraser called "sympathetic magic," mimesis should thus not be reduced to "the superstitious belief in the ability to have a direct impact on things."[24] Nor is it simply an appreciation of the uncanny similitudes that already supposedly exist in nature, those wondrous astrological, physiognomic or graphological correspondences, the "secret language of things" that Benjamin in his more anti-modern moods found so intriguing. In aesthetic mimesis in particular, what was preserved — as well as transformed — was the sedimented "material" of past artistic endeavors, which suggest a historical as well as natural "other" worthy of assimilation. Moreover, mimesis partakes of non-magical forms of knowing, in part through its preservation of some of the cognitive power of intuition, as opposed to conceptual appropriation, the intuition that Kant had seen as the hallmark of aesthetic experience.[25]

Its non-magical status also follows from the complicated relationship mimesis has to expression, by which Adorno meant something more than revealing the psychological interiority of the individual artist. Instead, what is expressed is a dissonant resistance to the harmonizing impulses of affirmative art, a resistance which is grounded in a remembrance of the sedimented suffering of the past and the continuing suffering of the present — the suffering of the object as well as the subject, of what might be called "nature" as well as humankind.[26] "Expression in art is mimetic," Adorno claimed, "just as the expression of living creatures is the expression of suffering."[27] Mimesis is thus a check to the ideological overcoming of real pain in the idealist art of consolation or the realist art of reconciliation,[28] which is why it remains so vital a part of the uncompromisingly dissonant modernist art, for example that of Beckett or Kafka, Adorno so vigorously championed (for reasons that were thus diametrically opposed to Barthes's semiotic celebration of the alleged free play of signifiers).[29]

But perhaps most importantly, the rational moment of mimesis paradoxically follows from its own need to be supplemented by — or, rather, placed in a force-field with — precisely that very conceptuality it seems to spurn. In aesthetic experience, Adorno insisted, mimesis was never sufficient unto itself, but always needed to be juxtaposed in a constellation with what he called the constructive impulse of "spirit."[30] "In art," he wrote, "mimesis is both inferior and superior to spirit: it is contrary to spirit and yet the cause of spirit's being kindled. In art works spirit has become the principle of construction. For spirit to live up to its *telos* means that it must well up from the mimetic impulses, constructing them by assimilation rather than external decree."[31] Spirit and mimesis, construction and expression, thus exist in a creative and unsublatable tension in works of art, a tension which should be preserved. Although they infiltrate each other — "To represent the mimesis it supplanted," Adorno wrote in *Negative Dialectics*, "the concept has no other way than to adopt something mimetic in its own conduct, without abandoning itself"[32] — the two cannot be simply identified at some higher level of unity.

Precisely because works of art preserve rather than falsely reconcile such tensions, they also stage what might be called a negative dialectic of imitation in relation to what exists outside their apparently self-enclosed boundaries. Adorno presents this negative dialectic as an unavoidable antinomy. On the one hand, works of art — or at least modernist ones that take seriously the art-for-art's sake credo — strive for autotelic self-sufficiency, which allows Adorno to say that "the mimesis of works of art is their resemblance to themselves."[33] As Lambert Zuidervaart points out, this claim implicitly answers the Platonic fear that art is duplicitous because it fails to imitate a higher reality; for Adorno instead, "similarity with itself separates the artwork from a false reality, where nothing is really real because everything obeys the law of exchange."[34] That is, by refusing to imitate or be assimilated entirely to a bad external reality — by paradoxically honoring, one might say, the Jewish taboo on graven images — works of art hold out the hope for the possibility of a more benign version of mimesis in a future world beyond domination and reification.

But on the other hand, the actual failure of such works to achieve absolute self-identity, a failure produced, *inter alia*, by their always being made for those who enjoy, exchange or consume them, bears witness to the still unredeemed quality of life in the social world. For that imperfection necessarily infiltrates the work and mocks the illusory claim to completion. As such, it also bears witness to bodily pain, the unhealed wounds of damaged life that are indirectly represented in the artwork's dissonant fissures. The very illusory quality of art, its deceitful claim to present the absolute in sensuous terms, is thus at once a protest against the inadequacies of the world it refuses to imitate and an expression of the inability to transcend those inadequacies through aesthetic means alone.

Adorno, to be sure, was aware that the delicate balance he admired in certain modernist works was threatened by the increasing hegemony of spirit and construction, understood in essentially instrumental rationalist terms, over mimesis or expression. The withering away of the sensuous moment in late modernist art meant that all that was being imitated was the reified social relations of the administered world, a conclusion he amplified in his critique of Schoenberg's move from atonalism to the twelve-tone row.[35] Its effects were felt outside the realm of art as well, Adorno insisted, for "the contemporary loss of any subjective capacity for experience is most likely identical with the tenacious repression of mimesis today."[36] And when the repressed does return, Adorno lamented, it often does so in the distorted form of a sadistic mimicry that shows its subordination to the ends of instrumental, dominating rationality.

To combat that repression was no easy task, but one modest effort has been discerned by Fredric Jameson in Adorno's own, idiosyncratic prose style. Without ever reducing philosophy to a variant of literature, Adorno sought to subvert the dominating, homogenizing power of conceptual thinking by introducing a mimetic element in his own writing. According to Jameson, this moment appears in those moves in Adorno's prose that can be called narrative. That is, his writing stages the conflicts and tensions of a story over time, with various theoretical terms and philosophical arguments playing the roles of actors, a procedure which tacitly undercuts the atemporal impulse of conceptual reason. Jameson writes:

> This micro-work of the sentence on the isolated concept is, then, what undermines its apparent rational autonomy and pre-forms it... for its multiple positions in the larger movement of the constellation or the "model." The mimetic or the narrative may be thought to be a kind of homeopathic strategy in which, by revealing the primal movement of domination hidden away within abstract thought, the venom of abstraction is neutralized, allowing some potential or utopian truth-content to come into its own.[37]

Whether or not the term narrative is fully appropriate here — it may suggest too linear an emplotment to capture the chiasmic logic Jameson himself recognizes as Adorno's main trope — the importance of Adorno's stylistic mimesis of mimesis is worth taking seriously, for it goes beyond a mere external staging of dialectical conflicts. Perhaps a more fruitful way to bring it to the surface would be to follow Adorno's own praise for the stylistic device that he found best resisted conceptual synthesis: paratactic rather than hypotactic syntax.[38] By resisting the imperative to arrange ideas hierarchically, parataxis both undercut the mediating logic of conceptual subordination and bore witness to the crisis of meaningful experience (*Erfahrung* in Benjamin's well-known sense, rather than *Erlebnis*) in the modern world.

In his discussion of Hölderlin, Adorno acknowledged, to be sure, that language, unlike music, cannot avoid some conceptual homogenizing: "by virtue of its significative element, the opposite pole to its mimetic-expressive element, language is chained to the form of judgment and proposition and thereby to the synthetic form of the concept. In poetry, unlike music, aconceptual synthesis turns against its medium; it becomes a constitutive dissociation."[39] In the late poetry of Hölderlin, this dissociation was especially "striking — artificial disturbances that evade the logical hierarchy of subordinating syntax."[40]

But precisely because he remained true to the unsublatable tension between the synthetic and the dissociative impulses in language — to what we have seen Adorno call elsewhere the spiritual/constructive and the mimetic/expressive moments in art — Hölderlin produced an aesthetic instantiation of negative dialectics. As such, he resisted the mythologizing reading based on the putative content of the poems alone that Heidegger wanted to force on him as the simple antithesis of idealism, the gnomic prophet of pre-reflective Being. The same resistance might be discerned in Adorno's own writing, which never one-sidedly pitted mimesis or sympathetic magic against conceptual rationality, synthetic domination or theoretical reflection in a non-dialectical opposition.

To invoke Adorno's admiration for and, indeed, arguably mimetic appropriation of Hölderlin's paratactic style provides a convenient bridge to Lacoue-Labarthe, who found in Hölderlin — albeit more in the dramatic works like *The Death of Empedocles* and the translations of Sophocles than in the late poetry — a profound lesson on the same issues. In "The Caesura of the Speculative," one of the central essays in *Typography*, Lacoue- Labarthe, in fact, approvingly cited Adorno's text, claiming that its author was justified in "comparing the 'parataxis' characteristic of Hölderlin's late style with the writing of Beethoven's last quartets."[41]

Lacoue-Labarthe's target in this piece is what he sees as the speculative dialectic at work in both tragedy, understood in a certain way, and absolute

Idealism, a speculative dialectic he identifies with what Heidegger called "the onto-theo-logical in its fully accomplished form."[42] Underlying that dialectic, he finds "the guiding thread of a primary and constant preoccupation, of a single question — none other than that of *mimesis*, at whatever level one chooses to examine it (whether it be that of 'imitation,' in the sense of the 'imitation of the Ancients,' of mimesis as a mode of *poiesis*, i.e. Aristotelian mimesis, or even — and this does not fail to enter into play — of mimesis in the sense of 'mimetism' or *imitatio*)."[43] According to Lacoue-Labarthe, only mimesis provides the means to transfigure negativity into positive being through representation, only mimesis allows the tragic pleasure that overcomes a visceral feeling of horror at the terrible events reproduced. This economy of specular transfiguration is precisely what underlies idealist philosophy as well, indeed philosophy in general. As such, it is the basis of what Derrida had called a "mimetologism," the imitation of the same in a closed system of ultimate higher reconciliation, a system in which what is mimetically re-presented is the putative unity of the logos itself, a logos which is identified with the truth.[44]

Lacoue-Labarthe is careful to deny that Hölderlin consciously transcended this economy, at least at the level of his own theoretical understanding, which was "speculative through and through."[45] Indeed, he implies that a complete extrication from the mimetological, speculative economy would be impossible.[46] But what Hölderlin's work does accomplish is a kind of internal dislocation of it, an exposure of a caesura in its smoothly working operation (as in the alexandrine), like the pause in poetic meter. And he does so by regressing behind Aristotle's affirmative understanding of mimetic representation to reveal what "*haunts* Plato under the name of mimesis and against which Plato fights with all of his philosophical determination until he finds a way of arresting it and fixing its concept."[47] Rather than expelling the troubling implications of the mimetic duplication of the same — an expulsion Lacoue-Labarthe calls the speculative "denegation" of mimesis — Hölderlin allows it to fester in the midst of his own tragic dramas, producing a kind of endless oscillation between proximity and distance that denies sublation and reconciliation, and cannot rest content at either pole.

More precisely, the dialectical structure of speculative recuperation *and* the infinite oscillation coexist in an uneasy equilibrium, the melodic and the rhythmic impulses of the work never coming completely together. The caesura in the work is thus mimetic representation itself, the space between the original and its duplicate, the hiatus rather than either pole. For this reason, Lacoue-Labarthe is able to conclude, with an implicit nod to Benjamin, by suggesting that Hölderlin's dramas come closer to the baroque *Trauerspiel* than to classical Greek tragedy.[48] Whereas the structure of speculative dialectics underlying the latter is like the completed work of mourning which in German is *Trauerarbeit*, the *Trauerspiel* keeps the "play" of mourning going forever without any final reconciliation or working through, keeping, that is, the "play" in the system from achieving any terminal stasis.[49]

If it follows any logic, it is that of paradox, which Lacoue-Labarthe dubs "hyperbologic." Expatiating in the other essays in his collection on its meaning, Lacoue-Labarthe points to the ambivalence at work in even Aristotle's notion of mimesis, at once a duplication or copy of what already exists, and a supplement or addition to fill the lack in what exists. Whereas the former is reproductive, the latter is productive. Whereas the former assumes nature is sufficient onto itself, the latter implies the need for a substitution. The paradox follows from the fact that mimetic substitution means both the need to imitate what already exists and the realization that what exists is itself insufficient and must be supplemented by the imitation. As Diderot showed in his discussion of actors who can imitate the identity of a character precisely because they themselves lack all fixed character, the result undercuts the notion of a proper, self-possessed identity. "The paradox," Lacoue-Labarthe writes, "states a *law of impropriety*, which is also the very law of mimesis: only the 'man without qualities,' the being without properties or specificity, the subjectless subject (absent from himself, distracted from himself, deprived of self) is able to present or produce in general."[50] Plato also grasped this paradox, but denounced the hypocrisy he saw as its issue, whereas Diderot — and Lacoue-Labarthe — appreciate it precisely for its destabilizing effect, its active unsettling of reified selfhood (indeed even of the fragile notion of the self underpinning Adorno's notion of mimesis as the expression of suffering).

Significantly, Lacoue-Labarthe connects the hyperbologic of the mimetic paradox to that of semblance or illusion (*Schein*) in general, a category Adorno also privileged in his writings on aesthetics.[51] "The division between appearance and reality, presence and absence, the same and the other, or identity and difference," Lacoue-Labarthe argued, "grounds (and... constantly unsteadies) mimesis. At whatever level one takes it — in the copy or the reproduction, the art of the actor, mimetism, disguise, dialogic writing — the rule is always the same: the more it resembles, the more it differs."[52] For Adorno as well, it was aesthetic illusion that resisted mimetological closure, or what he called the "general mimetic abandonment to reification, which is the principle of death."[53] Even certain variants of modernist art had succumbed to that principle through a simple presentation of external reality without aesthetic transfiguration into illusion: "Ever since the beginning of modernism art has absorbed objects from outside," Adorno remarked, "leaving them as they are without assimilating them (e.g. montage). This indicates a surrender by mimesis to its antagonist, a trend which is caused by the pressure reality exerts on art."[54] Lacoue-Labarthe's hostility to the ideology of the genuine or authentic original, which mimesis merely duplicates, was thus explicitly shared by Adorno, who warned in *Minima Moralia* against "the concept of genuineness as such. In it dwells the notion of the supremacy of the original over the derived. This notion, however, is always linked with social legitimation. All ruling strata claim to be the oldest settlers, autochthonous."[55]

But perhaps more than Lacoue-Labarthe, he was willing to retain an emphatic notion of truth in relation to works of art, for "the definition of art in terms of illusion is only half correct: art is true to the degree to which it is an illusion of the non-illusory (*Schein des Scheinlosen*). In the last analysis, to experience art is to recognize that its truth content is not null and void."[56] But it was precisely Adorno's point — and here he tacitly anticipated Lacoue-Labarthe's defense of the hyperbologic paradox — that such truth was manifest only in the non-sublatable, negative dialectic of illusion and non- illusion itself. As such, it could be understood as a comparable to a permanent allegory without symbolic reconciliation.[57]

Significantly, it was the yearning for such totalized reconciliation that Lacoue-Labarthe, in an essay jointly written with Jean-Luc Nancy, claimed was at the root of "the Nazi myth."[58] Myth, they claimed, "is *the* mimetic instrument par excellence,"[59] because it seeks absolute identification through typified existence (real "experience" through the realization of racial types). Although arguing that the Germans' need for mimetic mythologizing was stronger than elsewhere, because of the fact that their imitation of the Greeks was itself an imitation of an earlier French mimesis of the Ancients, they darkly conclude in a way reminiscent of Horkheimer and Adorno's *Dialectic of Enlightenment* that "this logic, with its double trait of the mimetic will-to-identity and the self-fulfillment of form, belongs profoundly to the mood or character of the West in general, and more precisely, to the fundamental tendency of the *subject*, in the metaphysical sense of the word."[60] Like the Frankfurt School theorists, they acknowledge the complicity of mimesis in one of its guises — in their case, that of the non-allegorical search for perfect identity, in that of Horkheimer and Adorno, the "organized control of mimesis"[61] by instrumental rationality — in the realization of nightmare politics. Even the Heidegger from whom Lacoue-Labarthe and Nancy had learned so much was not exempt from this critique: "an unacknowledged mimetology seems to overdetermine the thought of Heidegger politically," Lacoue-Labarthe admitted after the growing scandal about Heidegger's politics in the 1980s.[62]

The victims of Nazism, in contrast, are those who adhere to a non-mimetological variant of mimesis, which resists mythic closure. "All in all," writes Lacoue-Labarthe in his book *Heidegger, Art and Politics*, "the Jews are infinitely mimetic beings, or in other words, the site of an *endless mimesis,* which is both interminable and inorganic, producing no art and achieving no appropriation."[63] Although the claim that Jews have never produced art may seem perverse (as well as counter-factual), it is meant in a flattering way to the extent that "art" suggests symbolic sublimation of the unreconciled fissures of existence. Horkheimer and Adorno made a similar claim in *Dialectic of Enlightenment*, when they argued of the Jews that for all their complicity in the millenia-long process of dominating nature, "they did not eliminate adaptation to nature, but converted it into a series of duties in the form of ritual. They have retained the aspect of expiation, but have avoided the reversion to mythology which symbolism implies."[64]

Much more could be done to tease out the telling similarities between Adorno's and Lacoue-Labarthe's general notions of mimesis, but I want to turn now to the specific issue of the sensual element in their accounts. In the essay just discussed, "The Nazi Myth," Lacoue-Labarthe and Nancy claim that the Aryan type is the product of "a construction and conformation of the world according to a vision, an image, the image of the creator of forms.... the *anschauen* — 'seeing' as vision and intuition piercing to the heart of the things and *forming* being itself, the 'seeing' of an active, practical, operative dream — is the heart of the 'mythicotypical' process."[65] Privileging vision, in other words, is understood to be in the service of the speculative, theatrical, theoretical version of mimesis, which elsewhere Lacoue-Labarthe damns as mimetological.[66]

A similar argument informs his consideration of the psychoanalytic theory of the self in "The Echo of the Subject," included in *Typography*. Its targets are Lacan's privileging of vision in the mirror stage and the Imaginary and René Girard's notion of mimetic rivalry, both of which depend on a conceptualization of the subject in narcissistic terms. Preferring a notion of aural to visual mimesis — the Greek nymph Echo to that of her love object, Narcissus — he turns to the analyst Theodor Reik's discussion of voice and rhythm in *The Haunting Melody* for help in constructing a non-identical, uncanny version of the self. He calls it "allobiographical" — "the 'novel' of an other (be it a double)"[67] — rather than autobiographical. Such a self, he claims, is not based on specular reflection, on the imitation of the same, but rather on the *unheimliche* rhythmic repetition of an original that never existed in itself, a perpetual spacing without end. Rhythm, in fact, "establishes the break between the visible and the audible, the temporal and the spatial (but also the inscribed and the fictive), thus resisting the hold of such partitions and bearing a relation to *archi-écriture* in the Derridean sense of the term." As such, perhaps it remains, as Derrida himself says in his introduction to *Typography*, "outside the order of the sensible. It belongs to no sense."[68] And we might add, it rejects the Platonic realm of pure intelligibility as well.

Although one might discern a certain similarity between this argument and Benjamin's faith in "non-sensuous correspondences" — for example, those between heavenly constellations of stars and human destiny claimed by astrology — as the basis of a benign notion of mimesis, for Adorno, such a parallel is harder to discern. For despite his oft-proclaimed embrace of the Jewish taboo on graven images and his recognition that of all the senses, smell was perhaps the most mimetic, Adorno never completely denigrated visuality *per se* or sought a realm prior to both the senses and intelligibility.[69] As Gertrud Koch and Miriam Hansen have recently shown, even when it came to the mass cultural phenomenon known as film, Adorno could posit an emancipatory potential in the medium itself.[70] However much Hollywood films were part of the ideological Culture Industry, the cinematic mimesis of expressive bodies suggested a pre-linguistic experience prior to the conscious articulations of the ego.

In *Aesthetic Theory*, Adorno specifically defended the importance of a visual moment in art, which is another way to say the intuitive as opposed to the purely conceptual: "the desideratum of visuality seeks to preserve the mimetic moment of art."[71] But rather than fetishizing that moment into the essence of art *per se* or rigidly opposing sensuality to spirituality, Adorno also argued that "mimesis only goes on living through its antithesis, which is rational control by art works over all that is heterogeneous to them.... Art is a vision of the non-visual; it is similar to a concept without actually being one."[72] Once again, it is the constellation of mimesis and rationality, expression and spirit, that defines the unsublated aesthetic prefiguration of the utopia that Adorno refused to abandon.

Perhaps because of that refusal, Adorno never found rhythmic repetition without end, that infinite spacing and perpetual deferral so characteristic of deconstruction, as unambiguously congenial as did Lacoue-Labarthe. One of the central charges against Stravinsky in Adorno's celebrated invidious comparison of his music with Schoenberg's was directed precisely against the Russian composer's over-reliance on rhythmic composition: "even in those cases where the Schoenberg school operates with such rhythms, they are for the most part charged with melodic and contrapuntal content, while the rhythmic proportions which in Stravinsky dominate the musical foreground are employed solely in the sense of shock effects."[73] These shocks are simply absorbed by the numbed and overpowered musical subject, who no longer expresses the suffering of modern life, let alone has the will to resist it. Unlike Lacoue-Labarthe, Adorno never relegated the expressive moment of mimesis, which reveals the body — natural as well as human — in pain, to the margins of his analysis.

Adorno's suspicion against the value of rhythmic repetition derived, it might be speculated, from the link he saw between it and what Freud had understood as the functioning of the death drive. In fact, as Josef Früchtl has rightly argued, the ambivalence towards mimesis that can at times be detected in Adorno may be explained in part by his recognition that reconciliation and destruction were closely intertwined.[74] That is, the radically anti-narrative structure of the death drive, its compulsion to repeat in the service of restoring a state of undifferentiated stasis that can, however, never be realized short of actual death, lends to non-mimetological mimesis a melancholic tone that anti-utopian post-structuralists like Lacoue-Labarthe find congenial, but which Adorno did not.

Adorno, however much he may have been a practitioner of a "melancholy science," never gleefully embraced the masochistic self-shattering that defenders of the repetition compulsion claim is a release from the ideological mystifications of subjecthood.[75] He understood that the radical reduction of ego strength through the mimetic duplication of the inorganic world — what Caillois had called psychasthenia in his study of insect mimicry — could also mean the triumph of reification. As his frequent denunciations of Surrealism demonstrate, Adorno remained suspicious of an aesthetic based on the uncanny evocation of compulsive beauty by a depersonalized subject who ultimately revealed itself as "inanimate and virtually dead."[76] Although Jameson may overstate the case by saying that it was narration itself that Adorno hoped mimesis would rescue in its conflict with conceptuality, it is nonetheless true that he never damned narrative coherence *tout court* as merely another version of the speculative suppression of non-identity that was in Derrida's terms a version of mimetologism. He did, to be sure, acknowledge that any attempt to restore it under present circumstances was necessarily ideological — telling a story could only be based on the very continuity of experience (*Erfahrung*) that had been lost in the modern world — but he did not rule out the possibility of a future in which it might once again be meaningful.[77]

It is perhaps such historical hopes, which despite everything Adorno never lost, that most distinguish his meditations on this theme from those of Lacoue-Labarthe, who seems to defend an endlessly oscillating mimesis based on a paradoxical hyperbologic that steadfastly resists ontological stability, subjective integrity and speculative representation, all of which are seen as evidence of mimetological closure. In contrast, Adorno placed mimesis, also understood as susceptible to, but not identical with mimetology, in a tense constellation with its apparent opposites: rationality, spirit, narrative coherence, and subjective construction. Neither *Trauerarbeit*, in the sense of a fully triumphal mastery of otherness through a higher level sublimation like that of classical tragedy, nor *Trauerspiel*, in the sense of a perpetually melancholic resistance to any closure, defines his delicately nuanced position. Instead, Adorno practiced a *trauerliche Wissenschaft*, a "melancholy science," in which the noun was no less important than the adjective. As a result, mimesis may have been a necessary element in his utopian vision, but it was by no means sufficient onto itself.

What in conclusion have we learned by this comparison between the uses of mimesis in Adorno and Lacoue-Labarthe? First, it is clear that the most interesting contemporary debate over mimesis has little to do with the issue of referential representation versus the auto-referentiality of sign systems. Nor can it be reduced to a mere synonym for imitation. Despite the easy dismissal of mimesis by the thinkers cited at the beginning of this paper, it survives in important and unexpectedly similar ways in both post-structuralism and Critical Theory.

Second, it is no less obvious that the word itself is polysemic even catachrestic, with meanings that carry with them the residues of their separate origins in anthropological, psychological, aesthetic, philosophical and zoological discourses. So too, the value of the "original "model to be mimetically duplicated — variously identified with nature as a non-subjective other, the active producer of that nature, the cultural tradition of the Ancients, or the reified relations of the modern world — inevitably inflects the judgment about the process itself. If then, there is an economy of mimesis, what Derrida has called an economimesis, it is difficult to reduce it to a circulation or equilibrium of identical acceptations.[78] Instead, the term changes its meaning and often its evaluative charge depending on the context in which it appears. It is for this reason that even mimicry, which often seems to be related to the mocking and demeaning imitation of victims, can be turned around and become a tool of resistance, as post-colonial theorists like Homi Bhabha and post-modernist feminist artists like Cindy Sherman have recently demonstrated.[79]

Third, that context often involves the complex relation between mimesis and rationality or conceptuality. What the post-structuralists call mimetology involves the subordination of mimesis to a deadening logic of sameness or sublation, a theoretical/theatrical logic based on visual reproduction, which they see as typical of the Western onto-theological project in general. Mimesis understood as rhythmic repetition without closure, an infinite oscillation between original and copy, is posited as the — to be sure, never fully successful — hyperbological antidote to mimetology, as the uncanny caesura in a speculative system that seeks to stifle its playful uncertainties.

In the case of Adorno, mimesis becomes problematic when it is in league not with reason *per se*, but rather with the instrumental rationality of the modern world. Then what it imitates is the *nature morte* of a world of reified relations in which the suffering of both humans and nature is no longer expressed. But as his discussion of the interaction between mimesis and rationality in art indicates, Adorno felt that both were necessary to avoid surrendering to the potential in mimesis alone to ape the repetitive rhythms of the death drive. Despite his occasional adoption of a rhetoric of nostalgia for a lost paradise of mimetic affinities, Adorno posited a constellation in which reason and mimesis both make up for the deficiencies of the other.

Finally, we have seen that both Adorno and Lacoue-Labarthe share an appreciation for the function mimesis can play in decentering the strong constitutive subject, opening a place for otherness and non-identity and enabling a non-dominating relationship between the human and the non-human. Although Adorno never went as far as Lacoue-Labarthe in marginalizing the suffering subject or advocating the surrender of its ego strength, he recognized that such a subject had to be put in a constellation with the other victims of domination rather than given absolute pride of place. What in Roland Barthes produced feelings of nausea, in Lyotard a denunciation of the "master's law," and in Deleuze and Guattari a nomadic flight from paranoid despotism thus turns out in the two theorists we have examined to be a potential source of healing and solace. Which of these opposing attitudes we should ourselves imitate is a conclusion I will let each reader draw for him- or herself. Unlike concepts that coerce, mimetic affinities should, after all, operate only through sympathetic attractions whose power cannot be imposed by theorists from the outside.

NOTES

1 Roland Barthes, *S/Z* (Paris, 1970), 145.

2 Jacques Derrida, "The Double Session," in *Dissemination*, trans., Barbara Johnson (Chicago, 1982), 245.

3 Gilles Deleuze and Félix Guattari, *Milles Plateaux* (Paris, 1980), 144.

4 Jean-François Lyotard, "On the Strength of the Weak," in *Toward the Postmodern*, ed. Robert Harvey and Mark S. Roberts (Atlantic Highlands, N.J., 1993), 69.

5 Paul de Man, *The Resistance to Theory* (Minneapolis, 1986), 11.

6 For a useful comparison of the Platonic with the post-structuralist complaints against mimesis, see Christopher Prendergast, *The Order of Mimesis: Balzac, Stendhal, Nerval, Flaubert* (Cambridge, 1986), chap. 1.

7 Walter Benjamin, "On the Mimetic Faculty," in *Reflections: Essays, Aphorisms, Autobiographical Writings*, ed., Peter Demetz, trans. Edmund Jephcott (New York, 1978); "Doctrine of the Similar," *New German Critique*, 17 (Spring, 1979).

8 Roger Caillois, *Le mythe et l'homme* (Paris, 1938); see also his "Mimicry and Legendary Psychasthenia," *October*, 31 (Winter, 1984).

9 Max Horkheimer and Theodor W. Adorno, *Dialectic of Enlightenment*, trans. John Cumming (New York, 1972), for example, 180-181, 227.

10 In *Dialectic of Enlightenment*, however, the ambiguities of mimesis are perhaps more explicitly discussed than in later works like *Aesthetic Theory*. For a discussion that contends Adorno understood the impossibility of disentangling the reductive from the emancipatory moments in mimesis, see Alexander García Düttmann, *Das Gedächtnis des Denkens: Versuch über Heidegger und Adorno* (Frankfurt, 1991), 117f.

11 Theodor. W. Adorno, *Aesthetic Theory*, trans. C. Lenhardt, ed. Gretel Adorno and Rolf Tiedemann (New York, 1984), 453, 465. Herbert Marcuse, however, was less convinced. In *The Aesthetic Dimension: Toward a Critique of Marxist Aesthetics* (Boston, 1978), he wrote: "the realm of freedom lies beyond mimesis....mimesis remains re-presentation of reality. This bondage resists the utopian quality of art" (47). But he also acknowledged the role of aesthetic mimesis in preserving the memory of past happiness (67). In the later Critical Theory of Jürgen Habermas, mimesis plays a

much more marginal role, and when it appears, it is usually assimilated into his communicative notion of intersubjective rationality. See, for example, his remark in "Questions and Counter-Questions," in Richard J. Bernstein, ed., *Habermas and Modernity* (Cambridge, Mass., 1985), that "modern art harbors a utopia that becomes a reality to the degree that the mimetic powers sublimated in the work of art find resonance in the mimetic relations of a balanced and undistorted intersubjectivity of everyday life" (202).

12 Michael Taussig, *Mimesis and Alterity: A Particular History of the Senses* (New York, 1993), 45; Fredric Jameson, *Late Marxism: Adorno, or, The Persistence of the Dialectic* (New York, 1990) 64; for other discussions, see Martin Lüdke, *Anmerkungen zu einer "Logik des Zerfalls": Adorno-Beckett* (Frankfurt, 1981), chap. 5; Michael Cahn, "Subversive Mimesis: T.W. Adorno and the Modern Impasse of Critique," in *Mimesis in Contemporary Theory*, ed. Mihai Spariosu (Philadelphia, 1984); Karla L. Schultz, *Mimesis on the Move: Theodor W. Adorno's Concept of Imitation* (Bern, 1990); and, most notably, Josef Früchtl, *Mimesis: Konstellation eines Zentralbegriffs bei Adorno* (Würzburg, 1986).

13 A partial exception is Früchtl, who devotes some interesting pages to Julia Kristeva's relation to Adorno. See his *Mimesis*, 181ff.

14 See, for example, David Carroll, *Paraesthetics: Foucault, Lyotard, Derrida* (New York, 1987), 101f.

15 Philippe Lacoue-Labarthe, *Typography: Mimesis, Philosophy, Politics*, ed. Christopher Fynsk, intro. Jacques Derrida (Cambridge, Mass, 1989). The texts, translated by various hands, were chosen from his collections, *Le suject de la philosophie: Typographies I* (Paris, 1979) and *L'imitation des modernes: Typographies II* (Paris, 1986); and from *Mimesis: Des articulations* (Paris, 1975).

16 This second tradition is Kantian. See the critical discussion in Derrida, "Economimesis," *Diacritics*, 11 (1981), 9.

17 Adorno, *Aesthetic Theory*,162.

18 It is for this reason that Adorno explicitly repudiates the *verum-factum* principle adopted by Hegelian Marxists like Lukács. For a discussion, see Martin Jay, "Vico and Western Marxism," *Fin-de-Siècle Socialism and Other Essays* (New York, 1988). W. Martin Lüdke points out that for Adorno a more primitive adaptation to nature, which can be called mimicry, becomes true mimesis only when it turns into a conscious and intentional doubling of nature (*Anmerkungen zu "Logik des Zerfall,"* 58). This is true, it seems to me, only if the constructive impulse of this doubling is not understood to outweigh the assimilative

19 For a discussion, see Cahn, "Subversive Mimesis, " 6, n. 44.

20 W. Tatarkiewicz, "Mimesis," *Dictionary of the History of Ideas*, vol. III (New York, 1973), 226.

21 For example, by David Roberts, who claims that "Adorno's *utopia* of reconciliation in turn may be seen as the rational veneer for a profoundly arational *mysticism* of redemptive mimesis beyond and behind all civilization." *Art and Enlightenment: Aesthetic Theory After Adorno* (Lincoln, Neb., 1991), 70.

22 Jürgen Habermas, *The Theory of Communicative Action*, vol. 1, trans. Thomas McCarthy (Boston, 1984), 382. His attempt, like that of Albrecht Wellmer in *Zur Dialektik von Moderne und Postmoderne: Vernunftkritik nach Adorno* (Frankfurt, 1985), to relocate mimesis within an intersubjective, communicative sphere has been criticized by Früchtl, *Mimesis*, 190ff. Interestingly, it was conservative theorists like David Hume and Edmund Burke who first pointed to the positive role of mimesis in sociability. See the discussion in Terry Eagleton, *The Ideology of the Aesthetic* (Cambridge, Mass., 1990), 53. Imitation was also privileged by Gabriel Tarde and then criticized by Emile Durkheim in his classic study *Suicide*.

23 Adorno, *Aesthetic Theory*, 80, 453.

24 Ibid., 453. A major weakness of Taussig's *Mimesis and Alterity* is its failure to make this distinction. See my review in *Visual Anthropology Review*, 9, 2 (Fall, 1993).

25 For a helpful comparison of Adorno and Kant on this issue, see J.N. Bernstein, *The Fate of Art: Aesthetic Alienation from Kant to Derrida and Adorno* (University Park, Pa. 1992), 200f.

26 García Düttmann argues that in *Dialectic of Enlightenment*, the name "nature" stands metonymically for the relations with the other (118). If so, it would be important to recognize that it includes what in French is nicely differentiated as "*l'autre*" and "*l'autrui*," the objective and subjective "other."
27 Adorno, *Aesthetic Theory*, 162. Although the suffering of mute nature is expressed in mimesis, it takes human intervention to enable its appearance (an argument that in some ways parallels Heidegger's description of the relationship between *Dasein*, the being that cares for Being, and *Sein*).
28 According to Adorno, "Realism, which does not grasp subjective experience, to say nothing of going beyond it, only mimics reconciliation." "Trying to Understand *Endgame*," *Notes to Literature*, 2 vols., ed. Rolf Tiedemann, trans. Shierry Weber Nicholsen (New York, 1991), vol. I, 250.
29 Here the effects of Benjamin's anti-structuralist linguistics on Adorno can be discerned, for Benjamin saw the Saussurean insistence on the absolute arbitrariness of the sign as evidence of the Fall of language from its prelapsarian state in which a mimetic relationship between names and things prevailed. For a helpful account of the differences between Benjaminian and structuralist linguistics, see Irving Wohlfahrt, "On Some Jewish Motifs in Benjamin," in Andrew Benjamin, *The Problems of Modernity: Adorno and Benjamin* (London, 1989). For a suggestive gloss on Adorno's "mimetic" relationship to Benjamin, which goes beyond simple imitation through "influence," see Jameson, *Late Marxism*, 52. He argues, in fact, that on the question of mimesis itself, the two were by no means as unified as is often assumed (256).
30 For a lucid account of Adorno's argument about the dialectic of mimesis and rationality, see Peter Osborne, "Adorno and the Metaphysics of Modernism: The Problem of a 'Postmodern' Art," in Benjamin, ed., *The Problems of Modernity: Adorno and Benjamin*, 29f.
31 Adorno, *Aesthetic Theory*, 174.
32 Theodor W. Adorno, *Negative Dialectics*, trans. E.B. Ashton (New York, 1973), 14.
33 Adorno, *Aesthetic Theory*, 153.
34 Lambert Zuidervaart, *Adorno's Aesthetic Theory: The Redemption of Illusion* (Cambridge, Mass., 1991), 181.
35 Theodor W. Adorno, *Philosophy of Modern Music*, trans. Anne G. Mitchell and Wesley V. Blomster (New York, 1980), 64.
36 Adorno, *Aesthetic Theory*, 455.
37 Jameson, *Late Marxism*, 68. For another consideration of the relation between mimesis and narrative, see Prendergast, *The Order of Mimesis*, 216ff.
38 Still another possibility would be to follow his discussion of hieroglyphic writing and *écriture* in mass culture and modernist art, as Miriam Hansen has suggested in "Mass Culture as Hieroglyphic Writing: Adorno, Derrida, Kracauer," *New German Critique*, 56 (Spring/Summer, 1992).
39 Adorno, "Parataxis: On Hölderlin's Late Poetry," *Notes to Literature*, vol. 2, trans. Shierry Weber Nicholsen (New York, 1992), 130.
40 Ibid., 131.
41 Philippe Lacoue-Labarthe, *Typography: Mimesis, Philosophy, Politics*, ed., Christopher Fynsk, intro. Jacques Derrida, (Cambridge, Mass., 1989), 226. The comparison was made in Adorno, "Parataxis: Hölderlin's Late Poetry," 133. Lacoue-Labarthe's most extensive discussion of Adorno comes in a later piece, "The Caesura of Religion," in *Opera Through Other Eyes*, ed., David J. Levin (Stanford, Ca., 1994), which is a critique of Adorno's essay on Schoenberg's *Moses and Aron*, "Sakrales Fragment." Here he chastises Adorno for finding a redemptive moment in the music of the opera, which Lacoue-Labarthe claims reflects a failure to recognize the importance of the libretto in producing a sublime rather than redeemed work.
42 Lacoue-Labarthe, *Typography*, 208.
43 *Ibid.*, 214. Unlike Adorno, Lacoue-Labarthe emphasized the importance of the imitation of the Ancients as opposed to imitating nature, which emerged into prominence in the Renaissance. As Tartarkiewicz points out, "The watchword of *imitating antiquity* appeared as early as the fifteenth

century and by the end of the seventeenth century it supplanted almost completely the idea of *imitating nature.* This was the greatest revolution in the concept of imitation. It changed the classical theory of art into an academic one. A compromise formula was devised for the principle of imitation; nature should be imitated but in the way it was imitated by the Ancients." ("Mimesis," 229).

44 Derrida, like Adorno, generally denies the identity of mimesis and straightforward imitation. See his remarks in "The Double Session," 183. He is, however, far more eager than Adorno to uncouple mimesis from any notion of truth, defined either as unveiling (*alëtheia*) or agreement (*homoiösis* or *adaequatio*). See "The Double Session," 192 and 207.

45 Lacoue-Labarthe, *Typography*, 224.

46 As does Derrida in "The Double Session," 207.

47 Lacoue-Labarthe, *Typography*, 227.

48 Benjamin cites Hölderlin's Sophocles translations as evidence of a belated "baroque" confusion of Trauerspiel and Greek tragedy. See *The Origin of German Tragic Drama*, trans. John Osborne (London, 1977), 189. For a useful discussion of the more totalizing and harmonizing version of the baroque against which Benjamin and Lacoue-Labarthe warned, that of Hugo von Hofmannstahl and the Salzburg Festival, see Michael P. Steinberg, *The Meaning of the Salzburg Festival: Austria as Theater and Ideology*, 1890-1938 (Ithaca, 1990), 223f. Steinberg borrows Adorno's distinction between theater and drama from *In Search of Wagner* to set the ideological totalization of Hofmannstahl's baroque against Benjamin's critical version.

49 As Derrida puts it in his "Introduction: Desistance" to *Typography*: "A *Trauerspiel* plays at mourning, it doubles the *work* of mourning: the speculative, dialectic, opposition, identification, nostalgic interiorization, even the double bind of imitation. But it doesn't avoid it" (42).

50 Lacoue-Labarthe, *Typography*, 258-59.

51 For a helpful account of Adorno's thoughts on semblance, see Zuidervaart, *Adorno's Aesthetic Theory*, chapter 8.

52 Lacoue-Labarthe, *Typography*, 260.

53 Adorno, *Aesthetic Theory*, 193.

54 *Ibid.*

55 Theodor W. Adorno, *Minima Moralia: Reflections from Damaged Life*, trans. E.F.N. Jephcott (London, 1974), 155.

56 Adorno, *Aesthetic Theory*, 19. In his introduction to *Typography*, Derrida introduces the term "desistance" to signify Lacoue-Labarthe's playing with the relationship between mimesis and truth. "Mimesis 'precedes' truth in a certain sense;" he explains, "by destabilizing it in advance, it introduces a desire for *homoiösis* [adequation, similitude, resemblance] and makes it possible, perhaps, to account for it, as for everything, that might be its effect, up and including what is called the subject" (27).

57 For another way to approach the allegorical implications of this argument, see Terry Eagleton, who writes of Adorno's appropriation of Benjamin's notion of non-sensuous correspondences: "One might even name this mimesis *allegory*, that figurative mode which relates through difference, preserving the relative autonomy of a set of signifying units while suggesting an affinity with some other range of signifiers." *The Ideology of the Aesthetic* (Cambridge, Mass., 1990), 356.

58 Philippe Lacoue-Labarthe and Jean-Luc Nancy, "The Nazi Myth," *Critical Inquiry*, 16, 2 (Winter, 1990).

59 *Ibid.*, 298. For a critical gloss on this claim, see Jean-François Lyotard, *The Differend: Phrases in Dispute*, trans. Georges van den Abbeele (Minneapolis, 1988), 152.

60 *Ibid.*, 312. It is also evident, Lacoue-Labarthe claims in "Transcendence Ends in Politics," *Typography* (297), in Heidegger's pre-*Kehre* work, whose mimetological flaws help explain his political "error." For a critique of this argument, which sees it as a subtle way to exonerate the later

Heidegger, see Richard Wolin, "French Heidegger Wars," in Wolin, ed., *The Heidegger Controversy: A Critical Reader* (New York, 1991), 294f.
61 Horkheimer and Adorno, *Dialectic of Enlightenment*, 180.
62 Lacoue-Labarthe, "Transcendence Ends in Politics," *Typography*, 300.
63 Lacoue-Labarthe, *Heidegger, Art and Politics*, trans. Chris Turner (Oxford, 1990), 96.
64 Horkheimer and Adorno, *Dialectic of Enlightenment*, 186.
65 Lacoue-Labarthe and Nancy, "The Nazi Myth," 311.
66 Lacoue-Labarthe's critique of ocularcentrism is typical of many other recent French thinkers, as I have tried to demonstrate in *Downcast Eyes: The Denigration of Vision in Twentieth-Century French Thought* (Berkeley, 1993). See the similar discussion of sight in Derrida, "Economimesis" where the priviliging of vision is related directly to the symbolic recuperation he identifies with mourning because it is less directly affected by the unsublatable object than other senses (19). He claims that the disgust associated with vomit resists such a mourning process, because it produces objects that cannot be reabsorbed or symbolically represented. Derrida, to be sure, also strongly attacks hearing when it is a matter of hearing oneself speak, which implies auto-affection.
67 Lacoue-Labarthe, *Typography*, 179.
68 Derrida, "Introduction: Desistance," *Typography*, 33.
69 In fact, in *Dialectic of Enlightenment*, he and Horkheimer include the prohibition on images among the ways in which rulers prevented the subjugated masses from reverting to mimetic behavior (180-181). They do, to be sure, claim in that text that the sense of smell is superior in terms of the ability to assimilate to the other — "when we see we remain what we are; but when we smell we are taken over by otherness" (184) — but visuality plays a more critical role as the source of mimetic resistance to conceptuality in *Aesthetic Theory*.
70 Gertrud Koch, "Mimesis and *Bilderverbot*" *Screen*, 34, 3 (Autumn, 1993); Hansen, "Mass Culture as Hieroglyphic Writing."
71 Adorno, *Aesthetic Theory*, 141. For a discussion of the value of visuality in Adorno and its relation to Benjamin's notion of "dialectical images," see Susan Buck-Morss, *The Origin of Negative Dialectics: Theodor W. Adorno, Walter Benjamin and the Frankfurt Institute* (New York, 1977) 102f.
72 *Ibid.*, 141-42.
73 Adorno, *Philosophy of Modern Music*, 155.
74 Früchtl, *Mimesis*, 260.
75 See, for example, Leo Bersani, *The Freudian Body: Psychoanalysis and Art* (New York, 1986) chap. 3.
76 Adorno, "Looking Back on Surrealism," in *The Idea of the Modern in Literature and the Arts*, ed. Irving Howe (New York, 1967), 223. For a recent account of Surrealism that thematizes its debts to the uncanny and the compulsive repetitions of the death drive, see Hal Foster, *Compulsive Beauty* (Cambridge, Mass., 1993).
77 See, in particular, "The Position of the Narrator in the Contemporary Novel," *Notes to Literature*, vol. I.
78 In "Economimesis," Derrida, borrowing Bataille's distinction, argues that it is neither a "restricted economy" of circulation, not a "general economy" of waste, but something other (4).
79 Homi Bhabha, "Of Mimicry and Man: The Ambivalence of Colonial Discourse," *October*, 28 (1984); for a discussion of Sherman and mimicry, see Craig Owens, *Beyond Recognition: Representation, Power, and Culture*, ed, Scott Bryson, Barbara Kruger, Lynne Tillman, and Jane Weinstock (Berkeley, 1992), 70f. Both are indebted to Lacan's discussion of mimicry in *The Four Fundamental Concepts of Psycho-analysis*, ed. Jacques-Alain Miller, trans. Alan Sheridan (New York, 1981) 97f.

EXPOSITIONS OF THE MOTHER
A Quick Stroll through Various Museums
Werner Hamacher

Translation by Matthew T. Hartman

The tumult of metaphors which the museum has let loose since its historical appearance revolves with conspicuous constancy around its site. With equal constancy, it bears witness to the fact that this site appears to elude strict definition. Certainly, the museum is a mausoleum, a memorial and a cemetery. It is just as certainly a market-hall, a warehouse, a depot and archive of discarded cultural treasures, of what has been pulled from circulation, immunized or sterilized. It is the cave of Ali Baba and the robbers, a bourgeois-democratic den of thieves, no less than a place for the circulation of goods and the prime meridian of all artistic standards up to the fleeting now of the present. Repository of the master gauge of cultures, their viewing room and gymnasium, their sanatorium and morgue, a stockpile of munitions and spoils, a harem and a temple of the arts, a platonic cave and exit therefrom — certainly, it is all this and there is hardly anything that it would not be. No metaphor for the museum would be out of place, and there is none that could not for its part make its way into the museum. There is no word and no work, no analysis and no narrative, no story and no *aperçu* about the museum that would not for its part be ripe for the museum. And this means that there is nothing that could not be exposed in the museum, nothing that it could not surpass and survive. Everything can be a museum, and the museum is the site of everything that can be said about the museum, the site of everything that can be said about this site — about this site as an ideal, or ideological site; as a commercial and social, political and topographical site. It is thus the site about which never enough can be said or the site of which never enough can be shown — the site of art that no artwork and no art of theory can possibly saturate. Even if a museum were to become an object of its own exhibition, as happens now more than ever, even if there were a museum of museums — and, sooner or later, there will in fact doubtless be such a meta-museum, and presumably not just one — even then, that is to say, if museums make their way into the museum, there will always be the possibility of a further museum — a truly Borgesian museum of Babel in which its incompletion, its invisibility, its inconsistency and dystopy would make up the display.

The museum is not only the site of the inconsistency of the cultures and works it exhibits. Rather, it is a site of inconsistency; its time is inhomogeneous, ana- or dyschronic. Without simultaneously being larger and smaller than itself and thus precisely not itself, a museum cannot contain itself any more than a set according to the Cantor-Russell paradox. No assertion about the museum — and that means: no museum of the museum — can show us the truth of the museum. Every metaphor contrived to characterize the museum must transport it to something other than a site, to a non-site, to something other than chronometric time, a non-time, and expose it there where the museum does not exist. The museum is thus the displacement (*Entstellung*), the ex-position (*Aus-stellung*) of the museum, of everything that it can contain and everything that can be said about it.

Based on these, for the moment, formal findings, one might conclude that the museum is the institution of deinstitutionalization, the institution of — if I may — ekstitution and, consequently, also of the most conceivably radical de-ideologization. For the museum has the power, at least in principle, not only to archive and put to rest, but also to analyze and subject to further critical transformations all the productions of human history, its social formations and transformations. Though it has often been said, even to the point of having become topical and itself ripe for the museum, it is hardly debatable that the museum has the double function of conserving and, through isolation and analysis, of transforming; it upholds traditions and, through their decontextualization, finishes them off. The museum cashes in on the institutions it exhibits — it pockets the sum of their value and annuls them. The museum is tradition cashed-in. But does it still yield a profit for the cultural capital it pockets or does it lead to its bankruptcy? And what kind of profit can be gleaned from this bankruptcy? What is at stake in the economy of tropes and topoi of the metaphors and meta-metaphors of the museum?

One cannot decide these questions dogmatically and formally, but only by way of historical analysis. Yet since the structurally prominent traits of both history and the museum converge, one will perhaps not be able to decide upon them at all, or , if so, than only by way of exception. In order to approach an answer to these questions, one will have to enter the museum, or the library, and establish how, and as what, the museum was experienced at different times. In order to see the museum from the outside, one must already — or still — be in the museum. In order to bring the truth about the museum to light, one must be ready to bring it into the light of the museum. One will thus not be permitted to have any illusions about this truth: even it will still be a truth kept by the museum — even if it is one of the museums of the future. At this point, we can already say that one can only speak about the museum from, or at the threshold of, the museum. And the museum is itself perhaps nothing other than a threshold, an opening and a closing, a farewell and a greeting simultaneously. If it is thus an institution of de-institutionalization, then it is presumably also one of re-institutionalization — if an institution of de-ideologization, then presumably also one that remains susceptible to re-ideologization. But in what forms, or form, is this antinomy perceived? How is this form transformed and why, in the first place, is it susceptible to transformations and, moreover, to a farewell to forms in general ?

In order to give these and some other questions more contour, I will cite a series of passages from texts on the museum and, citing them, transpose them, as it were, into a small museum of the discourse on the museum. My commentaries on these texts will not advance very far and only seldom depart from the most salient details — they will be the observations of a passer-by.[1]

In his book of 1987 *Collectionneurs, amateurs et curieux: Paris, Venice XVIe - XVIIIe siècle*, Krzysztof Pomian set himself the task of accounting for the initial transformations that occasioned the emergence of the museum. Some sentences summarizing his investigations read:

> *La transformation en musée d'un trésor qui, même s'il garde son ancien nom, change de statut, ou d'une collection amassée dans un palais ou un château consiste toujours en la perte par les objets du rôle liturgique, cérémoniel, décoratif ou utilitaire qui fut le leur à l'origine. Cela se fait parfois de manière imperceptible et continue; des objets cessent de remplir leurs fonctions initiales soit parce qu'ils sont passés de mode, soit parce qu'ils ont été abîmés, soit parce que de nouveaux dévelopment techniques les ont rendus obsolètes, mais on les préserve à cause de leur valeur historique ou artistique jusqu'au jour où on décide de les exposer au public.*[2]

> [The transformation into a museum of a treasure, which, even if it keeps its old name, changes in status, or of a collection gathered in a palace or a castle, always involves

> a loss on the part of these objects of the liturgical, ceremonial, decorative or utilitarian role that had originally belonged to them. This transformation is sometimes an imperceptible and continuing process; some objects cease to fulfill their original function either because they are no longer fashionable, or because they have been damaged, or because new technological developments have rendered them obsolete, but, on account of their historical or artistic value, one preserves them all the same until the day when one decides to expose them to the public eye.]

The transformation of the private collection, the family gallery, the curiosity cabinet, or even of the public institution, the city, state, or church treasure, thus begins, Pomian argues, with a loss. It begins with a loss of context, of function, of the value and perspective in accordance with which the objects had been perceived. What Pomian characterizes as the loss of a "role" — *du rôle liturgique, cérémoniel, décoratif ou utilitaire* ["of the liturgical, ceremonial, decorative or utilitarian role"] — is however a loss, he is quick to concede, that is normal within the framework of social and technical development. For when technical innovations render an instrument obsolete, be it a weapon or a sculpture, then it withdraws from its former functional context and forfeits its utility. Once this happens, there are only two reasons why it might be considered for conservation: either on account of its "historical" or on account of its "artistic" value. Neither of these two forms of value, Pomian suggests, can be regarded as given, natural or originary. Both first arise out of a process of emancipation from use, whether ritualistic or of some other technical nature. Objects first emerge as artworks and historical documents — indeed, perhaps as objects in general — through a process of desacralization and detechnicization.

With this interpretation of the transformation from collection into museum, from liturgical or technical object of utility into artwork or historical document, Pomian, for his part, recycles a topos from the discourse of the museum. Indeed for some time now, the topos has belonged to the archive of the discourse-museum, to the museum of the museum. Works of art, this consideration maintains, are originally not meant for the museum, but for use. They first become candidates for the museum by way of their estrangement from custom and use, an estrangement inevitably interpreted by one as loss and by another as emancipation. The transformation makes the works autonomous at the expense of their world. They become useless for the purposes of religious and technical practices. Yet by virtue of their newfound independence, they can finally offer themselves as "themselves," according to their "own" law, as "artworks" or as testimony to "human history." This is the birth of art and of history, the birth, more precisely, of: *l'art pour l'art* and of *l'histoire pour l'histoire* out of the spirit of the museum. The weakness of this interpretation is obvious. Works and instruments do not make their way into the museum only once they have become unserviceable or useless, but, more often than not, even when they can still be of use; and furthermore, the museum is not the site of useless objects but rather the site of their altered use. If, however, they can be assigned this other use (for memory, education, the ostentatious display of symbolic capital), then this so-called estrangement from the primary usage must have already taken place within them, prior to their displacement. In their technical or liturgical use, they must be already qualified for their public exposition and already underway toward the museum. The talk of the "loss" of their "originary" status and their "primary" function, or "role," constitutes an idealization that is just as stereotypical as it is non historical.

I will turn now to some additional examples — further exhibits of the discourse-museum — that also interpret the museum as a site of the transformation from loss of world into profit for art and history. The first is a well-known and often cited passage from Walter Benjamin's study, "Das Kunstwerk im Zeitalter seiner technischen Reproduzierbarkeit" [The Work of Art in the Age of Mechanical Reproduction]. Benjamin writes:

> *Der einzigartige Wert des echten Kunstwerks hat seine Fundierung im Ritual, in dem es seinen originären und ersten Gebrauchswert hatte.... die technische Reproduzierbarkeit des Kunstwerkes emanzipiert dieses zum erstenmal in der Weltgeschichte von seinem parasitären Dasein am Ritual... Von der photographischen Platte zum Beispiel ist eine Vielheit von Abzügen möglich; die Frage nach dem echten Abzug hat keinen Sinn. In dem Augenblick aber, da der Maßstab der Echtheit an der Kunstproduktion versagt, hat sich auch die gesamte Funktion der Kunst umgewälzt. An die Stelle ihrer Fundierung im Ritual tritt ihre Fundierung auf eine andere Praxis: nämlich ihre Fundierung auf Politik*

> [...the unique value of the 'authentic' work of art has its basis in ritual, the location of its original use value.... for the first time in world history, mechanical reproduction emancipates the work of art from its parasitic dependence on ritual.... From a photographic negative, for example, one can make any number of prints; to ask for the 'authentic' print makes no sense. But the instant the criterion of authenticity ceases to be applicable to artistic production, the total function of art is reversed. Instead of being based on ritual, it begins to be based on another practice — politics.][3]

To the shift from the foundation of art in ritual to its foundation in politics — and this shift is for Benjamin an emancipation and a world-historical revolution — corresponds to a shift in the accent of the reception of its use value. The accent shifts, Benjamin argues, from its cult value to its diametrically opposed exposition value. The carvings abandoned in the cave by stone-age man and the *cella* of the mystery cults are exposed to the light of publicity. Benjamin writes:

> *Mit der Emanzipation der einzelnen Kunstübungen aus dem Schoße des Rituals wachsen die Gelegenheiten zur Ausstellung ihrer Produkte. Die Ausstellbarkeit einer Porträtbüste, die dahin und dorthin verschickt werden kann, ist größer als die einer Götterstatue, die*

> *ihren festen Ort im Inneren des Tempels hat. Die Ausstellbarkeit des Tafelbildes ist größer als die des Mosaiks oder Freskos, die ihm vorangingen*
>
> [With the emancipation of the various art practices from [the womb of] ritual go increasing opportunities for the exhibition of their products. It is easier to exhibit a portrait bust that can be sent here and there than to exhibit the statue of a divinity that has its fixed place in the interior of a temple. The same holds for the painting as against the mosaic or fresco that preceded it.][4]

With the emancipation from ritual — and in fact, as Benjamin writes, "out of the *womb* of ritual" — with this birth, this detachment from its mother, from its "originary" cult value, art becomes mobile. It distances itself from "festen Ort im Inneren des Tempels" [its fixed place in the interior of the temple]; displaced, it exposes itself and maximizes its exposition value. With the deliverance from the singleness (*Einzigkeit*) of its origin, it looses itself from its fixation on the singularity (*Einmaligkeit*) of its place (*Stelle*). It multiplies its appearance in space. From the magic of the cave it becomes the public, indeed, virtually democratic, exhibition and transforms the space of its appearance into an exposition (*Ausstellung*), a museum. For Benjamin, the exhibition of art is first of all its ex-position, its placing-outward (*Nach-Außen-Stellung*). In bringing about the dissolution of the cultic matrix, the absolution from the singularity of the "festen Ort[es]" [fixed place], it brings about the *reproduction* of artworks, multiplies their space and "sends" them into the museum of their, in principle, limitless visibility. The work of art in the age of its reproducibility is for Benjamin the dematernated, set-out (*nach Außen gestellte*) artwork: it is the work of art in the exposition. The museum, which Benjamin does not explicitly address in this context, would thus most likely consist for him in the exact opposite of the privileged cave of the magical cultic objects. It would much sooner consist in the multiplicity of the equal-ranking public sites on which these works realize their exposition value. Museum would then have to mean the dissolution of the originary, a fixed site of the interior, an exposition as tendentially unrestricted alienation from all magical and topical functions, a deposition (*Absetzung*) from the placental origo, and the detachment and distantiation (*Entfernung*) from and of the mother. Like film, the museum would have to be the ex-position (*Aus-stellung*), not only of every earlier, but of all possible positions* (*Stellungen*): their de-posing (*Entsetzung*).[5]

In discussing Benjamin's depiction of the world-historical transformation of art, I have drawn attention to the motifs of the "cave," the "cella," the "womb," and the "fixed place in the interior," as well as to the closely related motifs of the "ritual" and the "cult," as motifs of origin, in short, as motifs of the matrix and the mother, not only because they are topical, but also because they are topological or, more precisely, *archi*topological motifs. They constitute a recurrent and a fundamental figure in the museum of the discourse on the genesis of the museum. In a footnote,

Benjamin corroborates the paradigmatic rank he assigns to the figure of the mother through the choice of an example. In his elucidation of the functional change in art from ritual- to exposition-object, this particular example is the only one he explores in any detail. The example he gives is the Sistine Madonna. According to the analysis of Hubert Grimmes, the Madonna was originally painted, Benjamin writes, for the purpose of exhibition, namely, for the public laying-in-state of Pope Sixtus in a side chapel of St. Peter's Church. Since Roman ritual prohibited its exhibition on the high alter, the Madonna was "exiled" (it is Benjamin who uses the formulation "exile") from the chapel to the convent church of the Black Monks in Piacenza. In the Sistine Madonna, its cult value thus is conjoined with its exposition value. And Benjamin indeed presents it as an example of the fact that, in principle, every artwork establishes a link between these polar functions: *ein gewisses Oscillieren,* he writes, *zwischen jenen beiden polaren Rezeptionsarten prinzipiell für jedes einzelne Kunstwerk nachweisen* [a certain oscillation between these two polar modes of reception can be demonstrated for each work of art].[6] This means, however, that the artwork itself, even in the age of its technical reproducibility, can still perform a ritualistic function. It means that the emancipation of art as pure exhibition object has not yet been achieved. The process of dematernation, even the exile of the Madonna in the museum, even in film, will not succeed in bringing about this emancipation, as long as the means of production lie in the hands of capital. Even capital has a cultic use-value; even capital is still a mother as long as it is engaged in the aestheticization of the political. The techno-aesthetic of fascism, in particular, labors at the rehabilitation of genealogical codes oriented toward the imago of the mother. Based on Benjamin's observation about the "oscillation" of, in principle, every single artwork, one can conjecture that even the exhibition has not severed its connection to the paradigmatic figure of the mother. And this mother, it becomes clear from Benjamin's example, is Christian: it is the mother of God. Even the museum is still a "fixed place," a topos and not yet the U-topia of the unbounded democratic multiplicity of sites. Even it is not yet its unrestricted exposition. As long as this Utopia of exposition has not yet been reached, the museum, too, remains the site of a merely restrictive atheologization, atopization, dematernation. The museum remains a metaphor of the mother, her méterpher.

The next example from the library of the museum that I would like to point to, in a somewhat less cursory fashion, supports a series of similarities to the previous one — even if, in the end, it turns out to be its reverse image. In a brief, little known text of 1955, Heidegger, like Benjamin, also expresses his views on the Sistine Madonna and in the same context touches upon the question of the museum. He deals with it not so much in terms of world history as in terms of the history of being. *Daß die Sixtina zum Tafelbild geworden und museal: darin verbirgt sich der eigentliche Geschichtsgang der abendländischen Kunst seit der Renaissance*

[The proper historical course of Occidental art since the renaissance is concealed in the fact that the Sistine Madonna became a panel painting suited to the museum].[7] And Heidegger continues, substantiating the judgment with the following statements about the site, the display (*Aufstellung*) and the exposition (*Ausstellung*).

> *Wo immer künftig dieses Bild noch 'aufgestellt' sein mag, dort hat es seinen Ort verloren. Es bleibt ihm versagt, sein eigenes Wesen anfänglich zu entfalten, d.h. diesen Ort selber zu bestimmen. Das Bild irrt, verwandelt in seinem Wesen als Kunstwerk, in der Fremde. Dem musealen Vorstellen, das seine eigene geschichtliche Notwendigkeit und sein Recht behält, bleibt dieses Fremde unbekannt. Das museale Vorstellen ebnet alles ein in das gleichförmige der 'Ausstellung.' In dieser gibt es nur Stellen, keine Orte*
>
> [Wherever this picture might be 'displayed' (*aufgestellt*) in the future, there it has lost its site (*Ort*). It is prohibited from unfolding its essence in an originary way, i.e., from determining this site itself. Transformed in its essence as artwork, the picture errs, abroad in foreignness. This foreignness remains unknown to the mode of representation (*Vorstellen*) unique to the museum, a mode which, no doubt, retains its own historical necessity and right. This mode of representation (*Vorstellen*) levels everything into the uniformity of the exhibition (*Ausstellung*). In the latter, there are only places (*Stellen*), no sites (*Orte*)].[8]

The "covered" (*verborgene*), the "proper historical course of Occidental art," which Heidegger in these sentences claims to uncover, leads from the "site" (*Ort*), originarily determined by the picture itself, to "places" (*Stellen*), i.e., from what is proper to what is foreign, from truth to errancy, from the singularity of the advent to the uniformity of the object, from "essence" to representation (*Vorstellung*) and exhibition (*Ausstellung*). In short, the "proper course of history" leads to the museum. Heidegger leaves no doubt that the history of art's loss of site (*Ortsverlust*) and decline of essence (*Wesensverfall*) could not have come from without, as it were, by accident. On the contrary, he expressly grants this "mode of representation unique to the museum" "its own historical necessity and right." The essence of the picture, its proper site, one could thus argue, is "essentially" and "properly" menaced by the necessity of surrendering its "site" (*Ort*) to "places" (*Stellungen*) and "exhibitions" (*Ausstellungen*) and of loosing its singularity. Just as non-essence (*Unwesen*) is essential to essence, so the exposition would have to be essential to the picture it posited in itself. Already at its originary site and from, or out of, this site, the work of art would have to expose itself and thus expropriate "its proper essence." But it is exactly this consequence that Heidegger does not draw in his commentary on the Sistine Madonna.[9]

Heidegger can think of the museum as the ex-position of the originary position of truth, as atopization and errancy, only on the condition that he reserves the privilege of being the proper ex-positing (*Aussetzung*), the true site, the proper foreign (*eigene Fremde*), for positing (*Setzung*), the "setting-into-work of truth."[10] In the background of Heidegger's critique of the museum just as in the background of his "destruction" of the metaphysics of representation, the privilege of an originary positing (*Setzung*), or of an inaugural ex-posure (*Aus-setzung*), is strictly upheld. Heidegger can denounce the museum as a place (*Stätte*) of world withdrawal or world ruin only because he assumes the prior existence of an untransposed world and the originary figure of its presentation.

This figure — the proper, primary figure in which the world offers itself, the archetypical figure (*Urfigur*) of figuration — appears in Heidegger's text "On the Sistine Madonna" as the mother. It appears not just as any mother, but as the one and only mother, the mother of God, the Madonna, Mary. That is to say, it appears as *the* mother with *the* child — and, likewise, not just any child, regardless of sex, but the one and only male child, the infant Jesus. As astonishing as it may seem that this scene turns up in Heidegger's writing along with the privilege he thereby accords to Christian theology, without assuming any distance whatsoever, without a single gesture toward relativisation, without an attempt to situate it historically or, equally, in terms of the history of Being — and it is, to my knowledge, the sole text in the entire Heidegger corpus that explicitly and unreservedly speaks out for Christianity[11] — as astonishing as this fact may seem, more astonishing still must appear the vocabulary with which he characterizes the scene. It is none other than that of the ontological difference, of truth understood as *aletheia* and thus of the Setting-into-Work (*Ins-Werk-Setzens*) or the Bringing-into-Work (*Ins-Werk-Bringen*) of truth, as it occurs in the artwork. Heidegger writes, namely: *Maria bringt den Jesusknaben so, daß sie selbst erst durch ihn her-vor-gebracht wird in ihre Ankunft, die in sich jeweils das verborgen Bergende ihrer Herkunft mit-er-bringt* ["Maria brings the infant Jesus in such a way that she is herself first brought forth through him into her advent, which, in turn, brings forth with it the covered recovery of its provenance"].[12] The Madonna with the infant Jesus is for Heidegger a figure of A-letheia, in his translation: the recovering and covering discovery (*der bergenden und sich verbergenden Entbergung*) of what is and how it is. By the one discovered, the son, the one who brings him, in turn, is "brought forth" and made to appear: the one who brings is herself brought by the one whom she brings. The mother is mother only — according to Christian doctrine — insofar as she is the offspring of her child and thus the daughter of her son. It is the son who first makes the mother into a mother, and mother is she only as long as she remains the bearer and simultaneously the one brought forth (*Her-vor-gebrachte*). It is this double genealogical relation that first makes the mother into a mother, the son into a son, and both into an indissoluble pair.[13] It determines their relationship as one of reciprocal bearing, giving, and bringing. As the one who brings and as the one brought, however, the mother must withhold herself, hold herself back behind her son. That is to say, she must not only be the discoverer (*Entbergende*), but also, and for precisely that reason, the one covered and the one who covers herself (*die Verborgene und sich Verbergende*). Only as covered, withholding and holding herself back, can she be the mother at all, the one who holds, recovers and shelters (*Bergende*), and upholds (*bewahren*) the one she discovers (*Entbergen*). In bringing, she must hold herself back even as she holds on to the son she brought. For the sake of giving, she must withhold what she gives. From the repertoire of these maternal gestures — bringing, bringing forth, giving, holding, carrying, recovering and sheltering, in every thinkable inflexion and configuration — ensues for Heidegger the supposition that it belongs to the essence of the mother, to her advent and arrival, that she: *in sich jeweils das verborgen Bergende ihrer Herkunft mit-er-bringt* [always brings forth with her in herself the covered recovery and concealed concealment of her provenance].[14]

Mother and child bring themselves forth in the movement of aletheic truth, in the movement of the ontological difference. They hold up in it(*aufhalten*), mutually hold one another back (*zurückhalten*), and hold one another tight. This ontological difference, this difference between Being and beings, this difference between mother and child, and thus this difference of the pair, would not exist if the relationship that constitutes the pair were to dissolve, if the one discovered were not what was discovered by its discovery, if the child were not the child of his mother, beings not the beings of *their* Being. If the mother were not covered and if she were not covered by her son, and if she were not ensheathed and ensheathed by her son — the son is the sheath, the mother of the mother — then she would no longer be the one who recovers (*die Bergende*) and thus no longer be the mother. The pair would be in pieces. The difference would be no difference, no bearing to and no holding apart of the one toward the other; and the truth would be no truth, no self-holding and holding back It would no longer be the truth that upholds itself in its retention. That, however, the Sistine Madonna — the image of the mother-child-pair, the image whose very appearance adheres to the logic of the pairing of mother and child — is this truth, and thus the truth of the mother, Heidegger explicitly states in the following sentences: *So bildet das Bild den Ort des entbergenden Bergens (der* Aletheia*), als welches Entbergen das Bild west. Die Weise seines Entbergens (seiner Wahr-heit) ist das verhüllende Scheinen der Her-kunft des Gottmenschen* [The image forms the site of the discovering recovery (*aletheia*) as which discovering the image essentially is. The way of its discovering (its truth) is the veiling appearing of the provenance of God incarnate].[15] The Sistine Madonna is the figure of difference (*-ferre* means bringing and carrying) that carries out a being in such a way that this carrying out, the bringing, appears in what is brought and thereby simultaneously remains covered and concealed (*verborgen*) as arrival and carrying out. In another context, particularly in "Identity and Difference,"

Heidegger characterizes difference, the ontological difference, as a *carrying out* (*Austrag*) and, in turn, as a birth.[16] In the sketch on the Sistine Madonna, the event (*Ereignis*) of this difference between Being and beings (*Sein und Seiendem*) is likewise presented as the "bringing" and "bringing-forth (*Her-vor-bringen*) of the mother and the son of God and thus once again as a birth, as the event of motherhood. What happens — what happens but a single time and yet in this single occurrence happens once and for all: all that happens — is birth. Difference, its event, is birth. Still for Heidegger, it is not just any birth, but the birth of "God incarnate," the "incarnation of God." It is the *kat exochen* Christian event and defines the ontological as christological, as christo-ontological difference.

The difference, the ontological difference, has a name: it is called the Sistine Madonna; and she has a faith: she is Christian; and a historical region: the occident. Heidegger's ontology is a Christian meterology.[17]

I have spoken of the mother as a figure of *aletheia* and of difference. But she — and more exactly: the "essence" of the mother, her offering (*Darbringung*) of the son and her bringing forth (*Her-vor-bringung*) through the son — is not only one among other possible, historical or otherwise, figures of difference. It is not an ontic figure in the sense of something objective or present at hand, a figure of world or religious history. The mother — the "essence," the advent and the birth of the mother — is the only figure for Heidegger, the figure of difference as the matrix of figuration. He writes: *Das Bringen, worin Maria und der Jesusknabe wesen, versammelt sein Geschehen in das blickende Schauen, darein das Wesen beider gestellt, daraus es Gestalt ist* [The Bringing, in which Maria and the child Jesus have, and emerge as, their essence (*wesen*), convenes its happening in the gazing look in which the essence of both is formed and out of which it becomes a figure]. This figure is not interpreted by the image as something that would lie beyond it. It is not the imitation, or mimetic or depiction, of something that had already previously been at hand. This figure, this pair of figures (*Gestaltenpaar*) of mother and child, is the event of figuration itself; and the becoming figure of God (*das Werden zur Gestalt Gottes*), his becoming man, *happens as* this image.[18] *In the image*, and as *this image*, Heidegger writes, *geschieht das Scheinen der menschwerdung Gottes, geschieht jene Verwandlung, die auf dem Altar als 'die Wandlung', als das Eigenste des Meßopfers sich ereignet* [the appearance of the becoming man of God occurs, that transformation occurs that takes place on the alter as "transubstantiation," as that which is most proper to the sacrifice of the mass].[19] The Sistine Madonna is the transubstantiation and transformation of God into a visible form. In her and as her, formation happens as the convocation (*Versammlung*) of the Eucharistic happening (*Geschehen*) of difference into form. The mother in her offering (*Darbringung*), in her "essence," is the form of formation. And since she is herself the form of *aletheia*, she is the form of every possible formation, of every possible figuration, transformation or transubstantiation. She is not one among other possible or actual ontic-historical forms, but that single one in whose movement the happening of formation proceeds in general: the Sistine Madonna is the ontic-ontological matrix of the coming-to-form (*Gestaltwerdung*) par excellence. The matrix of every possible phenomenon, she is phenomenality in action. The God, who in her image becomes visible as a human form, can be neither a personal nor in general a phenomenologically thematizable entity before or outside of his offering. (Heidegger does not speak of this God presumably because he does not exist before or outside of his birth.) For Heidegger, God can be nothing else than the event of his offering, nothing else than his "transubstantiation," his formation and incarnation. He is *ferenz* to, and different from, form. Just as form is achieved in the Madonna with child and the Eucharist, so God is the event of birth and thus the event (*Ereignis*) of motherhood. God, this is his incarnation, his becoming figure, art, man. He is, in a word, the Sistine Madonna.

This is, one could argue, if not a heretical, then, at the very least, an idiosyncratic interpretation of Christianity, and one that bears scant resemblance to the Vulgate of official church doctrine. But as little as it can be doubted that it is an *interpretation* of the primal Christian scene (the anthropogenesis of God, the transubstantiation), so little can it be doubted that it is an interpretation of precisely this *Christian* and of no other scene. One could object further that, in order to think what mother, motherhood and birth mean, one would have first to think of the difference between Being and beings. One would have to think that the event of birth as such — this, as one supposes, empirico-historical happening — first determines itself in the "essence" of the event and thereby in the "transubstantiation" of the mere That of Being into the phenomenal What of beings and never the reverse. Heidegger, however, leaves no doubt that the ontological *difference* determines itself as a carrying out (*Austrag*), bearing (*Gebärde*), and further birth. As far as the Occidental epoch of thinking is concerned (the only one that for Heidegger can lay claim to this title), he leaves no doubt that the happening (*Geschehen*) of this difference in the history of Being is singular and thus, in accordance with the thought of monotheism, unrepresentable, unreproducible, and unrepeatable. He leaves, moreover, no doubt that the structure of aletheic truth is a historically determined and historically determining structure, i.e., a structure of dispensation (*Schickung*), of transmission (*Sendung*), of mission, and of messianism. He leaves just as little doubt that the structure of epochality itself — which is the structure of *aletheia* as the self-covering discovery (*sich verbergende Entbergung*) — has the structure of a convocation (*Versammlung*) to form and thus the form of the Messiah. Finally, he leaves no doubt — even if he should have only explicitly asserted this but a single time, in the text "On the Sistine Madonna" — that this form is that of Christ offered up (*darbringen*), held, and held back by his mother and that it is this form only in an image, in this singular image, of Christian art.[20] Yet this does not mean Heidegger discovered in the Sistine Madonna, say, the "expression," the coincidentally Christian "exemplification" or "illustration" of the "principle" of *A-letheia* or of the "fundamental structure" of the ontological difference. Nothing would contradict more blatantly everything that he had written on the subject. On the contrary, Heidegger thought that truth was the setting-into-work of truth, the carrying out of difference, and the historicallity of history, from the matrix of Christian messianism. What birth, what mother, what offering (*Darbietung*) and covering (*Verbergung*), what anthropogenesis and art, mean is not understood by Heidegger on the basis of what had previously, already and independently been understood as ontological difference. Rather, this difference is understood as birth — and indeed as Christian birth — as the "essence" of the mother — of the Christian mother — and as Christian anthropogenesis and transformation into art. The Sistine Madonna is nothing other than the advent out of the ontological difference; this advent is nothing other than the happening (*Geschehen*) of Christian-occidental history — and that means for Heidegger the happening of history in general. And this history is nothing other than its concentration (*Versammlung*) in the form of an image and in the society this image founds. The Sistine Madonna is "our" truth and, in truth, "our" mother.

What for Heidegger was both fulfilled and lost in the exposition of the Sistine Madonna, in her passage into the museum, becomes easier to understand. Not only was a world lost, but the world in general; not only a historical epoch, but the one and only epoch of the occidental "mission" (*Geschicks*). Not only was the one, the Christian *parousia*, lost, but, as this *parousia*, *parousia*, history, advent, "coming-to-presence" (*Anwesen*) as such was lost: the ontological difference, the mother and her birth. When the Madonna is transposed into the museum, she is exported from *her* site (*Ort*), from the site she herself determined, and drawn out into foreignness, into errancy. She becomes one object among a uniformity of others. She ceases to be the recovering (*bergende*) — and that means, also, the continuously pregnant — one. Having been leveled, she is flat: *Das museale Vorstellen ebnet alles ein in das gleichförmige der 'Ausstellung'* [The mode of presentation unique to the museum levels everything to the uniformity of the "exposition"].[21] In the museum, the mother ceases to be a mother. She dies there, even as she delivers (*bringt*) the infant Jesus who "brings her forth" (*her-vor-bringt*): the exposition is the miscarriage of the delivery; the museum is the "displacement" (*Versetzung*) of the "site" (*Ort*), the abortion (*Abort*) of the Christian-ontological difference, the abortion (*Abtreibung*) of God and thus the termination of the "transubstantiation" (*Wandlung*), the devastation of the sacrifice of the mass — a Good Friday at Christmas without Easter Sunday, Golgotha before its time and without resurrection. And worse yet: the museum is the ontotheological perversion *kat exochen*, in which God is still God and yet not, in which Being still delivers itself but as miscarriage, to the wrong site, into errancy — misbegotten God, erring mother, misplaced Being. Henceforth, there is only a uniform multiplicity of mothers, who are at the same time not mothers; of sons, who are not sons; of "singular happening[s] of this singular image" [einzigen Geschehnis[sen] dieses einzigen Bildes], which are neither singular, nor happenings, nor images. Henceforth, there is only a God decomposed into gods; henceforth, only gods disfigured into idols of representation (*Vorstellen*), only representations representing themselves in infinite uniformity and thus representing nothing at all: the era of the museum is that of a nihilism unconscious of itself. Heidegger not only hears, one could say, the Christian lament — God is dead, and you murdered him — crying out from the museum. He hears, as far as it is still to be heard, that the mother does not give, bear, or recover; that she is deposed and exposed, a mother in the exposition, a foreigner and thus no longer a mother: the mother is dead — the only one from whom a redeemer and redemption could have been expected — she is no more, she does not give herself, she — Being — gives not, is not (*gibt [es] nicht*).

As far as it is still to be heard — for, Heidegger says: *dem musealen Vorstellen, das seine eigene geschichtliche Notwendigkeit... behält, bleibt dieses Fremde unbekannt* [This foreignness remains unknown to the mode of presentation (*Vorstellen*) unique to the museum, a mode which, to be sure, retains its own historical necessity...]. Thus, outside of Heidegger, no one knows that she actually is the foreigner, that the mother is dead; the advent, terminated; that Being is not itself. No one knows that the image in the museum is a perversion of *parousia*, that this museum itself is a perversion of the altar and the church, whose structure, according to Heidegger, is "founded and fulfilled" by this image.[22] The "mother" church, the ecclesia, the congregation, the theopolitically organized society, displaced into the museum, is a church without church. She is a congregation that continually ungrounds and continually renders itself incomplete, a society that forsakes itself in its advent. In this society, no God can appear anymore, neither a social substance nor an existential being-with that would still know itself as such. In this society, in the mother who is not one, the mother is no longer even known and remembered as lost, not even as once having been. But this can mean two things: that she never did exist as a figure — in a way, Heidegger's talk about the self-*covering* discovery (*sich verbergende[.] Entbergung*) points to as much — and that, in the uniformity of the mode of presentation unique to the museum, her formlessness has usurped all power and dominion. It can mean that she was never there and that she never was a mother in the first place, and that, precisely in her absence, she is unconsciously omnipotent.[23]

The museum, it would appear, is regularly interpreted as a site of abandonment by the mother: "our" abandonment by every matrix of relating (*Verhalten*), "our" abandonment by "us"; abandonment by the one orienting and originary figure, by history, by the history that could safeguard a provenance and open a future; abandonment by the mother, whether it be interpreted as emancipation from use — as Benjamin and Pomian would have it — or as loss of world and essence — as Heidegger would have it — abandonment once more of the mother by the mother. An abandonment, a forsakeness, of the most extreme ambiguity: for it is abandoned to abandonment and thus, perhaps, no abandonment at all. I continue on in this small gallery of the discourse on the museum and turn to another scene, a scene revealing that the poetry of forsakeness is not only pervasive in theoretical conceptions of the museum, but that it is also conjured up in literature, indeed, already in the literature of the nineteenth century. It reveals, above all, that the tradition cashed in by the museum still lives on in the museum — or, more precisely, on its borders and as museum — and that the spent religious capital can further maximize. The scene I have in mind bears the title "The Emptiness of Picture-Galleries" and is to be found in "The Marble Faun" by Nathaniel Hawthorne, which, concurrent with its American publication, came out in England under the title "Transformation." I shall once again overlook the scene's context and restrict myself instead to highlighting some of its details. Though they testify, as is clear on the first glance, to the iconoclasm of a very American Puritanism, they nevertheless have constant recourse to the European *vanitas*-tradition. Hawthorne writes:

> Then there is such a terrible lack of variety in their [the Old Italian Masters'] subjects! The churchmen, their great patrons, suggested most of their themes, and a dead mythology the rest. A quarter-part, probably, of any large collection of pictures, consists of Virgins and Infant Christs, repeated over and over again, in pretty much an identical spirit, and generally with no more mixture of the Divine than just enough to spoil them as representations of Maternity and Childhood, with which everybody's heart might have something to do. Half of the other pictures are Magdalens, Flights into Egypt, Crucifixions, Depositions from the Cross, Pietàs, Noli-me-tangeres, or the Sacrifice of Abraham, or Matyrdoms of Saints, originally painted as altar-pieces, or for the shrines of chapels, and woefully lacking the accompaniments which the artist had in view.[24]

Here, all of the by now well-know elements of museum criticism come together. The museum is a public institution for pictures in the age of their reproducedness. Through the repetition of their subject matter, their cultic and liturgical character is hollowed out. All works of art have sunken into an incurable melancholy over the loss of their originary site, of their world. "Virgins and Infant Christs," which lay claim to the greater statistical part of museum exhibits, have forfeited their holiness. Through the admixture of sacral elements, "Maternity and Childhood" have suffered the loss of their humanity: "just enough to spoil them." For

Hawthorne, the museum is also the site (*Stätte*) of the distantiation (*Entfernung*) of, and from, the mother — and, worse yet, the site of her ambiguity. In Christian tradition always virginal, the mother is sexualized and profaned in the eyes of the puritan through the proximity of mythological nudities:

> These impure pictures [of Venuses, Ledas, Graces] are from the same illustrious and impious hands that adventured to call before us the august forms of... the Blessed Mother of the Redeemer, and her Son, at his death, and in his glory.... If an artist sometimes produced a picture of the Virgin, possessing warmth enough to excite devotional feeling, it was probably the object of his earthly love, to whom he thus paid the stupendous and fearful homage of setting up her portrait to be worshipped, not figuratively, as a mortal, but by religious souls in their earnest aspirations towards Divinity. And who can trust the religious sentiment of Raphael...after seeing, for example, the Fornarina![25]

The reproach uttered in this attack on Raphael and his Madonna with child reads, when clearly stated: Not only does the museum transform the church into an institution of repetition, the repetition of the eternal return of the same emptiness, but also, and precisely because of this, into a bordello. It makes of the church a brothel, and of the brothel, a church. The exhibition carries out the profanation of the sacral, and the sacralization of the profane, to the point where both the Heavenly Mother and the Sensual Venus effect their mutual ruin: "just enough to spoil them." What remains, in Hawthorne's words, is "lack," "deficiency," "hollowness," "emptiness," "monotonous misery," "the exile's pain." What remains is "the emptiness of picture-galleries."[26]

But this emptiness, that of the assault of the sensual on the godly — and that means, for Hawthorne, the human — this pain, which the idolatry of catholic aestheticism leaves behind, must for its part be captured in an image and displayed in the picture-gallery. The forsakeness from all true forms must itself become form — the emptiness of the picture-gallery must be displayed in the picture-gallery itself. After the profanation of art has shown that art can no longer be experienced, the only experience that still remains is the experience of the no-longer of art, the experience of God-, of man- and of art-forsakeness, of the abandonment of art. What remains after the end of art — and that means, after the end of religion — is the museum. The museum is the end of art: all works are bound to end up there, even when they remain in place. In the museum, art ceases to be the *parousia*, the real-presence or -advent of a better future. The museum is the end of art as the site (*Stätte*) of the abandonment by art, by all that might be represented in it of what was formerly human and of what is still possibly human, of what is godly. If this final, aporetic experience of art, the experience of its end, is to remain capable of yielding an experience of *art*, or an experience at all, then it must be an experience of the museum. The final, the proper, object of art must be the experience of the museum — and of the museum as the site of art-forsakeness, of God- and man-forsakeness. In the emptiness of the picture-gallery, at least one — a single — picture, or image, must still hang: one that displays the emptiness of the picture gallery.

Catholic, Heidegger's "single" image is that of the Christian Advent. Protestant, the single image that Hawthorne, though not letting her see it, allows his protaganist to long to see again is Sodoma's Sienese fresco of the martyred Christ. The description of the fresco in a passage following the elegiac criticism of the idolatrous art-corruption carried out by the museum makes it into an image of the latter: one could say, into its allegory, if allegories were not always signifying something other than itself and if it were not always, indeed, signifying. Suffering does not signify — and for Hawthorne, the museum, in every one of its images, is a site of sacrilege, of aesthetic corruption, of melancholy and of pain. Hawthorne describes the suffering Christ as follows: "One of the most striking effects produced, is the sense of loneliness. You behold Christ deserted both in Heaven and earth; that despair is in him, which wrung forth the saddest utterance man ever made — 'Why hast Thou forsaken me?'"[27] In this single, utmost, and final sigh and in this single, this *matchless picture*, Christ is abandoned, left alone, "deserted," and "forsaken" by God and man because he is abandoned by the art that should link God and man and thus bring forth the majesty of humanity in the first place. In Hawthorne's Christ (God and man and the image that makes them into God and man) is the art in which he is supposed to incarnate himself. Christ, God incarnate in the image, dies in the museum, his omnipresent Golgotha. No image can succeed, none can really be an image, except for the one that shows the impossibility of the image, its disappearance and destruction.[28] The only possible image is that of the suffering and death of the image: the final image is the literally *executed* image. That the representation of forsakeness (forsakeness by God,man, and art and the representation of this forsakeness as *testimony* to God as well as to man and to art) succeeds in the single case of the tortured and dying Christ is not simply the work of art. Sodoma's fresco, like the paintings of Fra Angelico, is "a visible prayer... Sodoma, beyond a question, both prayed and wept, while painting his fresco...."[29] Sodoma's image not only shows the forsaken Christ, it is itself this Christ in his forsakeness, and as this selfsame Christ, weeping and praying, his painter painted it. The painter and his image are embodiments of God incarnate because they are incarnations of God- and man-forsakeness, of the abandonment of God and man by God and man: they deplete themselves even as they complete themselves (*erschöpfen sich*) in the sigh of de-incarnation "Why hast Thou forsaken me": Christian negative art-theology of the museum.[30]

Hawthorne's image of the god- and man-forsaken picture-gallery — this final, iconoclastic image still susceptible of being displayed in the museum and of which the museum is itself the exhibition — remains within the horizon of the Christian religion. Christianity lives from the death of God. In its final image, even the museum reveals itself as a Christian institution. The devil — this demon of unfaithfulness, of forsaking and forsakeness — is not far off: "that icy Demon of Weariness, who haunts great picture-galleries. He is a plausible Mephistopheles, and possesses the magic that is the destruction of all other magic."[31] Accordingly, the mother is not far off, and this time not as the one who brings (*Bringende*) or sacrifices (*Darbringende*), who bears and gives birth (*Gebärende*), but as the one who mourns her birth, as the *mater dolorosa* or the *Pietà*. Directly in front of the entrance into the museum, Hawthorne depicts a scene of prayer addressed to her as "Divine Womanhood, afar in bliss, but not remote, because forever humanized by the memory of mortal griefs — ...a Mother!"[32] Even this mother mourning her son and her own motherhood is still in Hawthorne's narrative a figure of the museum that grieves for its children and its childlessness. It is a figure of miscarriage, of empty gesture and interrupted gestation (*leeren Gebärde*), a departure (*Abschied*) of the mother from motherhood. The museum that comes out empty-handed and mournful of the fact that god no longer appears in it is not despite this fact, but precisely because of it, the proper Christian site. It is the site of "memory" and "bliss," the site of blissful mourning. It is the only site where humanness and godliness touch. The museum is a *Pietà*.

We have not left the gallery of Christianity: The mourning for the museum, the mourning of the museum for the museum, the mourning of the mother for herself, the lost mother of the lost son, make it clear that even the image of the empty museum, be it the final and only one, is still susceptible of being displayed in the museum. They make it clear that the figure of the forsaken mother, of dematernation, is still a figure, a Christian figure, and awaken the suspicion that the Christian gallery of abandonment cannot be abandoned at all. The discourse on the end of the museum, like the discourse on the end of art, is still christological. Mourning has no end; it is, as Hawthorne's text suggests, melancholia with all the symptoms of self-destruction because it holds fast to what is lost and surrenders the figure of infinite incorporation for that of a destructive incarnation. This is the scene sketched out in Hawthorne's text: the melancholia of the museums over a lost Messiah or a lost mother is still itself this Messiah or the mother in their lostness. The museum presents itself as the metaphor — as Metaphor — of a forsaken mother. This scene is not, as one is want to say, historical, datable to around the middle of the nineteenth century, as if it were firmly implanted there, in "its" "place," in its maternal fabric. It migrates. Even so-called postmodernism, which proclaims the end of the great myths, becomes recognizable as the maniacal reverse of its great depression, as post-, and thus, still in agreement with the Christian model, as maternism.

The question gradually taking shape in these observations is that of the possibility of a mourning for mourning, of the forsaking of forsakeness, of a no longer, or not yet, Christian *Pietà.* If there were to be such a mourning, then it would have to be older and more powerful — or more powerless — than the one it leaves behind. It would have to be a "mourning" preceding every mourning that orients itself on the image of the mother. It would have to be a "fore-mourning" (*Vor-Trauer*), in whose trajectory this image of the mother could first emerge. A further scene points to just such an abandon, to a forsaking that fore-mourns for a time immemorial, *for*gotten, prehistoric and pre-originary. It points to a mourning before every possible loss — to something other than mourning, or fore-mourning, and something other than loss. Signed by Proust and written some sixty years after that of Hawthorne, this scene, located at the beginning of the second part of "A l'ombre des jeunes filles en fleurs" [Within a Budding Grove], records no meditations on an image, no observations and no elegies, not even a stroll through the museum, but just a mention of it. Adorno drew attention to this short passage in his essay, "Valéry Proust Museum."[33] I will highlight the motifs he passed over. The question addressed on the sparse page of the *Recherche* to which I turn concerns the experience of travel and thus also the time and space of experience in general. "La différence entre le départ et l'arrivée" [The difference between departure and arrival], this difference, in which the experience constitutes itself and which is itself this experience, becomes palpable for Proust in the distance, in the departure, in "départ." Its emblem, indeed its "schema," is "l'opération mystérieuse qui s'accomplissait dans ces lieux spéciaux, les gares" [the mysterious operation performed in those peculiar places, the railway stations].[34] In order to be able to undergo an experience, one cannot wish to inhabit the world of habit. One must rather bid it farewell. Against this possibility of experiencing, not only time and space, but also phantasy and language, the present epoch has developed the mania, Proust notes, for showing every imaginable thing in its original surroundings. But in so doing, it suppresses the essential thing: the act, namely, that separates and isolates them from precisely these surroundings. The example Proust gives of this experiential impediment consists in the custom of "presenting" images only in their markedly antiquarian, contemporary contexts — and he isolates, here, the word "presenting" with ironic quotation marks to signal, as it were, that this procedure of "presentation" itself strips them of their surroundings.

> *On 'présente' un tableau au milieu de meubles, de bibelots, de tentures de la même époque, fade décor qu'excelle à composer dans les hôtels d'aujourd'hui la maîtresse de la maison la plus ignorante la veille, passant maintenant ses journées dans les archives et les bibliothèques, et au milieu duquel le chef-d'oeuvre qu'on regarde tout en dînant ne nous donne pas la même enivrante joie qu'on ne doit lui demander que dans une salle de musée, laquelle symbolise bien mieux, par sa nudité et son dépouillement de toutes particularités,*

les espaces intérieurs où l'artiste s'est abstrait pour créer

> [A picture is nowadays 'presented' in the midst of furniture, ornaments, hangings of the same period, stale settings which the hostess who but yesterday was so crassly ignorant but who now spends her time in archives and libraries excels at composing in the houses of today, and in the midst of which the masterpiece we contemplate as we dine does not give us the exhilarating delight that we can expect from it only in a public gallery, which symbolises far better, by its bareness and by the absence of all irritating detail, those interior spaces into which the artist withdrew to create it].

Pomian and Benjamin, Heidegger and Hawthorne — the historians, the philosophers, and the writer — whose images of the museum we have been viewing up to now, all agree that the image must be sought out at its site — in the cave, in the "womb," in the original surroundings, in its liturgical or cultic function, in its use — in order to still be visible as this image; and they all agree that it loses its proper, original substance, as soon as it strays into the museum. To Proust, this is the ideology of the bourgeois "maîtresse de la maison." It is the ideology of the housekeeper, the economist of experience, who insists on keeping everything in its place, in her and its "milieu," and who does not abide a "changement d'habitude, c'est-à-dire la cessation momentanée de l'Habitude" [the change of habit, that is to say, the momentary cessation of Habit]. But these images and the experiences set loose in them cannot be enjoyed, *tout en dînant* [as we dine], in the maternal habitat, but only where they have distanced themselves from her, where they have abandoned the "milieu," the house, the habitat, where they have broken through the continuum of their surroundings and their time and have taken leave of their world. And this departure — here is Proust's decisive insight — must precede this world. Not only does art not belong to the hostess of the house, but there would not be any art for her to "present," there would be no house and no hostess, if the distance from art were not given in the first place. The space of this distance, of this departure, is the railway station. It does not *present* itself, but "presents" itself — and presents itself, in the first place, in the museum. The museum, like that railway station for Proust, is distance and thus the atopic, achronistic and in every respect heterogeneous condition of all topo-, chrono- and genealogical orders.[35] Before art, the museum must already have been there. Before the arrival, the departure. Before the mother, the outset from her — and it is only out of this *départ* that she can be experienced at all. The beginning is not the mother, but the experience that a mother is not there.

The museum is for Proust the site of outset before every possible arrival. It is a railway station, a way station, and art sets out from it. Art is art at all only because it is the art of setting-out and going-wayward (*Kunst des Abschieds*), of isolation, of abstraction, of disenchantment, of *dépouillement.* "Dépouillement" — divestment of all characteristic properties (*Eigentümlichkeiten*), excoriation, skinning (from *spolium* and spolaz — skinned hide, stolen panoply of the enemy), denudation — is the gesture, the gesture before every possible gestation, with which art detaches itself from all that could belong to it and from all to which it could belong.[36] Heidegger's sentence, "The Sistine Madonna belongs in the one church of Piacenza" [Die Sixtina gehört in die eine Kirche zu Piacenza], would be impossible for Proust. For Proust, she does not "belong" at all, and the space of this non-belonging is the museum: the space of absolute alienation, of, as Proust writes, "nudité." If for Proust there can still be a husk and a house, then only from *dépouillement.* If there can still be a mother, then only from the distance of the mother; if there can still be presence, then alone from the *différence entre le départ et l'arrivée,* from difference and outset: a setting out, paradoxically, prior to that from which it parts. The pit of forgetting is first the well of remembering — but only of an arbitrary, non-intentional remembering.[37] Thus, it is, here, in a very unchristian manner that the absence of the mother antecedes the mother. One fails to understand what is at issue in the word "mother" — or *mère* — before one encounters it in a railway-station or a museum. (At what price? One knows since Bergotte's encounter with that one detail of that one painting of Ver Meer.) The parting (*Abschied*) with the imago of the mother, which for a long time had defined the concept and experience of the museum, seems first to succeed with Proust and with the move into a museum, that is itself a space of parting and of setting out — of a departure before every possible arrival, of a setting out, not from the mother, but *before* the mother.

Yet the marvels and terrors of Christianity still live on in this anteroom. They do not define it, but they are cited in it (just as the word "présente" is cited by Proust). The *lieux merveilleux* that railway stations and museums constitute for Proust are also, he says, *lieux tragiques.* For, in such places, one has to leave all hope of return behind. And he cites the verse embossing the entrance of Dante's Inferno (*Il faut laisser toute espérance* [It is necessary to cast aside all hope]) so as to continue, ironically but also quite bitterly: *de rentrer coucher chez soi, une fois qu'on s'est décidé à pénétrer dans l'antre empesté* [of going home to sleep in one's own bed, once one has decided to penetrate into the pestiferous cavern] — the railway station is the Dantean hell — *par où l'on accède au mystère...* [through which one gains access to the mystery]. The bizarre conjunction of hell and modern industrial architecture makes the Christian myth displayed in the museum of tragic antiquities into a citation just as much as it immerses the Parisian railway station into the citation of the pestiferous cavern. With this connection, the reality of modernity becomes no less a citation and museum-like than the literary tradition in whose light it is dramatized. This double estrangement also affects the privileged site of departure — the railway station and the museum. They do not remain, as often first "presented," the fixed points and schemas of the city and of artistic creativity. Rather, they are exposed to a movement over which they can no longer exercise control. Of a sky unfolding over glass-roofed sheds, Proust writes, namely, that it can only be compared to those on the canvases of the Italian renaissance painters: the railway station vaunts an image that does not stand in it — or in the museum — but under which — railway station or museum — it itself stands. The museum is the effect of the image it made possible. Of Saint-Lazare, Proust writes:

> [*Il*] *déployait au-dessus de la ville éventrée un de ces immenses ciels crus et gros de menaces amoncelées de drame, pareils à certains ciels, d'une modernité presque parisienne, de Mantegna ou de Véronèse, et sous lequel ne pouvait s'accomplir que quelque acte terrible et solennel comme un départ en chemin de fer ou l'érection de la Croix*
>
> [[It] extended over the eviscerated city one of those bleak and boundless skies, heavy with an accumulation of dramatic menace, like certain skies painted with an almost Parisian modernity by Mantegna or Veronese, beneath which only some terrible and solemn act could be in process, such as the departure by train or the erection of the Cross.][38]

The sky, unfolding over the railway station and its equivalent, the museum, is comparable to the sky of a painting that could hang in this very museum. And thus the museum strays into its pictures. It is, like the image it houses, simultaneously larger and smaller than itself, never containing, or "belonging" to itself, but rather separating itself in a final movement of *dépouillement* even from its "proper" space: the space of departure, which is itself exposed to the movement of departure. Parting even with parting, and parting first of all with the momentous, cultic, Christian talk of parting, makes Proust's "image" of the museum also a parting with the "image" and with the "museum" and likewise with what he cites as the "symbol" of those *espaces intérieurs* [interior spaces] of artistic creation. There is no interior space. Like its images, the museum is open, not a separate space, but rather time and space as the movement of setting apart. The museum stands in the image that stands in the museum: a *mise en abîme*, for which there are only ever further museums of museums. There is never a last and thus never a museum and never a *museum* — neither an interior nor an imaginary one, neither a distinctive object nor the conceptual unity or the proper name "museum," neither the metaphor "museum" nor the metaphors for the "museum." The "museum," beneath the almost Parisian sky of Mantegna or Veronese, no longer belongs to the register of meternymies — as Hawthorne's image of the *mater dolorosa* does. It is one of the elements of a pre-maternal, open metonymy, of a metonymic movement that brings each of its elements into a never substantial, always external relationship to others, and thus, marks each one, *a limine*, as catachresis. In Proust's image of the museum, the museum takes leave of itself: it is an image without museum, a museum without image, a museum without museum.

Beyond what Marcel explicitly says about the museum (that it is the site of the stripping of all contents, memories, and meanings that might precede or adhere to the art work), the rhetoric of the deliberations in which these thoughts were unfolded reveals a structure of greater complexity. The museum is not only the site in which something is stripped bare, it is the stripping bare of the site, the stable topos, the secure foundation, the logically, or historiologically, fixable locality. With this *mise en abîme*, the museum has slid into an abyss and has itself become an abyss, an aporetic topos of atopia, a museum that ceases and always has ceased to be founded on the semantics of its concept and whose tropes are swept up into the vertiginous syntagmatics of an impossible figure, the figure of the impossible determination and representation of every figure. "Museum" does not simply mean the site of *dépouillement*, but, more precisely, the *auto*-dépouillement of every site, every topos, every place, position and figure. Its slogan can no longer run "museum, (ergo) sum," but, at best, "museum nec sum." This fundamental inconsistency, this inconsistency of the fundament, which the museum is to offer art as birthplace and end, dictates the movement of the last legerdemain of Proust's sentence. It is a zeugma in which the paradox of self-distantiation achieves its comical climax. The heavens, he writes, "under which only a horrid and sinister act could be carried out, [are] like a departure in the train or the erection of the cross." The juxtaposition of "departure in the train" and "erection of the cross" asserts a correspondence between two elements that, because of their incompatibility, are torn apart even as they are juxtaposed; and since each element of the comparison first receives its new determination in the zeugma, not only the pair, but each of its members is torn. The zeugma is a *sparagmos:* parting with Christian parting, absolution from the Christianly determined, the ontological difference, de-paring, departure of the train before a Pietà could commence her mourning.

It is a museum thus without museum: a museum that is only a museum because it is not one, that only coincides with itself because it never arrives at itself, that only abstains because it cannot restrain and maintain itself, neither as concept nor as trope, or as topos; a museum that is always more and less than itself and that has a *self* only *as* this "more or less;" a museum that is only *open* to *possible* museums but that, precisely by virtue of its openness, does not allow a single one of these museums to establish itself and that rejects every "actual," every accomplished possibility; a museum thus as the infinite virtualization of the museum and as an equally infinite depositivization, deposition, ex-position. It withholds itself only as that in which it is withheld: it withholds itself as another does not hold but, rather, breaks its hold; it does not bear or bear out but remains unbearable. Not a matrix of itself, not a model, not a mother — not a gestating or a gesturing one, nor one that mourns herself and her loss — it is rather the mere possibility of maternation, never the presence or presentation of a mater, but always an *ammaternation* that only admits the figure of the mother as exposed, this side of both her position and her negation, "her" *affiguration* this side of every figure and its disavowal, her *afference*, yet therefore no longer "hers," in which the carrying out and through of difference, the ontological and Christian, to which Heidegger and Hawthorne cling, would be left to the movement of its opening, its possibilization and the impossibilization of its "actuality." For Heidegger, the mother was the figuration of the figure, pre-origin and delivery in a difference that could still be determined as the bearing and maintaining of a messianic form; for Hawthorne, the allegorist of god-forsakeness, it was the residual figure of figuration that preserved the possibility of representation on the mourning-borders of its ruins. In Proust's paradoxes, the *mise en abîme* and the zeugma, the metaphor of the mother and of the museum, her meterphors and meternyms, her bearing, bearing out, and her carrying over : her difference is exposed to another movement in which they, of course, do not disappear, but in which they can no longer figure as the ground or "truth," the guarantor of stability or the messianic essence of history: their "difference" is left to another that does not belong to them but to which they owe their existence: an opening of bearing and holding, in which the question remains open whether or not it will ever be borne out and whether in what is borne out a figure can ever take shape. An *afference*, therefore, in whichever difference, the ontological too, is laid open. Museum without museum also means — but "means" only insofar as "to mean" itself is in question — that the museum is not a consistent site, nor is it even a consistent movement. It cannot be borne nor does it bear. Strictly speaking, it is itself never the museum of a museum that it could shelter, pass on and conserve. The "museum without museum," is, thus, also not a formula that for its part could be exhibited and detained in a museum, even if it were a discourse museum. For the interminability and beginninglessness of the museum, and thus not a historical epoch thereof, but the *epoché* of the museum and of every possible sentence spoken about it is declared in this paradoxical syntagm, this ana- and atagm. "Museum without museum" is the proposition of its *de-posing* (*Entsetzung*).

The visitor quits the museum. This is the scene — the last I can mention here — that Paul Valéry sketched in his essay of 1923, "Le problème des musées," which appeared shortly after the publication of Proust's text, though it is unlikely he knew it.[39] He begins with the dry observation, *Je n'aime pas trop les musées* [I don't much like museums]. The principles of classification, of conservation, and of public utility represented by the museum he deems well and good, yet they bear positively no relation whatsoever to what he loves in art, namely, pleasure. Upon entering the museum, he is obliged to hand over his walking stick and asked to extinguish his cigarette. He compares the museum to a temple — *Mon pas se fait pieux* [my gait becomes pious] — and to a salon, to a cemetery and a school; he feels depressed and bored, weary and fatigued. Above all, he feels exhausted on account of the jealousy and murderous clash raging between the individual paintings and sculptures, each one averring more vehemently than the other a monarchical claim to exclusivity and thus challenging the existence of the others. However, the claim to absolute sovereignty Valéry observes in the individual works of art, he finds again in the institution of the museum itself, which rallies them together in democratic turbulence. For, he explains: *Le musée exerce une attraction constante sur tout ce que font les hommes. L'homme qui crée, l'homme qui meurt, l'alimentent. Tout finit sur le mur ou dans la vitrine.... Je songe invinciblement à la banque des jeux qui gagne à tous les coups* [The museum exerts a constant attraction on everything that men do. The man who creates, the man who dies feed it. Everything ends on the wall or in the glass-case. I cannot but think about the gambling bank which wins everytime].[40] Everything is destined for the museum. The cultural capital amassed by museums is, to be sure, *un capital excessif et donc inutilisable* [an excessive and therefore unusable capital], a capital, one could add, that continually decapitalizes and decapitates itself, that turns its jealousy against itself and contests its own existence. *L'homme moderne...est appauvri par l'excès même de ses richesses* [modern man is impoverished by the very excess of his riches]. And he is tired, this modern museum-goer, the modern who defines himself as museum-goer. After quitting the exposition, he speaks twice of fatigue, of the fatigue of the museum — *Quelle fatigue, me dis-je, quelle barbarie!* [What a weariness, I said to myself, what barbarity!] — and of his own — *l'extrême fatigue.... Je sors la tête rompue...* [Extreme weariness...I leave with a shattered head]. Finally, already in the streets, the "elucidation" of the "Problem of the Museums" finally dawns on him. The *démon de l'explication* ["the demon of explication"] — other than Hawthorne's *Demon of Weariness* — whispers to him: *Peinture et Sculpture...ce sont des enfant abandonnés. Leur mère est morte, leur mère Architecture. Tant qu'elle vivait, elle leur donnait leur place, leur emploi, leur contraintes. La liberté d'errer leur était refusée.... Tant qu'elle vivait, ils savaient ce qu'ils voulaient...* [Painting and Sculpture...these children are abandoned. Their mother is dead, their mother Architecture. As long as she was alive, she gave them their place, their use, their constraints. The freedom to err was denied them. As long as she lived, they knew what they wanted].[41] Valéry, who, as one knows, harbored a certain sympathy for anarchism, once more has recourse to the myth of the one-time arché, architecture, the mother of the plastic arts. She is dead, and her children, abandoned. There is a museum for works of art only because there is no longer a mother for them. Such is the counsel the museum-goer takes from the demon of explication, from whom he knows that he is often just as inimical to pleasure and thus to art as the museum itself. Even the explanation of the exposition is a part of the exposition; even the talk about the loss of proper place, of architecture, is without place; even the memory of the mother is abandoned by her. With this ironically archaizing memory, Valéry's demon takes his leave: *Adieu, me dit cette pensée, je n'irai pas plus loin* [Farewell, said this thought to me, I will go no further]. The thought could go further, but it would not know where, would not be able to determine its site and would have to, as it has already begun to, make way in errancy, since even it is no longer denied *la liberté d'errer* [the liberty to err]. And this possibility is expressly conceded by Valéry when he says about the malaise that whispered his thoughts to him: *Il remarque ou il invente, — je ne sais quelle relation entre cette confusion qui l'obsède et l'état tourmenté des arts de notre temps* [It observes or invents, — I do not know which relation between this confusion that obsesses it and the tormented state of the arts of our times]. The explanation of the demon is that the confusion of modernity and the tribulation of art were borne of the death of the mother; this explanation could be an observation and it could be an invention. It could hit the mark or it could lead astray. The decision as to whether the absence of the mother does, or does not, elucidate something, as to whether this mother, this arché, ever was and as to whether she is lost, or as to whether it is only an error that there is talk of her at all, regardless: this decision can only remain open.[42]

Valéry's thought comes to him only once he has reached the street. The thought about the mother comes to him only once he has quit the museum, abandoned the site of her presumed absence. Proust could possibly have said: the mother is only she who she perhaps will have been. Without advancing much, Valéry would have to have said: the mother is perhaps she who she can no longer have been. The step out of the museum, the parting of the museum from the museum, is the utopia of this experience.

NOTES

1. Here, in the first niche of the discourse-museum, we should already make allusion to the existence of its outbuildings, its wings and subterranean archives, to those magazines that now and then, *très en passant,* may catch the reader's attention. To be sure, no one can be certain just how far he gets in a museum or its vaults, even on a flying visit. Vladimir Nabokov warned of this in his story, "The Visit to the Museum." Fleeing from the rain, the visitor of a small French provincial town takes refuge in a museum that he had wanted to avoid and rediscovers himself at the end, after a tour through a labyrinthine collection of trivialities and nightmares, on a snow-bound street in Russia. (It is worth noting that the curator of the museum goes by the name of "M. Godard" and that the visit, as involuntary as it is, concerns the portrait of a father, of the grandfather of a friend: *Several years ago--the story begins--a friend of mine in Paris--a person with oddities, to put it mildly--learning that I was going to spend two or three days at Montisert, asked me to drop in at the local museum where there hung,*

he was told, a portrait of his grandfather by Leroy. (Vladimir Nabokov, *Nabokov's Quartett* New York: Phaedra1966, 91)
2. (Paris: Gallimard 1987) 298.
3. (Frankfurt/M.: Suhrkamp 1963) 20-21. English translation in: *Illuminations.* ed. Hannah Arendt, trans. Harry Zohn (New York: Schocken 1978) 223-24.
4. L.c., Germ., 21-22; Eng., 225. (Note slight modification of the translation.)
* Translator's note: the German word "Stelle" (meaning generally "place," "position," "situation," and "posture") will sometimes be translated as "place" and sometimes as "position," or alternatively, "positioning," depending upon the demands of the context. The word is to be distinguished from the German word "Ort," also meaning place, but which, for the sake of clarity and consistency, will be translated as "site." For Heidegger, as Werner Hamacher later points out in his commentary, "Stelle," in the sense of "place," comes to designate a place divested of its properties, a generic place, while "Ort," translated here as "site," designates the space of an event or happening, a proper place: the site of an appropriation (*Ereignis*).
5. In the Artwork-essay, Benjamin's treatment of the lexicon of "Stellungen," positions; "Einstellungen," settings (in the sense of "focus"); "stellen," to place or position; and "Standpunkte," standpoint or point of view, hardly permits another reading. He deploys this vocabulary with striking insistence when he notes the disappearance of that place (Stelle) which, for its part, cannot be viewed from the standpoint of another place (Stelle): *Eine Film- und besonders eine Tonfilmaufnahme...stellt einen Vorgang dar, dem kein einziger Standpunkt mehr zuzuordnen ist, von dem aus die...Aufnahmeapparatur ...nicht in das Blickfeld des Beschauers fiele.... Dieser Umstand--er mehr als jeder andere--macht die etwa bestehenden Ähnlichkeiten zwischen einer Szene im Filmatelier und auf der Bühne zu oberflächlichen und belanglosen. Das Theater kennt prinzipiell die Stelle, von der aus das Geschehen nicht ohne weiteres als illusionär zu durchschauen ist. Der Aufnahmeszene im Film gegenüber gibt es diese Stelle nicht* ["The shooting of a film, especially of a sound film.... presents a process in which it is impossible to assign to a spectator a viewpoint which would exclude from the actual scene such extraneous accessories as camera equipment, lighting machinery, staff assistants, etc.--unless his eye were on a line parallel with the lens. This circumstance, more than any other, renders superficial and insignificant any possible similarity between a scene in the studio and one on the stage. In the theater one is well aware of the place from which the play cannot immediately be detected as illusionary. There is no such place for the movie scene that is being shot"](l.c., Germ., 35; Eng.,.232-33). With this, Benjamin claims that the film--and one can add: its functional equivalent, the museum--is not only ex-position (*Ausstellung*) in the sense of exhibition and placing-outward, but also in the sense of the dissolution of all places and standpoints for which there might still be a hidden or withdrawn place. When, however, such a place is suggested in film, Benjamin continues, then it is *a result of the editing,* thus of that which also can destroy the illusion of this invisible place. The film differs principally from previous procedures of representation in that it presents a world without the blind spots that permit one to maintain the illusion of authenticity and the illusion of illusion. Thus, in principle, it is a revolutionary procedure of representation since it does not link up with re-presentations, but rather exposes the paradigm of re-presentation as a whole. (On Benjamin's political theory of de-posing (*Ent-setzung*) cf. my "Afformative, Strike," in: *Walter Benjamin's Philosophy - Destruction and Experience* (ed. Andrew Benjamin/Peter Osborne, [London: Routledge 1994] 110-138.)
6. L.c., Ger., 55; Eng., 245.
7. Martin Heidegger, *Aus der Erfahrung des Denkens,* (Gesamtausgabe Bd 13), (Frankfurt/M: Vittorio Klostermann 1983) 119.
8. .c., p. 120. Heidegger continues--Benjamin would have been amused--: "The Sistine Madonna belongs in the one church at Piacenza." [*Die Sixtina gehört in die eine Kirche zu Piacenza.*] Just as everywhere, so also in the question concerning the "essence" of art, this "belonging" (*Gehören*) is

decisive for Heidegger. In his treatise, "The Origin of the Work of Art," he writes: *Wohin gehört ein Werk? Das Werk gehört als solches einzig in den Bereich, der durch es selbst eröffnet wird. Denn das Werksein des Werkes west und west nur in solcher Eröffnung* ["Where does a work belong? The work belongs, as work, uniquely within the realm that is opened up by itself. For the work-being of the work occurs essentially and only in such an opening"] (M.H.- "Holzwege," Frankfurt/M.: Vittorio Klostermann 1950; 30. English translation in: *Martin Heidegger: Basic Writings,* ed. D.F. Krell [Harper: San Francisco, 1993,] 167).

9. He avoids this consequence likewise in the two other texts where he, indeed somewhat more extensively, asks the question concerning the museum. In the short existential-ontological phenomenology of the museum, which he sketches in § 73 ("The ordinary understanding of history, and Dasein's historizing") of *Being and Time,* Heidegger departs from the question that the historian of museums, Pomian, took to be unquestionably resolved: from the question, namely, of what it actually means that something "passes away," becomes "past," falls "out of use." Faced with this question, he comes across a peculiar aporia: *Im Museum aufbewahrte 'Altertümer', Hausgeräte zum Beispiel, gehören einer 'vergangenen Zeit' an und sind gleichwohl noch in der 'Gegenwart' vorhanden.... Aber in dieser Vergänglichkeit, die auch während des Vorhandenseins im Museum fortgeht, liegt doch nicht der spezifische Vergangenheitscharakter, der es zu etwas Geschichtlichem macht.... Was waren die 'Dinge', das sie heute nicht mehr sind?.... Ob im Gebrauch oder außer Gebrauch, sie sind gleichwohl nicht mehr, was sie waren. Was ist 'vergangen'? Nichts anderes als die* Welt, *innerhalb deren sie, zu einem Zeugzusammenhang gehörig, als Zuhandenes begegneten.... Die* Welt *ist nicht mehr.* ["The 'antiquities' preserved in museums (household gear, for example) belong to a 'time which is past'; yet they are still present-at-hand in the 'Present'.... But that specific character of the past which makes it something historical, does not lie in this transience, which continues even during the Being-present-at-hand of the equipment in the museum. .... What were these 'Things' which today they are no longer? .... All the same, whether they are in use or out of use, they are no longer what they were. What is 'past'? Nothing else than that world within which they belonged to a context of equipment and were encountered as ready-to-hand.... That *world* is no longer"]. (M.H. *Sein und Zeit* [Niemeyer: Tübingen, 1967] 380. Eng. *Being and Time,* trans. by J. Macquarrie and E. Robinson [Harper: San Francisco, 1962] 431-32). Regardless of whether a thing is still in use or not, Heidegger thus says, its world is continually passing away. The museum is the place for things whose world is passing away and, even while in the museum, does not stop passing away. Things are, as it were, their own museums: although their world is already "past," they are still at hand in the "present." The museum assumes a special place in Heidegger's considerations not merely because it is the site where the world passes away--for it is always passing away--nor merely because it is the "site" where the site passes away, but rather because it is that site where the passing away of sites and of world is exposed. The museum is thus the proper "world-historical" site: the site where the historicality of what Heidegger calls "World" or "entities other than Dasein" are put on display. (l.c., Eng. 433; Ger. 381). But the historicality of the world, he insists, is merely of a secondary nature. It derives from the proper historicality of existing Dasein. Since Dasein is then "primarily historical," essentially temporalizing, and since this temporalizing is such that it projects itself into its future and only first from hence determines its past, or its having-been (*Gewesenheit*), it would have to be said that the museum, as the space of "world-history," defines itself from the future of Dasein, that the exposition of the museum defines itself out of a more "primary" ex-position, namely, *Ek-sistenz* as the ex-posure (*Aus-setzung*) of Dasein to its futuricity. In the museum, the world of its exhibits passes away--but it passes away only out of the possible future and possible futures of the already previously ex-posed Dasein. In the museum, possible pasts come to meet us from future possibilities. Every museum would thus have to be from the future, a museum of possible, future pasts. It would have to be a museum of the future.

Heidegger does not arrive at this consequence. In the museum, he sees only the institution of the suspension (*Stillstellung*) of history and of the vulgarization of its "proper," its temporalizing temporality. This becomes clearer in another text, which incidentally forms the backdrop of his reflections on the Sistine Madonna, namely, the "Origin of the work of Art." Here, in a short passage dedicated to the museum, Heidegger attends to the question of whether or not the "pure standing-in-itself (*Insichstehen*) of the work," or its "pure self-subsistence," can show itself, and how the work as a "setting-itself-into-work" (*Sich-ins-Werk-Setzen*) of the truth of beings can represent itself. "Setting" (Setzen) means here: *bringing to a standstill* (*zum Stehen bringen*) (*Holzwege*, l.c., 25). Can this setting, or placing (*Setzen*), this bringing-to-a-standstill and this positing of truth (*Stellen der Wahrheit*), can this position be seen in the exposition and its exhibits? Like the work of art, is the museum a site of truth? Heidegger writes: *So stehen und hängen denn die Werke selbst in den Sammlungen und Ausstellungen.... Die 'Ägineten' in der Münchener Sammlung, die 'Antigone' des Sophokles in der besten kritischen Ausgabe sind als die Werke, die sie sind, aus ihrem eigenen Wesensraum herausgerissen. Ihr Rang und ihre Eindruckskraft mögen noch so groß, ihre Erhaltung mag noch so gut, ihre Deutung noch so sicher sein, die Versetzung in die Sammlung hat sie ihrer Welt entzogen. Aber auch wenn wir uns bemühen, solche Versetzungen der Werke aufzuheben oder zu vermeiden, indem wir z.B. den Tempel in Paestum an seinem Ort und den Bamberger Dom an seinem Platz aufsuchen, die Welt der vorhandenen Werk ist zerfallen* ["Well, then, the works themselves stand and hang in collections and exhibitions.... The Aegina sculptures in the Munich collection, Sophocles' Antigone in the best critical edition, are, as the works they are, torn out of their own native sphere. However high their quality and power of impression, however good their state of preservation, however certain their interpretation, placing them in a collection has withdrawn them from their own world. But even when we make an effort to cancel or avoid such displacement of works--when, for instance, we visit the temple in Paestum at its own site or the Bamberg cathedral on its own square--the world of the work that stands there has perished"]. (l.c., Germ., 29-30; Eng., 166). In the exposition, works no longer stand in themselves, because they no longer stand in their world. The setting-into-work of truth no longer appears in them, because they and their truth--it is Heidegger who stresses this word by constantly repeating it--have fallen victim to a displacement, or transposition (*Versetzung*). This setting, or positing (*Setzen*), is itself, sur place, transposed, displaced (*versetzt*). The temple, the cathedral and the truth of their setting, or positioning (*Setzung*), are their own museum. Yet even when the displacement (*Versetzung*) of the temple "to its site (*Ort*)," of the cathedral "to its place (*Platz*)," happens immediately, this historical-topological withdrawal of place (*Stellungs-Entzug*)--withdrawal and decomposition of world--is not merely irreversible, but also, as Heidegger insists, a result of the setting, or positing(*Setzung*). That the works in the exhibition become objects of the "art industry," of "art appreciation," of "tradition and conservation," of "cultivation" and the "market," is a result of their self-subsistence (*Insichstehen*). *Ihr Entgegenstehen ist zwar noch eine Folge jenes vormaligen Insichstehens, aber nicht mehr dieses selbst. Dieses ist aus ihnen geflohen. Aller Kunstbetrieb, er mag...alles um der Werke selbst willen betreiben, reicht immer nur bis an das Gegenstandsein der Werke. Doch das ist nicht ihr Werksein* ["Their standing before us is still indeed a consequence of, but no longer the same as, their former self-subsistence. This self-subsistence has fled from them. The whole art industry, even if carried to the extreme and exercised for the sake of works themselves, extends only to the object-being. But this does not constitute their work-being"](l.c., Germ., 30; Eng., 166). The metaphysics of objectivity and of representation (*Vorstellung*) is the metaphysics of the exhibition and the museum. This may be, Heidegger says, a "result" of the original emplacement (*Stellung*) and setting-into-work of truth, but it is no longer this itself. With the concept of the "result" (*Folge*)--aligned in Heidegger's text with that of the "still" (*noch*), the "former" (*vormals*), and the "no longer" (*nicht mehr*)--a category of what he calls "vulgar" temporality is, to be sure, introduced into the discussion--and thereby also a category of the metaphysics of representation (*Vorstellungsmetaphysik*) that, as Heidegger sees it, is incapable of thinking its proper provenance (*Herkunft*). The exhibition is a "result" of the "former" standing-in-themselves, or self-subsistence, of works. This sentence means that the standing-in-itself inaugurates and permits its displacement into the exhibition, though it is not yet itself this displacement.

10. Here, I present only two from a legion of references Heidegger makes to the affinity between the words "existence" and "ex-position," or ex-posure, (*Existenz and Aussetzung*). The first is to be found in "Vom Wesen der Wahrheit" ["On the Essence of Truth"]: *Als dieses Sein-lassen setzt es sich dem Seienden als einem solchen aus und versetzt alles Verhalten ins Offene. Das Sein-lassen, d.h. die Freiheit ist in sich aus-setzend, ek-sistent* ["As this letting-be it exposes itself to beings as such and transposes all comportment into the open region. Letting-be, i.e., freedom, is intrinsically exposing, ek-sistent"] (*M.H. Wegmarken,* [Vittorio Klostermann: Frankfurt/M, 1967] 84. English translation in. *Martin Heidegger: Basic Writings,* ed. D.F. Krell, [Harper Collins: San Francisco, 1993] 125-6).). The second is located in "Kants These über das Sein ["Kant's Thesis on Being"]: *Statt 'Dasein' sagt die Sprache der Metaphysik auch Existenz. Es genügt, an diese Wort zu erinnern, um in dem sistere, dem Setzen, den Zusammenhang mit dem ponere und der Position zu erkennen; die existentia ist der actus, quo res sistitur, ponitur extra statum possibilitatis* (cf. Heidegger, Nietzsche, 1961, Bd. II, p. 417 ff.) ["Instead of 'Dasein' the language of metaphysics also says existence. It suffices to recall this word in order to recognize in the word sistere, to set [*setzen*], its affinity to ponere and the position; the existentia is the actus, quo res sistitur, ponitur extra statum possibilitatis"] (l.c.; 302). Superfluous though it may be, we might also point out that, besides positing (*Setzen*), *ponere* also means "placing" (*Stellen*); sistere also, "to bring to a stand" (*zu Stande bringen*), "to emplace" (*hinstellen*), "to erect" (*aufrichten*), "to remain standing" (*stehenbleiben*); *Ek-sistence* thus also "to ex-pose" (*Aus-stellung*), ex-position. Heidegger's open aversion to the "exhibition" (*Ausstellung*) in the museum is thus all the more conspicuous. One would have to link it up with the sentence, likewise from "On the Essence of Truth," that characterizes the structure of "comportment" (*Verhalten*), which is also the structure of "epoché,"and that thus characterizes the epochality of the epoché: *Ek-sistent ist das Dasein insistent* (l.c., 132) ["As ek-sistent, Dasein is insistent" (l.c., 91).]. For Heidegger, "insistence," along with all of its institutional affiliations, is one of the two elements constitutive of what he calls "relationship" (*Verhältnisse*) or, alternatively, the "openness of comportment" (*offenständiges Verhalten*), namely: the insistence on self-security. "Insistence" is thus a form of "errancy." Accordingly, in his sketch on the Sistine Madonna, he writes: *Das Bild irrt...in der Fremde* ["The image errs in the foreignness"]. So conceived, the museum-exhibition is an existential of Dasein. It belongs to the epochality of the epoché and hence to the happening of aletheic truth as "recovering discovery" (*bergender Entbergung*). It is only in this way that Heidegger can grant the mode of representation unique to the museum its proper historical necessity. Yet because the "errancy" of "insistence" is not only recovery and covering (*Bergung und Verbergung*), but also, following the essay on the "Work of art," the displacement (*Verstellung*) of this covering (*Verbergung*), Heidegger must denounce the museum as an institution of world-eclipse and of the metaphysics of representation. In the museum exhibition, the ek-sistent ex-position, one could thus say, is "displaced" (*verstellt*).

11. With the exception, to be precise, of his Trakl-essay in *On the Way to Language,* in particular the elucidation of Trakl's poem, "Ein Winterabend" with its Eucharistical theme in "Das Gedicht" (1950). (I hope to be able to discus this text at a later time.)

12. "Aus der Erfahrung des Denkens" [*From the Experience of Thinking*], l.c., 120. Instead of the formulation "setting-into-work" (*Ins-Werk-setzen*), Heidegger uses the formulation "Bringing-to-work of truth" (*Ins-Werk-Bringen der Wahrheit*) in his essay, "Die Kunst und der Raum" [*Art and Space*], of 1969 (ibid., 206).

13. The pair in the only other image to which Heidegger, insofar as I know, has dedicated an extensive commentary has been analyzed by Jacques Derrida in *Restitutions* - "de la vérité en pointure" (in: *La vérité en peinture,* [Flammarion: Paris 1978]). There, he departs from the question of whether the

issue is a pair of shoes or merely a couple of shoes--the issue thus of what constitutes a pair. If one were to submit the mother-child-pair of the Sistine Madonna to a similiar question, then the consequences would be no less distarous than those brought to light by Derrida. (I have examined the rending of the Christian pair and Christian family through the doubling and exchange of the child in Kleist's story "The earthquake in Chili" in "Quaking Presentation," forthcoming in: W.H. -- *Premises: Essays on Philosophy and Literature from Kant to Celan,* [Harvard University Press: Cambridge, 1996]. - Incidentally, Kleist numbered among the few authors cherished by Heidegger.)
14. A fund of maternal gestures: it is hardly an exaggeration to say that all of Heidegger's late work was dedicated to the tracing, sifting through, and archivization of such gestures--beginning with the gesture, the bearing (*Gebärde*) itself. He writes in the Trakl-essay: *Die Dinge tragen, "Die Sprache," of 1950, indem sie dingen, Welt aus. Unsere alte Sprache nennt das Austragen: bern, bären, daher die Wörter 'gebären' und 'Gebärde.' Dingend sind die Dinge Dinge. Dingend gebärden sie Welt* ["By thinging, things carry out world. Our old language calls carrying *bern, bären*; hence the words *gebären,* to carry, gestate, give birth, and *Gebärde,* bearing, gesture. Thinging, things are things. Thinging, they gesture--gestate-world"] (*Unterwegs zur Sprache,* Neske: Pfullingen, 1959. English translation in: M. Heidegger, *Poetry, Language, Thought*, trans. A. Hofstadter [Harper and Row: New York, 1975] 200). On occasion of the "verhaltenen Gebärden" ["subdued gestures"] in "Rashomon [L.c., 104; English translation in: M. Heidegger, *On the Way to Language,* trans. P.D. Hertz, Harper and Row: New York, 1982, p.16], it is said in the "Dialogue on Language" (1953/54): *Gebärde nennen Sie demnach: die in sich ursprünglich einige Versammlung von Entgegentragen und Zutrag* ["Thus you call bearing or gesture: the gathering which originarily unites within itself what we bear to it and what it bears to us"] (Germ., p.108; Eng., p.19). Just as the entire vocabulary of carrying (*des Tragens*) assembles into a lexicon of bearing (*des Gebärens*), so too does the vocabulary of recovery (*des Bergens*), up to and including the famous "Gebirg des Seins" ("the mountain-burrow-of-Being"). The interest, not only in provenance, advent, future (*Herkunft, Ankunft, Zukunft*), in origin, outset and beginning (*Ursprung, Anfang und Beginn*), in tools, testimony and productions (*Zeug, Bezeugung, und Erzeugnissen*), in the throw, the project, throwness (*Wurf, Entwurf und Geworfenheit*), in physis as coming up and forth and as coming forth before (*Aufgang und Hervorgang*) etc., but also explicitly in birth, is not of course articulated for the first time in Heidegger's latter writings, but at the very latest in *Being and Time: Das faktische Dasein existiert gebürtig, und gebürtig stirbt es auch schon im Sinne des Seins zum Tode* ["Factical Dasein exists as born; and, as born, it is already dying, in the sense of Being-towards-death"] (Germ., p. 374; Eng., p. 426). "What is that--birth?" or: "What is called bearing?"--under this title one could subsume large parts of Heidegger's oeuvre, entirely without the intent of thereby denouncing them as so-called children's questions on the order of "where do children come from?"
15. L.c., 121
16. One should read, for example, the sentences from *Identität und Differenz: Sein im Sinne der entbergenden Überkommnis und Seiendes als solches im Sinne der sich bergenden Ankunft wesen als die so Unterschiedenen aus dem Selben, dem Unter-Schied. Dieser vergibt erst und hält auseinander das Zwischen, worin Überkommnis und Ankunft zueinander gehalten, auseinander-zueinander getragen sind. Die Differenz von Sein und Seiendem ist als der Unter-Schied von Überkommnis und Ankunft der entbergend-bergende Austrag beider* ["Being, in the sense of a discovering overwhelmed in handing over, and beings as such, in the sense of an arrival that recovers itself, springs forth in essence as the thus differentiated out of the same, out of the dif-ference. That differentiation alone cedes and holds apart the 'betweeen,' in which the overwhelming handing over and the arrival are held toward one another, are borne away from and toward each other. The difference of Being and beings, as the differentiation of overwhelming handing over and arrival, is the carrying out (*Austrag*) of the two in *discovering recovering*"] (*Identität und Differenz,* [Neske: Pfullingen, 1957] 56; English translation: *Identity and Difference,* trans. J. Stambaugh [Harper and Row: New York, 1974] 65. English

translation modified.). In the same text, "Die onto-theo-logische Verfassung der Metaphysik" ["The Onto-theo-logical Constitution of Metaphysics"], Heidegger embarks upon an answer to the question of how "the deity" entered philosophy with the following sentence: *Der Gott kommt in die Philosophie durch den Austrag, den wir zunächst als den Vorort des Wesens der Differenz von Sein und Seiendem denken.... Der Austrag ergibt und vergibt das Sein als her-vor-bringenden Grund, welcher Grund selbst aus dem von ihm Begründeten her der ihm gemäßen Begründung, d.h. der Verursachung durch die ursprünglichste Sache bedarf. Dies ist die Ursache als die Causa sui, so lautet der sachgerechte Name für den Gott in der Philosophie. Zu diesem Gott kann der Mensch weder beten, noch kann er ihm opfern* ["The deity comes into philosophy as the carrying out that we in the first place think as the precinct of the essence of the difference of Being and beings.... The carrying out yields and cedes Being as the ground that brings forth out in front, which ground, in turn, itself needs to be appropriately grounded by what it grounds, that is to say, it needs to be caused through the most originary cause. This is the originary cause as causa sui, the name, most faithful to the source, of the deity in philosophy. Man can neither pray nor sacrifice to this deity"] (Germ., 64; Eng. 71-2. English translation modified.). The portion of Heidegger's Minima Theologica that offers "Über die Sixtina" does not interpret "the deity" in terms of the Cartesian formula of the *causa sui*, but as the offering (*Darbietung*)--in the literal sense of the word as gift and sacrifice--of difference. It remains thus pre-Cartesian, in Heidegger's sense of the term, pre-philosophical and speaks of a God to whom "man" (*der Mensch*) can pray and sacrifice.

17. "Heidegger's Mother"--this theme and anathema require, of course, more extensive treatment. Here, only three or four further remarks:

The movement of the Madonna in Raphael's painting is described in the "Ursprung des Kunstwerks"--in the text thus that offers the foil, as it were, to "Über die Sixtina"--as the movement of the "earth" (*der Erde*). There, it is said: *Die Erde ist das, wohin das Aufgehen alles Aufgehende und zwar als solches zurückbirgt. Im Aufgehenden west die Erde als das Bergende* ["Earth is that whence the arising brings back and shelters everything that arises as such. In the things that arise, earth occurs essentially as the sheltering agent"] (l.c., Germ., 31; Eng., 168) *Sie zeigt sich nur, wenn sie unentborgen und unerklärt bleibt. Die Erde läßt so jedes Eindringen in sie an ihr selbst zerschellen* [It shows itself only when it remains undisclosed and unexplained. Earth, thus, shatters every attempt to penetrate it] (l.c., Ger., 36; Eng., 172). *Die Erde ist das zu nichts gedrängte Hervorkommen des ständig Sichverschließenden und dergestalt Bergenden* [The earth is the spontaneous forthcoming of that which is continually self-secluding and to that extent sheltering and concealing] (l.c., Ger., p37; Eng., 174). The earth is for Heidegger, in a word, the mother. For pages, the characterizations he chooses for her read as though lifted from a draft of one of Hölderlin's hymns, namely, "Der Mutter Erde"--a text Heidegger nowhere else commented upon but certainly knew. I will cite some formulations out of the Hellingrathian edition, which was available to Heidegger in the thirties: *O Mutter Erde!... hüllest du nicht so.... Gemildert ist seine macht, verhüllt in den Stralen und die Erde birgt vor ihm die Kinder ihres Schooses <in> den Mantel...und im Verborgenen haben, dir, sich selbst geheim, in tiefverschlossener Halle dir auch verschwiegene Männer gedient...und sollst indes er fern ist und alte Ewigkeit verborgener und verborgener wird, statt seiner seyn den sterblichen Menschen, wie du Kinder gebahrest und erzogst für ihn....* (Cited here from the third edition: Hölderlin, *Sämtliche Werke*, Bd IV; [Propyläen-Verlag: Berlin, 1943] 238-9.) As Heidegger himself continually stresses, the motif of the earth is closely connected to that of physis. In his writings on Aristotle, on Hölderlin, and explicity in the Artwork-essay, this motif is invariably dealt with in the same vocabulary with which he deals with that of the "earth." The relationship in the mother-child-pair discussed in "Über die Sixtina" corresponds to the "conflict" between the earth-world-pair in the Artwork-essay.

In *What is Called Thinking?* of 1951-52, the motif of hearing is linked to the mother. Refraining from commentary, I restrict myself to citing: "*Warte, ich werde dich lehren, was gehorchen heißt*"--*ruft die*

Mutter ihrem Buben nach, der nicht nach Hause will. Verspricht die Mutter ihrem Sohn eine Definition über den Gehorsam? Nein.... Sie wird vielmehr dem Sohn das Gehorchen beibringen. Oder noch besser und umgekehrt: sie wird den Sohn in das Gehorchen bringen.... Es glückt umso einfacher, je unmittelbarer die Mutter den Sohn ins Hören bringt. Nicht erst so, daß er sich dazu nur bequemt, sondern so, daß er vom Hörenwollen nicht mehr lassen kann. Weshalb nicht? Weil er hörend geworden ist für das, wohin sein Wesen gehört ["'You just wait--I'll teach you what we call obedience!' a mother might say to her boy who won't come home. Does she promise him a definition of obedience? No. Or is she going to give him a lecture? No.... Rather, she will convey to him what obedience is. Or better, the other way around: she will bring him to obey. Her success....will be easier, the more directly she can get him to listen--not just condescend to listen, but listen in such a way that he can no longer stop wanting to do it. And why? Because his ears have been opened and he now can hear what is in accord with his nature"] (Niemeyer: Tübingen, 1971; 19. English translation: *What is Called Thinking?*, trans. J.G. Gray, [Harper and Row: New York, 1968,] 48). (For a plausible connection between this scene and the Sistine Madonna, one ought consider Max Ernst's painting "La vierge corrigeant l'Enfant-Jesus devant les yeux de trois témoins: A.B., P.E. et l'artiste" [Die Jungfrau Maria verhaut das Jesuskind im Beisein von drei Zeugen"] 1926.)
And a final remark: on the mother tongue as Mother Language. I cite, once more, without commentary. *Der Mensch spricht aus jener Sprache heraus, der sein Wesen zugesprochen ist. Wir nennen diese Sprache: die Muttersprache.* ["Man speaks out from that language to which his essence is bespoke. We call this language the mother tongue"] ("Hebel--der Hausfreund" in: *Aus der Erfahrung des Denkens*, l.c., 148). *Sprache ist Sprache als Muttersprache.... Die Mundart ist nicht nur die Sprache der Mutter, sondern zugleich und zuvor die Mutter der Sprache.* ["Language is language as mother tongue.... Dialect is not only the tongue of the mother, but at the same time the mother of the tongue"] ("Sprache und Heimat," l.c., 156).

18. Even the most recent work of an art historian on the Sistine Madonna is not far off from the Heideggerian assessment. Hans Belting, who, in comparing Raffael's earlier "Madonna of Foligno" with the Sistine Madonna, writes: *Das ältere Bild* enthält *eine himmlische Erscheinung. Die "Sixtinische Madonna"* ist *eine solche.... Die Präsenz der Hauptfiguren ist davon* [von einem meßbaren Ort im Bild] *unabhängig, als seien diese zu "absoluten" Bildern im wörtlichen Sinne geworden.* ["The older painting *contains* a heavenly apparition. The Sistine Madonna *is* just such a one.... The presence of the principal figures are independent [independent of a measurable point in the painting], as if they had become "absolute' in the literal sense of the word"] (Belting, Hans, *Bild und Kult: Eine Geschichte des Bildes vor dem Zeitalter der Kunst*, [C.H. Beck Verlag: München, 1990] 535). Belting's cultic presentism, for which the Sistine Madonna *is* a heavenly appearance, obscures the techniques he himself deems responsible for producing, as their effect, the suggestion of presence. The major figures of Raphael's picture are precisely *not* independent from its mariginal figures, rather the latter are what in the first place *stage* this independence.

19. L.c., 121

20. Heidegger speaks explicitly and repeatedly of this singleness: *dem einzigen Geschehnis dieses einzigen Bildes* ["the single happening of this single image"](p.120); the *einzigen Geschehnis des Bildes...; dem einzigen Fenster dieses einzigen Bildes* ["single happening of the image...; the single window of this single image"] (p.121). Just as there is only one image of the one Christ of the one mother, so there is also only one window and one frame. Departing from the art-historical concept of the "window-painting," Heidegger asks: *Was ist ein Fenster? Sein Rahmen grenzt das Offene des Durchscheinens ein, um es durch die Grenze in eine Freigabe des Scheinens zu versammeln. Das Fenster als Einlaß des nahenden Scheinens ist Ausblick in die Ankunft* ["What is a window? Its frame delimits the open expanse of a shining-through in order to gather it through the limit in a setting free of shining. The window as the inlet of the nearing shining is an outlook into the advent"] (120).

21. L.c., 120.
22. Heidegger writes: *Der Ort ist je ein Altar einer Kirche. Diese gehört in das Bild und umgekehrt. Dem einzigen Geschehnis des Bildes entspricht notwendig seine Vereinzelung an den unscheinbaren Ort der einen unter den vielen anderen Kirchen. Diese Kirche wiederum, und d.h. jede einzelne ihrer Art, rufen* [sic!] *nach dem einzigen Fenster dieses einzigen Bildes: Es gründet und vollendet den Bau der Kirche* ["The site is always the altar of a church. The latter belongs in the image and vice versa. The single happening of the image necessarily corresponds to its having been singled out at the inconspicuous site of the one church among the many others. These churches, in turn, and that means every one of their kind, call for the single window of this single image: it founds and completes the building of the churches"] (l.c., 121). The talk of the "founding" of the church through the image corresponds, evidently, to Heidegger's conviction, especially as articulated in his writings on Hölderlin, that the poet "endows" and "founds" (*stiftet*) Being and the epochal appearance of the people.
23. Between dismay and the certainty of salvation lies the gaze that Schopenhauer apprehends on the Jesus of the Sistine Madonna. He dedicated a short poem to her, dated "Dresden, 1815" and carrying the title: "Auf die Sixtinische Madonna" [On the Sistine Madonna]:

Sie trägt zur Welt ihn: und er schaut entsetzt
In ihrer Gräu'l chaotische Verwirrung,
In ihres Tobens wilde Raserei,
In ihres Treibens nie geheilte Thorheit,
In ihrer Qualen nie geheilten Schmerz,--
Entsetzt: doch strahlet Ruh' und Zuversicht
Und Siegesglanz sein Aug', verkündigend
Schon der Erlösung ewige Gewißheit.

In this gazing, this dismay and confidence, Schopenhauer perhaps discerned that representation of the world that never quite expels the turbulence of the will, but that at least announces mitigation and, in fact, its "salvation:" the salvation of the world thus in that contemplation in which the work of art observes the world. In Jesus, the gaze of art is borne to the world. It is thus the announcement of a salvation that delivers from dismay only insofar as it observes this dismay-- pain remains "never to be assuaged," foolishness "never to be overcome": Christian aesthetics of redemption, the redemption of the world as representation. (Schopenhauer's poem is here cited from A.S. -- "Sämtliche Werke," Parerga und Paralipomena", vol. 2; [Brockhaus: Wiesbaden 1947] 695.)
24. Nathaniel Hawthorne, *Novels*. ed. Millicent Bell (New York: Literary Classics 1983)1129 sq.
25. L.c., p. 1132.
26. Since the eighteenth century, the great motif of the literature on the museum, the disclosure of the private, the exposition of the secret, secretive or discrete--what one could thus call the principal *indiscretion* of the museums--transforms images into *bijoux indiscrets* in the imaginary world of the observer. American Puritans and French libertines were particularly sensitive to this quality. Their observations on the sexualization of the museum and the musealization of sexuality are anything but marginalia in the experience of the museum in the last centuries. Published for the first time in 1939 in "L'Age d'Homme," a text of Michel Leiris, entitled "Lupanars et Musées," attests to the mixture of voyeurism and exhibitionism accompanying this experience. Here an excerpt, in which, incidently, it is easy to detect the same technique of juxtaposition and serialization employed by Hawthorne in his representation of the museum: *Rien me paraît ressembler autant à un bordel qu'un musée. On y trouve le même côté louche et le même côté pétrifié. Dans l'un, les Vénus, les Judith, les Suzanne, les Junon, les Lucrèce, les Salomé et autres héroïnes, en belles images figées; dans l'autre, des femmes vivantes, vêtues de leurs parures traditionnelles, avec leurs gestes, leurs locutions, leurs usages tout à fait stéréotypes. Dans l'un et dans l'autre endroit on est, d'une certaine manière, sous le signe de l'archéologie; et si j'ai aimé longtemps le bordel, c'est parce qu'il participe lui aussi de l'antiquité, en raison de son côté marché d'esclaves,*

prostitution rituelle ["To me, nothing seems to resemble a bordello as much as a museum. One can find there the same shady side and the same petrified side. Here, the Venus, the Judith, the Suzanne, the Junon, the Lucrèce, the Salomé and other heroïnes fixated on beautiful images. There, live women, clothed in their traditional attire, with their gestures, their locutions, their entirely stereotyped manners. In both places, one is placed, in a way, under the sign of archeology; and if I have long loved the bordello, it is because it belongs to antiquity as well, with its ties to the slave market, to ritual prostitution]". (Gallimard: Paris, 1946, 67). By way of its juxtaposition with ritual prostitution, the comparison between the two public institutions--the bordello and the museum--leads back to antiquity, world-historical antiquity as well as the antiquity of one's own childhood. The museum leads not only to the fusion of institutions, but also of diverse spaces and times. Whoever enters, steps into the cave of his own prehistory, even when it exhibits all the traits of the most recent present. It is perhaps for this reason that the bordello--and from a certain point of view also the museum--is for Leiris, above all, a threshold phenomenon. In his youth, it meant for him portel...--et, de fait, ce qui me paraît aujourd'hui encore le plus émouvant *quand on va au bordel, c'est l'acte de franchir le seuil, comme on lancerait les dés ou passerait le Rubicon* ["gate...--and, in fact, what seems to me, today still, the most moving when one goes to the bordello, is the act of stepping over the threshold, as one would throw the dice or cross the Rubicon"](L.c.; 68).

In the opening pages of *Finnegans Wake*, with its kaleidoscopic museum of all languages and literatures, Joyce formulates the connection between sexuality and the museum--what he could have called "museux"-- even more drastically than do both Leiris and Hawthorne. After having spoken of a *mounding's mass in front of the Wallinstone national museum, he says: Penetrators are permitted into the museomound free* (London: Faber and Faber 1975, p. 8). And after having established this connection between the museum, the mouth of the womb, the tomb, and the alter of mass and having recalled *redismembers invalids of old guard* and the *janitrix*, the female doorkeeper and progenitor, the stroll through the museum of the battle of Belle Alliance is open with a *This way to the museyroom.* In this *Willingdone Museyroom* with the defective armature of soldierly virility warehoused, each item is presented with a "This is": ... *This is big Willingdone mormorial tallowscoop Wounderworker .... Sexcaliber hrosspower. ... This is mistletropes. ... This is the bissmark of the marathon merry....* (8-9).

What impresses Hawthorne and Leiris, as well as Joyce, about the structure of the museum is not only the transposition of the sacral into the profane sphere and vice versa, but the juxtapositions that go hand-in-hand with this transposition. The museum is for them a Faszinosum or a Horrendum because it breaks up what is, at any given time, singular into virtually endless series: "Virgins and Infant Christs..., Magdalens..., Crucifixions..., Pietàs;" "Les Venus, les Judith, les Suzanne, les Junon,...." The museum turns its visitor into a Don Juan. In the first of his "Beiträge zur Psychologie des Liebeslebens" of 1910, entitled "Über einen besonderen Typus der Objektwahl beim Manne," Freud offered, as explanation for the passion of collecting directed toward women, the theory that through this passion a series of surrogates are sought for the one, irreplaceable and nonrepeatable mother and that these surrogates enable the afflicted to remain true to her. He writes: *Wenn die Liebesobjekte bei unserem Typus* [Don Juan or the collector] *vor allem Muttersurrogate sein sollen, so wird auch die Reihenbildung verständlich, welche der Bedingung der Treue so direkt zu widersprechen scheint. Die Psychoanalyse belehrt uns auch durch andere Beispiele, daß das im Unbewußten wirksame Unersetzliche sich häufig durch die Auflösung in eine unendliche Reihe kundgibt, unendlich darum, weil jedes Surrogat doch die erstrebte Befriedigung vermissen läßt* ["If we are to understand the love-object chosen by our type [Don Juan or the collector] as being above all mother-surrogates, then the formation of a series of them, which seems so flatly to contradict the condition of being faithful to one, can now also be understood. We have learnt from psycho-analysis in other examples that the notion of something irreplaceable, when it is active in the unconscious, frequently appears as broken up into an endless series: endless for the reason that every surrogate nevertheless fails to provide the desired satisfaction"]

(GW VIII; p. 71 sq.; English translation: *Standard Edition of the Complete Psychological Works of Sigmund Freud in 24 Volumes*, Vol. XI, Hogarth Press, 1962, p.169). Freud's reflections offer grounds for generalizing the observations he devotes to a particular "type." With the formulation "das im Unbewußten wirksame Unersetzliche," he declares "mother" to mean what in another context he designates as an unconscious concept. The mother is unconscious. The conscious forms in which she announces herself are all surrogates of what remains irreplaceable in the unconscious. The irreplaceable itself, however--the rigorous analytic concept of the mother--cannot as such become an object of the imagination (*Vorstellung*) or of consciousness. But this means that the production of surrogates already begins with consciousness itself and that for consciousness and its intuitional and representational forms the irreplaceable never announces itself except in the form of substitutions. The conscious, imagined or represented mother is the prothesis of the unconscious one. But this means further that the work of consciousness consists in nothing else than "dissolving" what is irreplaceable and nonrepeatable into a series of surrogates and repetitions: consists in taking it to pieces, sharing it out and causing it to vanish. The announcement of the unconscious concept of the mother is understood by Freud thus as its dissolution. Both the announcement and the dissolution, however, must be "endless"--take place in an "endless series"--since they are dealing with something not susceptible to being reproduced in any finite form, something unconscious and singular. The unconscious is coextensive only with the infinite, the inappropriable, the unreachable. Where something only "announces" (*kundgibt*) itself infinitely, there in the form of paradoxes, at the threshold, subliminally--or sublimely--as something that promises satisfaction, but grants none; that announces itself to the extent that it withdraws; that can be touched only as the untouchable; that represents itself only in its irrepresentability; that remains unrepeatable only in its repetitions. This experience--or, more precisely, the experience of this non-experienceability--is that of the collector. In the age of the museum, and that is the age of democratization, this experience has taken on institutional forms, has even itself become an institution and has placed itself time and again disappointingly under the curatorship of a figure: the figure of the mother, of the lost, the recuperated or promised. Freud's observation on the structure--or destructure--of the Don Juanian museum not only makes clear that little is to be expected from this curatorship, that it can only ever constitute one among a virtually "endless series" of possible others and is thus itself but a phenomenon of the "dissolution" it wishes to banish. Politically inflected, his observation also makes clear that political collectives and collective movements, all of which have placed themselves under the protection of a mother-imago, have the character of surrogates and are bound to break up. The politics of the museum is the politics of the "endless series"--and that means also of the impossible linearity and homogeneity of the series, the impossible series. It is the Politics of endless democratization, of the di-stanciation (*Ent-fernung*) of the mother. (Similar to the Heideggerian usage, "Ent-fernung," *di-stanciation*, designates here that movement in which something brings itself nearer while keeping, and alone while keeping, its distance. What brings here, however, is not the mother. She is herself what is brought. "Ent-fernung" of the mother is not dematernation, but her announcement (ad-maternation) and her withdrawal (a-maternation) at once, her announcement out of the withdrawal: ammaternation.)

27. L.c., 1134.

28. To characterize the disappearance of the image in the museum, Hawthorne, as though in a wing of his exposition, finds an image in which only the imagelessness of white--less than white--remains: *And as for these galleries of Roman palaces, they were... drearier than the white-washed walls of a prison corridor* (l.c., 1135). As punishment for his crimes, Hawthorne condemns the ghost of the architect to wander aimlessly through these prison corridors and, for ever and ever in comtemplation of the master-pieces hanging there--these works "drearier than white-washed walls"--to be dispossessed more and more of its life's warmth: the museum as a penitentiary of infernal mercilessness. (A familiar

passage, certainly not unknown to the bible-versed Hawthorne, in Peter 3:18-20; 4-6--in fact the only passage that explicitly deals with hell--speaks of Christ's "preaching" to "spirits in prison." C.f. Hans Urs von Balthasar, "Abstieg zur Hölle" in: *Pneuma und Institution*, Johannes Verlag, Einsiedeln, 1974.) Even the ghost is a perverted Christ figure: resurrected, returning from the dead, yet not the Redeemer, but the redeemed. (The image of hell is certainly a perversion of the Christian doctrine of grace, though it is indeed a very Christian perversion, not only as it represented in Hawthorne but also in the cardinal texts of inferno-literature, those of Aquinas and Dante. This would have to be elaborated elsewhere.) Even hell is a museum, the museum a hell. Within the scope of negative theology (and there is no other), a redemption is evidently only possible if the Savior himself enters the realm of the unredeemed. Hence, the fascination with ghosts and images of hell that runs throughout European literature: the epoch of Christianity and of all the religions and theologies it has touched, digested or left undigested, whether one likes it or not, is the epoch of Holy Saturday.

This also means that it is the epoch of perversions, inversions, persiflages, and travesties that do not cease to act in collusion with what they blacken in Black Masses and with what they whiten in white-washed prison halls. In Hawthorne's empty gallery only a series of images are left over by the "Demon of Weariness" --*He annihilates colour, warmth, and, more especially, sentiment, and passion, at a touch*--which arouses the suspicion that they are heretical travesties: herrings instead of Christus piscus, a long-stalked wineglass instead of the chalice and the monstrance, bread and cheese instead of panis vivus: *If he [the wicked Demon] spare anything, it will be some such matter as an earthen pipkin or a bunch of herrings by Teniers; a brass kettle, in which you can see your face, by Gerard Douw;...or a long-stalked wine-glass, transparent and full of shifting reflections, or a bit of bread and cheese, or an overripe peach with a fly upon it, truer than reality itself, by the school of Dutch conjurors* (l.c., 1131).

29. L.c., 1134.

30. On the last page of the *Phänomenlogie des Geistes*, Hegel makes this theology of abandonment into one of the two moments through which the becoming of spirit moves toward itself. He grasps this side of the history of knowledge with the image of the museum: *Dies Werden stellt eine träge Bewegung und Aufeinanderfolge von Geistern dar,* eine Galerie von Bildern, *deren jedes mit dem vollständigen Reichtume des Geistes ausgestattet, eben darum sich so träge bewegt, weil das Selbst diesen ganzen Reichtum seiner Substanz zu durchdringen und zu verdauen hat* ["This way of becoming presents a slow procession and succession of spiritual shapes..., *a gallery of pictures*, each of which is endowed with the entire wealth of Spirit, and moves so slowly just for the reason that the self has to permeate and assimilate all this wealth of its substance"](My emphasis. W.H.). Some lines later, this same history is designated as the *Schädelstätte des absoluten Geistes* ["Golgotha of Absolute Spirit"] that, without its philosophical recognition, would be das leblose Einsame ["the lifeless lonesome one"]; *nur--aus dem Kelche dieses Geisterreiches/ schäumt ihm seine Unendlichkeit* ["Only--The chalice of this realm of spirits/foams forth to God his own infinity"] (*Phänomenologie des Geistes*, [Ullstein: Berlin, 1973] 446-47. English translation: *Phenomenology of Mind*, trans. J.B. Baille, Harper Torchbooks, [Harper and Row: New York, 1967] 807-08. Translation modified). A "gallery of pictures," the "Golgotha," the "lifeless, solitary, and alone," the "chalice"--this is the history of a knowledge that does *not* grasp itself, revive or sublate (*aufheben*) itself in the concept. The museum of the spirit is Golgotha but only so long as the spirit therein does not recall itself and only so long as it resurrects itself as "the spirit knowing itself as spirit." Thus, Hegel does not simply leave the museum behind the resurrective concept of absolute knowledge. Rather, he lets it overflow as a Eucharistic chalice. Its superfluity, however, flows back into the museum; and in the picture gallery, it must continue to surrender itself to the "sluggish" ("*träge*") digestion, the Golgotha, the "lifeless, solitary and alone." given over to the *lifeless lonesome one*: infinite circulation of the museum that is a museum of museums and that can only be a museum to the extent that it abandons itself and can only abandon itself in order to return to itself.

Blanchot's two very rich texts on the museum--"Le Musée, l'Art et le Temps" and "Le mal du musée"--in which he attempts to establish a connection between Heideggerian and Hegelian themes, also revolve around the motifs of loss of world and absence. But this absence and this loss designate for Blanchot the origin of the picture as well as the museum. They are embedded in them as categories of their (de)constitution and from the very beginning distantiate the one as well as the other from themselves. It is for this reason that Blanchot, in his critique of André Malraux' "Musée imaginaire," speaks of a *puissante et impuissante dialectique* ["powerful and powerless dialectic"] to which those works already destined from the moment of their production for the museum must be subjected: *l'oeuvre est sa propre absence: à cause de cela en perpétuel devenir, jamais accomplie, toujours faite et défaite*" ["the work is its proper absence: because of this it is perpetually becoming, never accomplished, always done and undone"](in: *L'Amitié*, [Gallimard: Paris, 1971] 48). It is for exactly this reason that Blanchot, in a peculiar coupling of Hegel's Christian and Nietzsche's para-Christian doctrine of the return, must speak of a ressassement éternel ["an eternal recycling"] as the movement of the museum: *tout se répète à l'infini parce que rien n'y a jamais lieu vraiment* ["everything repeats itself to infinity because nothing has ever truly taken place"](44). The absence of world, the museum, the desert grows. For Blanchot, however, unlike Hegel and Hawthorne, there is no privileged figure in which this endless flight from museums and worlds could still be represented, for it is the movement of representation itself as an unstoppable evacuation, for which, in truth, there has never been a site and a place: *rien n'y a jamais lieu vraiment-* : Representation is here nothing other than the desertion from and of truth, place, and protection.

31. L.c., 1131 *The touch seemed like ice,* Hawthorne says of his contact with the collector in his narrative "A Virtuoso's Collection." His soul is *dead within him* and no spirit lives under his *frozen mass of earthly life.* (N.H. "Tales and Sketches", [New York: The Library of America 1982] 713). What his collection contains is, like the collector himself, *cut off from natural sympathies* and *ceases to be human* (712-13), even though--and herein lies the radicality of Hawthorne's construction--it is comprised of requisites from all of the wisdom, myths, literatures, art treasures, and the political exploits of mankind: *the original fire which Prometheus stole form Heaven* (707) and *the identical scissors of Atropos* (706), *the missing treatises of Longinus, the original manuscript of the Koran, Alexander's copy of the Iliad as well as the tub of Diognes, Medea's cauldron, and Psyche's vase of beauty* (702), the wolf that ate Red Riding Hood and her grandmother, Alexander's Bucephalus, Don Quixotes' Rosinante, and Coleridge's Albatross, Aladdin's Lamp and Franklin's asbestos cap, *the long, hairy ears of Midas and the bowl which a sculptor modelled from the curve of [Helen's] perfect breast* (702), *the lyre of Orpheus, and those of Homer and Sappho, Dr. Franklin's whistle as well as a phial of the tears into which Niobe was dissolved and some Egyptian darkness in a blacking jug* (705), *the blood-encrusted pen of steel with which Faust signed away his salvation* (706), not to mention, *the picture of the Old Woman [by Zeuxis], and which was so ludicrous that he himself died with laughing at it* (710). In short, the cabinet of the "Virtuoso" contains the history of literature, art, and religion; of science and of politics in the condition of its historicist fetishisation since they can only be objects of curiosity or contempt. "*I had learned to despise all things,*" the collector says of his relationship to the world. At the end of the tale, Hawthorne dedicates to him, and it becomes clear--in accordance with the logic of puritanical Antisemitism--that the crude materialist, to whom the soul of things as well as his own is dead, is in fact *the Wandering Jew,* and the museum he inhabits, a *Hades* (713). Yet the tale of this world becomes allegory, of this world, pointing to nothing but its own spirit-, feeling-, and senselessness, does not exempt itself from its own Christian condemnation. In his collection of tales "Mosses from an Old Manse," Hawthorne placed it last, thereby conferring upon it the function of telling the tale both of *this* collection--and thus its own tale--as well as that of another "Virtuoso's Collection." In the spirit of puritanical self-mortification, the "mise en abîme" denounces its own denunciation of the shadow world of the museum by making itself part of the museum; the allegory of the Hades of dead

collectibles, as a dead collectible itself; the writer as a double of the ice-cold virtuoso and even of Mephistopheles, this *Demon of Weariness.* (I owe the reference to "A Virtuoso's Collection" to a remark by Robert Stockhammer.)

32. L.c., p. 1128

33. In: Theodor W. Adorno, *Prismen: Kulturkritik und Gesellschaft*, dtv: München, 1963; pp. 176-189. English translation: *Prisms*, trans. Samuel and Shierry Weber, The MIT Press: Cambridge, 1982.

34. Marcel Proust, *A la recherche du temps perdu I*, ed. Pierre Clarac, André Ferré [Gallimard: Paris, 1954] 644 All citations in the text are located on this and the following page. Therefore, they will not be individually footnoted. [English translations from: *In Search of Lost Time II: In a Budding Grove*, trans. by C.K. Scott Moncrieff & Terence Kilmartin [Chatto & Windus: London, 1992] 255-6.]

35. In the first story of his collection, "Deshoras" [*Untimes*], in which a woman--not a mother--disappears in a museum and its images, Julio Cortázar plays out the displacement of time and space, dystopies and achronies, in a way very different from that of Proust.

36. In Henry James', "The Spoils of Poynton," "spoils" refers, on the one hand, to the captured treasure, or winnings, that the protagonist had stored up in her villa, and, on the other, to the second meaning that "spoil" can have in English, namely, that these very treasures get "corrupted" and "wasted." "The Spoils of Poynton" is the story of a mother who, upon the death of her husband, loses the artworks she collected to her son and the woman he took as bride. In the end, the small museum she had assembled in the course of her life goes up in flames and is reduced to ashes. The two motifs--the museum and the mother--which turn up with striking regularity in conjunction with one another, are thus conjoined by James too--and are conjoined again under the aspect of the distancing of the mother, of dematernation and *dépouillement.*

37. A page before the passage dedicated to railway stations and museums, it is said: *C'est grâce à cet oubli seul que nous pouvons de temps à autre retrouver l'être que nous fûmes.... ...nous ne le retrouverions plus, si quelques mots (comme "directeur au ministère des Postes") n'avaient été soigneusement enfermés dans l'oubli, de même qu'on dépose à la Bibliothèque Nationale un exemplaire d'un livre qui sans cela risquerait de devenir introuvable* ["It is thanks to this oblivion alone that we can from time to time recover the person that we were.... ...we shall never recapture it had not a few words (such as this 'head of the Ministry of Posts') been carefully locked away in oblivion, just as an author deposits in the National Library a copy of a book which might otherwise become unobtainable"] (l.c., Fr., 643; Eng., 254). Hence, this also says that the museum--like the library--is a site of forgetting before every possible present.

38. The city is called here, I repeat, *éventrée*: through the skylights of Saint-Lazare, its body opens onto a sky that for its part is characterized as gross, pregnant--indeed, pregnant with a crucifixion, or the departure of a train: Pregnant thus with death. I do not wish to further comment on this peculiar double-opening and this communication (between city and heaven) in the medium of death, but merely--and just as cursorily--to point to another place in Paris that historically, as well as literarily, has become a place of rotation between regeneration and musealisation. "Les Halles," the "ventre de Paris," have been torn down and on their site the Centre Beaubourg" has been erected. In their description and evaluation of this transformation, massively anti-emancipatory forces, flirting with a culture-critical vocabulary, still today avail themselves of a rhetoric that hardly leaves any room for doubt that they were not talking about "les Halles" but about "Les PHalles" in the center of the mother city and about her presumptive castration. Allen Ginsberg, already in 1958, long before the city market place was replaced by a museum, described these halls as a slaughterhouse and museum, in which the figure of an old woman appears at regular intervals. Without further commentary, I shall limit myself to citing a few verses from Ginsberg's "Apocalypse of Les Halles": *Carts full of lungs carts full of liver carts full of hearts .... An old woman stained with blood... corpses identical hanging in hundred*

perspective under the staring light bulb... Fat butchers clutching their corpse breasts split down the middle with an ax... Six wheeled carts rumbling empty over Rimbaud's grave/ Sweet lady in an apron what're you doing here... Here come mummies of Egypt for breakfast ... A whiff of mammal smell in the atmosphere a peep of blue gowns of angels' bloody aprons. / Fellow conspirators, Eat! ("Antaeus", The Final Issue, Autumn 1994; 256-57).

39. Paul Valéry, *Oeuvres II*, 9Gallimard (Pléiade): Paris, 1960) 1290 sqq.

40. With this note, Valéry not only repeats the metaphor of the cemetery; he also suggests that humans can themselves become the objects of collections and museums. Seventeen years prior, Joseph Conrad expressed this idea in his anarchist-tale "The Informer: An Ironic Tale." It is said there: *My friend in Paris is a collector, too.... He collects acquaintances. It is delicate work. He brings to it the patience, the passion, the determination of a true collector of curiosities.... He observes them, listens to them, penetrates them, measures them, and puts the memory away into the galleries of his mind. He has schemed, plotted, and travelled all over Europe in order to add to his collection of distinguished personal acquaintances (The Complete Short Fiction of Joseph Conrad: The Stories*, vol. II, ed. Samuel Hynes; The Ecco Press: Hopewell, NJ, 1992; p. 21). Based on these sentences alone, it already becomes clear that even the narrator of this tale constitutes one of the curiosities in his friend's collection. It may be tempting to conclude that all literature is occupied with the establishment of "galleries of the mind"--and with their ironic--all too ironic--dissolution.

41. In "Valéry Proust Museum," Adorno comments upon what he calls a "coquettish allegory" with the following sentences: *Wenn Valérys kokette Allegorie Malerei und Skulptur den Kindern vergleicht, welche die Mutter verloren haben, dann wäre daran zu erinnern, daß in den Mythen die Helden, in denen das Menschliche dem Schicksal sich entringt, allemal die Mutter verloren. Zur vollen promesse du bonheur werden Kunstwerke erst losgerissen von ihrem Nährboden, auf der Bahn zum eigenen Untergang* ["If Valéry's coquetish allegory compares painting and sculpture to children who have lost their mother, one must remember that in myths the heroes, who represent the emancipation of the human from fate, always lost their mothers. Works of art can fully embody the *promesse du bonheur* only when they have been uprooted from their native soil and have set out along the path to their own destruction"] (*Prismen*, l.c., p. 188; Eng. pp.184-85). With this, Adorno says: the mother is fate; her loss--indeed clearly also a fateful one--the emancipation from fate. And this emancipation is, as for the heroes so for the artworks, the path to destruction. The only other place in his museum essay where he speaks of the mother stands in a certain contrast to this mythologization, heroicization, and tragicization of both artworks and emancipation--a procedure Adorno employed as often as he denounced it. It reads: *Übrigens war es um diesen Genuß, an den Valéry und Proust glauben wie an die Versicherung einer bewunderten Mutter, immer schon fraglich bestellt* ["This aesthetic pleasure, furthermore, in which Valéry and Proust have as much faith as in a revered mother, has always been a questionable matter"] (l.c., Ger., p. 181; Eng., p. 179). In Proust and Valéry, such a "faith" is not the issue--entirely apart from the fact that in order to enjoy pleasure, one need not first have faith in it and entirely apart from the fact, moreover, that to have faith in a revered mother is itself a pleasure, indeed, the pleasure of her pleasure. But if Adorno "always already" finds this pleasure--that of the artworks--questionable, then he simultaneously suggests that the reverence for the mother, that the mother herself, was always already questionable--and certainly not the native soil, which he biologistically summons up some pages later.

42. Whether an invention or an observation, it is worth noting that Valéry allows the murderous and suicidal inclinations of the museum, in which each painting strives to extinguish the other, the diadocho-battle of the works--*Ce tableau, dit-on quelquefois, TUE tous les autres autour de lui....*--to come into play only after the death of the *mother*, unlike Freud who dated such clashes to the period following a *patricide*. Wherever ones speaks of the museum, one speaks at the same time of society, of its structure and its destructure.

THE HYPOTHESIS, THE CONTEXT, THE MESSIANIC, THE POLITICAL, THE ECONOMIC, THE TECHNOLOGICAL — ON DERRIDA'S *SPECTERS OF MARX*[1]

Simon Critchley

> I once said, perhaps rightly: The earlier culture will become a heap of rubble and finally a heap of ashes, but spirits will hover over the ashes.
>
> Wittgenstein, *Culture and Value*

To begin with, let us try to be quite clear about what Derrida is affirming in *Specters of Marx* (SdM[2]). Although he claims from the beginning to the end of SdM that Marxism is *plus d'un* (both more than one and no longer one), and that deconstruction has neither been Marxist nor non-Marxist (SdM 126-7/75), and that, as Marx said before him, "What is certain is that I am not a Marxist"(SdM 145/88), Derrida's affirmation in this text is the following:

> Deconstruction has never had any sense or interest, in my view at least, except as a radicalization, which is also to say *in the tradition* of a certain Marxism, in a certain *spirit of Marxism.*(SdM 151/92)

Although Derrida has understandable reservations about the felicity of the word "radicalization," he elsewhere speaks, to use another word he has problematized, of the *position* (SdM 92/53) he is going to defend in terms of assuming the Marxist heritage, "one must [*il faut*— with all the force that the *il faut* commands in a whole series of Derrida's texts] assume the heritage of Marxism..."(SdM 93/54).

Deconstruction is marxism, it would seem. A formula that we will have to put alongside Derrida's other hyperbolic formulations, that "deconstruction is justice," or, more awkwardly, "America is deconstruction."[3] I don't know how shocking this identification of deconstruction with Marxism might appear. To Derrida-watchers it shouldn't exactly come as news, particularly regarding a number of elements in his career: his early interest in Tran Duc Thao's attempted reconciliation of phenomenology and dialectical materialism, his radicalization of the thought of economy from his earliest work, particularly in his essay on Bataille, and his revealing comments on Marxism during the "Political Seminar" of *Les fins de l'homme.*[4] However, if deconstruction is a certain reception, continuation and continued radicalization of the Marxist heritage, then we are still no closer to understanding what this might mean. To do this I would like to begin by briefly discussing *the hypothesis* advanced in SdM and making a couple of remarks about *the context* for the book. I will then go on to discuss what I see as the central theme of SdM: *the messianic.* As a way of unpacking this theme, I will address a number of sub-themes in SdM: the injunction of *différance,* democracy to come *(la démocratie à venir*), justice, religion and the *es spukt* (it spooks). As a consequence of this discussion, I would like to turn to the theme of *the political* and address the sub-themes of hegemony, the decision and the New International. I conclude, more speculatively, with brief discussions of two more themes: *the economic,* specifically the relation of deconstruction to capitalism, and *the technological,* where I focus on some of Derrida's hints on the relation of spectrality to technicity and try to approach Derrida as a thinker of originary technicity.

The Hypothesis

Derrida's hypothesis in SdM has a structure that will be extremely familiar to readers of his work. He spells it out schematically in the concluding pages of the text,

> On the one hand (*D'une part*), Marx insists on respecting the originality and the proper efficacity, the autonomization and automatization of ideality as finite-infinite processes of *différance* (phantomatic, fantastic, fetishistic, or ideological)... But, on the other hand *(d'autre part)*...Marx continues to want to ground his critique of his exorcism of the spectral simulacrum in an ontology. It is a — critical, but pre-deconstructive — ontology of presence as actual reality and as objectivity. This critical ontology means to deploy the possibility of dissipating the phantom, let us venture to say again of conjuring it away as the representative consciousness of the subject, and of bringing this representation back to the world of labor, production and exchange, so as to reduce it to its conditions. Pre-deconstructive here does not mean false, unnecessary, or illusory. (SdM 269/170)

D'une part... d'autre part— this is the double gesture, the rhythm of double or what I call elsewhere *clôtural* reading that has *haunted* Derrida's work since the 1960's, of which the examples are legion, and which is the most distinctive motif of deconstruction as a way of reading.[5] As always, Derrida reads with two hands, following assiduously and indefatigably the unstable limit that divides what we might call the logic of a text, its fundamentally aporetic or undecidable basic concepts and distinctions, from the intentions that attempt to govern that text, the author-ity that tries to dissolve or control those aporias. As is so often the case, Derrida focuses this double gesture in the ambivalent usage of a specific word by the author he is considering, in this case *Spectre, Gepenst.* Previous examples, of course, are *Geist* in Heidegger, *pharmakon* in Plato, *supplément* in Rousseau, and so on. So, at the formal level at least, SdM "c'est du bon Derrida, n'est-ce pas?" Always the same, yet always different in each particular instance of reading; a singular event and the eternal return of the same. But, after all, could we or should expect Derrida not to be Derrida?

However, to operate strategically with a pre-deconstructive distinction, if the double gesture gives us the *form* of Derrida's reading of Marx, then what of the *content* to his hypothesis? To introduce detail that will only become clear later on, the basic claim that Derrida makes is that, on the one hand, Marx respects the spectrality of *différance* at the basis of any conceptual order, political regime or mode of economic organization. For Derrida, this is exemplified in a number of specific ways: in Marx's treatment of technology and the media, his thinking of the spectrality of communism ("A spectre is haunting Europe — the spectre of communism"), and the spectrality of capital itself: the fetish character of the commodity form, the non-phenomenologizable mystery of exchange value, and the subtle evasiveness and tendency-to-invisibility of ideology. This leads Derrida to one side of his hypothesis, that the figure of the spectre or phantom is not just one figure amongst others in Marx's text, it is rather "la figure cachée de toutes les figures"(SdM 194/120). The basic task of Derrida's reading in SdM is to survey this *phantomachia peri tes ousias* that runs through Marx's texts, which is traced through a partial reading of the *Communist Manifesto*, the Second Chapter of Volume I of *Capital* and, most impressively, a reading of Marx's critique of Stirner in *The German Ideology*.

This leads Derrida to the claim that there is, to use his neologism, a *hantologie* in Marx's text, a certain irreducible spectrality and *différance* at work, a logic of haunting that, for Derrida, is the condition of possibility and impossibility of any conceptual order.[6] One of the crucial distinctions in SdM turns, characteristically for Derrida, on a homonym, namely the difference between *ontologie* and *hantologie*, a difference that can only be marked grammatologically in writing, that by-passes phoneticization. I will specify ontology in a moment, but let it be noted that Derrida's claim early in the book is that this *hantologie* is not only more powerful and ample than any ontology or thinking of Being, i.e. Heidegger's, but contains within it, as a secondary effect, any eschatology or teleology linked to such ontology, whether that be an eschatology of Being, of class struggle, of divive revelation, or whatever (SdM 31/10). In a gesture that will be familiar to Derrida-watchers, *ontologie* is a apocalyptic discourse on or of the end, whereas *hantologie* is a discourse on the end of the end.[7]

Marx is therefore, according to Derrida, a *hantological* thinker. This is what his texts *say*. This is the logic that governs them, that makes them possible, *despite themselves*. However, following the other side of the double gesture — *d'autre part* — if Marx's texts respect a logic of spectrality that is, as Derrida implies in the above quote, deconstructive, then, as Derrida makes crystal clear in his reading of the critique of Stirner in *The German Ideology*, Marx also wanted to be rid of phantoms and specters. Of course, Marx shares this tendency with the Young Hegelians

(Bauer, Feuerbach, Stirner) — and, I would claim, with Hegel himself — insofar as they wanted to free philosophy and consciousness of the illusions to which it had subjected itself in history, in particular the illusory spectrality of religion. However, as is well known, the young Marx's problem with the Young Hegelians was that they concerned themselves with "German philosophy and not German reality," and restricted their critique of spectrality to the realm of consciousness and its objects. However, Marx's discourse was not only directed against the spectrality and *Vorstellungsdenken* of the Young Hegelians, but also against the spectre of ideology, that is, "the legal, political, religious, aesthetic or philosophical"[8] forms through which the ideas of the hegemonic class become the ideas of the epoch, and also against the spectrality of bourgeois economy characterized by the fetish character of the commodity form and the phantom nature of exchange value.

Furthermore, Marx wanted to found his critique of spectrality on what Derrida refers to as an *ontology*, which is critical but pre-deconstructive. Why pre-deconstructive? Because, to echo Derrida's words, it is a critique of political economy that has as its horizon or foundation a conception of presence as effective reality or objectivity, what Derrida elsewhere refers to as the living present of life, praxis, production and labour. The unstable limit that Marx's text criss-crosses at various points is that between the deconstructive and the pre-deconstructive, between *hantologie* and *ontologie*. Thus, the general hypothesis here is that Marx's analysis and critique of the Young Hegelians, of the German Ideology, and of bourgeois political economy is deconstructive and *hantological*, but it becomes pre-deconstructive when that critique is referred to or founded upon an ontology of presence, effectivity, praxis and objectivity. Derrida's characteristically quasi-transcendental claim is that *hantologie* is the condition of possibility for *ontologie*, that is, although Marx makes a decision to refer the critique of capital to an ontology of presence, this decision cannot repress what we might call the *spectral drive* or *différance* which would ruin any such ontology *avant la lettre*. Thus, although Derrida is reading with two hands, his reading is not even-handed, he is not offering an even choice between *hantologie* and *ontologie*, rather he is showing how this ambivalence is structured or staged in Marx's text, but *hantologie* has theoretical priority, it is from this spectral drive that something like thought is born (SdM 260/ 165)

(I have a parenthetical worry here about what counts as Marx's ontology: Derrida refers to an ontology of presence in Marx, but how are we to understand this? I take it that Marx's "ontology" is located in what, at the beginning of *The German Ideology*, he refers to as the "presuppositions" of his approach, namely that "we begin with real individuals, together with their actions and the material conditions of life, those in which they find themselves, as well as those which they have created through their own efforts".[9] That is, we begin with an insight into the fundamentality of the social production of life — "As individuals express their life so they are" — in terms of a dialectic between individual forces of production and the arrangement of the relations of production into which those forces are born, and which constitutes the economic structure of society. I take it that Marx's ontology is located in his insight into the dialectic of forces and relations of production, which generates both the materialist conception of history and an agenda for political action, — let's call it communism. Two thoughts on this: is this an ontology? To my knowledge, Marx doesn't use this word in this sense and I imagine that many scholars of Marx would be suspicious of this terminology. For example, J. O'Malley in his recent helpful edition of Marx's *Early Political Writings* calls this "ontology" a "materialist guideline".[10] Thus, the notion of ontology here would seem to presuppose the hermeneutic grid of a Heideggerian conception of metaphysics which is not, as Derrida has shown better than anyone, exempt from deconstruction. Secondly, and more importantly, if the elements of Marx's "ontology" are somehow "pre-deconstructive," then what does this mean? Derrida is careful to point out in the above quote that pre-deconstructive does not mean "false, unnecessary or illusory," but presumably neither does it mean 'true, necessary or real'. If the elements of Marx's "ontology" are pre-deconstructive, then what remains that we might call (pre-deconstructively) *substantive* or at the level of *content* in a deconstructive Marxism? What force does Marxism retain if we set to one side its materialist account of life, production, praxis and history? I completely agree with Derrida that there are certain ontologies that we can do without, for example the Marxist-Leninist economic determinism of dialectical materialism, and we must constantly resist the temptation to ossification and dogmatism into which Marx's discourse can fall, but does this qualification disqualify all ontologies? Can we do without ontology or, better, an ontological *moment* if we are Marxists, even deconstructive Marxists? And what remains of Marxism when we set to one side this ontological baggage? I will return to this question below in my discussion of the political.[11])

The Context

However, if Derrida's hypothesis in SdM claims a theoretical argument for the primacy of spectrality, then is this Derrida's only reason for writing SdM? Is there not, to use another pre-deconstructive paleonym, a *normative* claim running through SdM which allows us to establish something like the *context* for this text. Why read Marx now?

In the paragraph that follows the statement of the hypothesis that we have been commenting on, Derrida remarks,"that the ontological and the critical are pre-deconstructive, has [and have] political consequences that are perhaps not negligible. And they are doubtless not negligible, to say it too quickly here, as concerns the concept of the political, as concerns the political itself".(SdM 270/ 170-71)

To express a thought telegraphically and in a way that I will try to make good below, the normative drive of SdM, and what I find so impressive about the text — so urgent and so clear — is its attempt at a politicization or, better, re-politicization (SdM 144/87) of deconstruction, an attempted reinvention of the political in terms of a Marxist *hantologie.* But what is Derrida arguing against? That is, what are the political consequences of a pre-deconstructive ontology and critique? They are twofold, or rather there are at least two elements to the context for SdM, one within Marxism, one outside of Marxism, the latter being much more important for Derrida. What they have in common is a refusal of spectrality.

1. Within Marxism, a strong point of Derrida's reading is the link he draws between what he rather euphemistically calls "the totalitarian heritage of Marx's thought"(SdM 170/104) and the refusal of spectrality. Totalitarianism, or what Jean-Luc Nancy calls "immanentism," in all its recent and less-recent guises, is a political form of society governed by a logic of identification, where "everything is political" that is, where all areas of social life are claimed to represent incarnate power: the proletariat is identified with the people, the party with the proletariat, the politburo with the party, the leader with the politburo, and so on. Totalitarianism is the phantasy of a completed and transparent social order, a unified people among whom difference or social division is denied. In terms of SdM, totalitarianism is premised upon a refusal of spectrality, it is, as Derrida puts it, a "panic before the phantom in general," that is, before something which escapes, transcends and returns to haunt the social order. Although totalitarianism is a grotesque distortion of Marx's thinking, particularly of what I would see as its fundamentally democratic ethos (which is, of course, powerfully and rightly critical of the formalism of bourgeois liberal democracy, of the latter's attempt to have political equality without economic equality), it is clear how totalitarianism inherits a certain conception of "the end to politics" within Marx's text, what he called the abolition of the state and which Engels referred to as its "withering away." Against the troubling tendency to subordinate the political to the socio-economic within Marx's "ontology," which was transformed into the economism of the Second International, Derrida's argument for a logic of spectrality within Marxism can be linked to the claim for the irreducibility of the political understood as that moment where the sedimented meanings of the socio-economic are contested. Following Ernesto Laclau's radicalization of Gramsci, one might link the logic of spectrality to the logic of hegemony; that is, if one renounces — as one must — the communist eschatological "a-theodicy" of the economic contradictions of capitalism inevitably culminating in revolution, then politics and politico-cultural-ideological hegemonization is indispensable to the possibility of radical change. I will come back to this below.[12]

2. Outside of Marxism, and here we come to the real context for SdM, if there is a refusal of spectrality within totalitarianism, then there is an equal refusal of it in that anti-Marxist consensus that celebrates the "collapse of communism" in terms of the uncontestable triumph of liberal democracy. The context for SdM is the hegemony of the teleological discourse on the death or end of Marxism, which, as I mentioned above, Derrida rightly sees with a sense of *déjà vu*, as a rehearsal of the 1950s end of ideology thesis. Derrida detects a three-fold thread to this hegemony in the recent behaviour of the political class, the media and intellectuals (SdM 91-92/52-53). As an example of this anti-Marxist hegemony, Derrida chooses Fukuyama's *The End of History and the Last Man*, which is the focus of the engaging second chapter to SdM. Derrida quite rightly and very persuasively places Fukuyama's end-of-history thesis in the tradition of American Straussianism continued by Fukuyama's teacher, Allan Bloom, and going back, via Leo Strauss, to Kojève's interpretation of Hegel. In a way that recalls Derrida's discussion of an apocalyptic tone in philosophy, he shows how Fukuyama's neo-liberal euphoria of the end of history is essentially a Hegelian-Kojèvian theodicy where liberal democracy, allegedly rooted in a recognition of the dignity of human beings and economic effectivity, is the realization of the kingdom of God on earth. Thus, the end of history would be the final eradication of the spectre of communism and the universal *incarnation* of liberal democracy. Thus, Fukuyama opposes the spectre of Marxism with a certain Hegelian/Kojèvian Christian logic of incarnation as the end of history.

Although seemingly diametrically opposed, both elements of the context for SdM (and these two elements by no means exhaust its context) follow a logic that is premised upon a refusal of spectrality; they are both discourses on and of the end: apocalyptic discourses. We could go further and claim that both discourses are *Christian* in Hegel's sense of the word, that is, discourses of *incarnation*[13] and *revelation*, ultimately the incarnation of community, absolute knowing as community, the system as socio-political comedy (of course, there are other, and perhaps more persuasive, readings of Hegel than the *comic* reading). This thought can be linked to an opposition that runs throughout SdM, and which is particularly important in the final chapter, between spectrality and *phenomenology*. The specter is precisely that which refuses phenomenologization, that retreats before the gaze that tries to see it, like the ghost of Hamlet's father. The specter is the apparition of the inapparent.[14] Phenomenology is here conceived in its Hegelian rather than Husserlian sense,[15] as that *active experience (Erfahrung)* where objects become objects for consciousness. In this sense, phenomenology is always a phenomenology of spirit (subject becoming spirit and spirit becoming subject), or a becoming-phenomenologizable of the specter, in a logic which is both Christian, insofar as Christ is the phenomenologization of the spectrality of the divine, and, as the

Young Hegelians were perfectly aware, post-Christian insofar as Christianity is the self-alienation of consciousness or human essence. For Derrida, the irreducibility of the spectral is thematically linked to the irreducibility of the religious. But, in order to understand what this means we must turn to the central theme of SdM: *the messianic.*

The Messianic

First, a word on ghosts. In the characteristically elliptical opening to SdM, entitled "Exordium" (possibly an allusion to Kierkegaard's *Fear and Trembling*), Derrida suggests that without speaking to, and of, ghosts, we would not be able to be responsible either to the living or to the not-yet or no-longer living. Thus, the discourse on specters is the condition for what, with Benjamin, we would call an anamnesic solidarity with the dead of history and for those as yet unborn.[16] Thus, the discourse with and on specters proceeds in the name of justice, as this word is presented in the essay "Force of Law," which is in many ways the Ur-text for SdM, although the former presents the barest bones of the latter.[17] Indeed, in SdM — as in "Force of Law" — Derrida cites Levinas and employs the latter's conception of justice from *Totality and Infinity* to illustrate his own account (SdM 48-49/23).[18] Justice here defines and is defined by the ethical relation to the other, *"la relation avec autrui — c'est à dire la justice."* In Derridian terms, Justice is the undeconstructable condition of possibility for deconstruction, the "for-the-sake-of-which" deconstruction takes place, "but," Derrida notes, "we can call it by other names". The messianic will be one of those other names.

Thus, SdM proceeds in the name of justice, whether ethical or political, and speaks of specters in order to try and do justice to the living, the dead and the unborn. Running through Derrida's opening remarks is a critique of any account of justice that would restrict responsibility only to the living, to the presently living, or to the living present. In a manner that is difficult to present cogently outside the dense allusiveness and performative compression of the opening pages of SdM, Derrida is weaving together his account of justice with his early deconstruction of the *lebendige Gegenwart* in Husserlian phenomenology, to suggest that justice is somehow constituted by *différance.*

Before unpacking this claim, we should note that there are two prime candidates for accounts of justice that would restrict responsibility to the living. Firstly in Marx himself, recall the famous words from *The German Ideology* cited above — "as individuals express their life, so they are" — where Marx's thinking would seem to be rooted in an ontology of life. Secondly, we can also note an oblique debate with Michel Henry's reading of Marx, for whom *life*, for Henry the subjective praxis of living individuals, is the foundation upon which economic and meta-economic reality can be constructed.[19] Against Marx's and Henry's primacy of *la vie*, an approach that the latter would call phenomenological, Derrida posits a notion of *la sur-vie* (living-on, sur-vival), which one could trace back to his readings of Blanchot.[20] This notion, which only occurs, to my knowledge, on three occasions in the text (SdM 17, 179, 235-36/xx, 187, 147), plays a quiet but organizing function. The nearest one gets to an explanation of *sur-vie* is when the debate with Henry surfaces in a long footnote (SdM 177-79/186-88). For Henry, Marx's metaphysical determination of reality in terms of praxis, production and, ultimately, life, gives rise to an entirely novel conception of subjectivity as "une puissance immergée en soi et qui s'éprouve soi-même sans distance,"[21] that is to say, as radically immanent subjectivity constituted through affectivity. Although Derrida might be said, in principle, to grant the *ontological* plausibility of Henry's reading of Marx, as "the hyper-phenomenological principle of the flesh-and-blood presence of the living person..."(SdM 230/191), Derrida opposes this reading with his own *hauntological* approach. After posing some persuasive critical questions to Henry, Derrida writes revealingly:

> We are attempting something else. To try to accede to the possibility of this very alternative (life and/or death), we are directing our attention to the effects or the petition of a living-on or survival [*une sur-vie*] or of a return of the dead (neither life nor death) on the sole basis of which one is able to speak of 'living subjectivity' (in opposition to its death).(SdM 179/187)

By following the path of the specter and the logic of spectrality in Marx's text, Derrida is obviously seeking to deconstruct the limit between the living and the non-living and show that the seeming priority of life in fact presupposes a *sur-vie* that undermines this priority. We speak of ghosts in the name of justice.

However — and this is an extremely difficult thought to get to grips with, but it is a *capital* idea — to claim that justice is constituted by *différance* is not to imply that justice is deferred, delayed or indefinitely postponed: *"demain on rase gratis"*, "it's jam tomorrow". *Différance* is falsely accused of procrastination or of evading the pressing needs of the present with the so-called *luxury* of undecidability. On the contrary, Derrida's whole effort in SdM is in thinking the *injunction*, be it the injunction of Marx (the title of the first chapter) or the injunction of *différance*. As Derrida remarks in an interview given at the time of the publication of SdM, "There would be no *différance* without urgency, emergency, imminence, precipitation, the ineluctable, the unforseen arrival of the other, to the other to whom reference and deference are made."[22] With an urgency and precipitation that marks the whole tone of the book, making its prose restless and light,[23] Derrida writes, and I quote at length:

> In the incoercible *différance* the here-now [*l'ici-maintenant*] unfurls. Without

> lateness, without delay, but without presence, it is the precipitation of an absolute singularity, singular because differing, precisely, and always other, binding itself necessarily to the form of the instant, in *imminence and in urgency*: even if it moves toward what remains to come, there is the *pledge* [*le* gage] (promise, engagement, injunction and response to the injunction, and so forth). The pledge is given here and now, even before, perhaps, a decision confirms it. It thus responds without delay to the demand of justice. The latter by definition is impatient, uncompromising, and unconditional. No *différance* without alterity, no alterity without singularity, no singularity without here-now. (SdM 60/31)

A full commentary on this compressed and rich passage would constitute a separate lecture in itself. It would at the very least cause us to link the urgency and injunction of Marx to the theme of *le gage* which, as I have shown elsewhere, is the key to an understanding of Derrida's reading of Heidegger in *De l'esprit*.[24] However, the central thought here is that the injunction of SdM — of *différance* and Marxism — is *l'ici maintenant sans présence*, that is, the absolute singularity of justice happening now without presence. We should hear in the "here and now" both the classical and theological *hic et nunc* and the semantic richness of the *maintenant*, understood both as the now, but also as the "maintaining," that is, the act of *maintenance* or maintaining/sustaining/bearing, where the present participle connotes an *act* of presencing irreducible to the present (*Gegenwart*). We might even hear the thought of the hand-holding (*manutenere* — *manus, tenere*) of the now which appears in Derrida's reading of Heidegger.[25]

For Derrida, the ethico-political imperative of Marxism happens *now*, it is maintained at this very moment and is not postponed to a utopian future.[26] It would seem to me that the entire plausibility of SdM rests upon this difficult thought of the *here and maintaining-now without presence as an impossible experience of justice*. If this thought proves absolutely unintelligible, then one can perhaps follow Derrida no further.

Derrida associates the injunction of *différance*, or the injunction of Marx, with his notion of *democracy to come* (*la democratie à venir*), which has been an increasingly persistent theme in Derrida's recent work (SdM 110-111/64-65). Once again, Derrida is anxious to distinguish *la démocratie à venir* from any idea of a *future* democracy, where the future would be a modality of the *lebendige Gegenwart*, namely the not-yet-present. Derrida's discourse is full of negations at this point: democracy is *not* to be confused with the living present of liberal democracy, lauded as the end of history by Fukuyama, *neither* is it a regulative idea or an idea in the Kantian sense, *nor* even a utopia, insofar as all these conceptions understand the future as a modality of presence (SdM 110/65). It is a question here of linking *la démocratie à venir* to *différance* understood in the above-mentioned sense as *l'ici maintenant sans présence*, as an experience of the impossible without which justice would be meaningless. In this sense, *la démocratie à venir* does not mean that tomorrow (and tomorrow and tomorrow) democracy will be realized, but rather that the experience of justice as the maintaining-now of the relation to an absolute singularity is the *à venir* of democracy, the temporality of democracy is *advent*, it is arrival happening now. As I have hypothesized elsewhere, democracy is the future of deconstruction, but this future is happening now, it is happening as the now blasting through the continuum of the present.[27] In this sense, we might speak of *la démocratie à venir* not as a fixed political form of society, but rather as a process of *democratization*. Although, I cannot go into the requisite detail here, it would be a question of developing at least three further points:

(i) To show how the time of justice, that is, the time of the injunction of *différance*, of Marxism and *la démocratie à venir*, can be understood as messianic time in the sense developed by Benjamin in the "Theses on the Philosophy of History"[28]; that is, as that *Jetztzeit*, which Derrida translates as "l'à-présent"("the at-present") (SdM 96/181), that *now* which is not the empty and homogenous flow of objectivist history governed by the *Gegenwart*, and which Benjamin assimilates to a notion of historical materialism.

(ii) To show how the Benjaminian notion of messianic time can be thought in relation to Levinas's notion of ethical time or the temporality of what he calls, with great discretion in the Preface to *Totality and Infinity*, messianic eschatology.[29] Levinas opposes the time of justice to the ontological or economic notion of time and history that reduces and reifies individuals, determining them in terms of their works, relations of exchange and productivity. When Levinas claims that "When man truly approaches the Other he is uprooted from history,"[30] I think "history" here refers to the objective history of the victors, or "barbarism" in Benjamin's sense of the word. At least on my reading, Levinas's work attempts to rub history against the grain, to find the "ruptures in history,"[31] to produce a history for those without works or texts, what I have elsewhere called *ethical* history.[32] The historical materialist, in Benjamin's sense, blasts open the continuum of objectivist history in the name of another history, in the name of justice, which would not be — for Benjamin, Levinas or Derrida — an end to history, but the continual working over of history as a work of infinite mourning, a politics of memory, the insomniac experience of being haunted by the specters of the past. Levinas writes, "Of peace there can only be an eschatology.(...) That peace does not take place in the objective history disclosed by war, as the end of that war or as the end of history."[33]

(iii) To show how the time of justice in Derrida, as the maintaining-now without presence, can be productively linked to the temporality of the ethical relation in Levinas. Levinas's later work proceeds from a distinction between two orders of time: synchrony and diachrony. Synchronic time is a linear, infinite series of punctual moments spread along the axes of past, present and future — what one might call, with Bergson, the spatial representation of time or, with Heidegger, the vulgar Aristotelian concept of time. Diachrony, on the other hand, is — literally — the coming apart of time, it is time as the punctual present falling out of phase with itself (*le déphasage de l'instant*) or the time of the lapse (*le laps*). In Bergson's sense, diachrony is the real time of subjectivity: the unique, unrepeatable and mobile temporality of *la durée;* in Heidegger's sense, it is the temporalisation of time (*die Zeitigung der Zeit*), the authentic experience of time from which the inauthentic time of synchrony is derived. Levinas's basic and astonishing claim is that the concrete case in which time temporalizes itself as diachrony is in the everyday event of my reponsibility for another.[34] Time is accomplished in a relation to the other. This relation is not an experience of presence for Levinas, but is rather a relation to the other that is underwritten by an experience of the trace, the trace of the infinite as that past which has never been present. For Levinas, the essence of time is *temporisation*: postponement, patience, the undergoing of time as senescence, the passivity of ageing. Time establishes a relation to the future that is not achieved through laying hold of the future, as Heidegger attempts in his analyses of *Verstehen* and *Entwurf*, but in a "lack of any hold upon the future."[35] The enigma of time — the time of justice — for Levinas lies in an experience of time that differs from the present, both as an absolute past and an ungraspable future, precisely as trace and as *différance*. And yet, this experience of time happens *now*, blasting through the continuum of the present in a relation to the other, the experience of justice. Interestingly, this temporal and ethical structure is what Levinas would call (and would Derrida call it?) *témoignage* testimony or witness.[36]

However, we are still a little distant from the theme of the messianic, although it has been presupposed in everything that has been said in the last few pages. Something is rotten in the state of Denmark, the time is out of joint. The lesson that Hamlet learns from the political assassination of his father, according to Derrida, is that the order of law, of the state, is based on violence, vengeance and injustice. Given this identification of law and violence — which, Derrida rightly claims, is Shakespeare's question before it is Nietzsche's, Heidegger's or Benjamin's (and whose is it before Shakespeare? Homer's?) — how is one to think of justice at this time of disjuncture? Derrida asks, and it is here that the messianic is introduced for the first time, qualified by a characteristically coy "quasi,"

> If right or law stems from vengeance, as Hamlet seems to complain... can one not yearn for a justice that one day, a day belonging no longer to history, a *quasi messianic* [my emphasis] day, would finally be removed from the fatality of vengeance. (SdM 47/21)

In these fascinating pages, Derrida is weaving together a dense fabric of allusion and argument, where he associates (i) the experience of *disjuncture* (a crucial word in these pages), of Hamlet's sense of the time being out of joint — the order of law as vengeance — with (ii) the disjuncture of the ethical relation in Levinas, which is precisely that which cannot be assembled into a totality and (iii) Heidegger's meditation on time and justice in *Der Spruch der Anaximander*, where *dike* is translated as jointure or *Fug*, and which is thought together with *a-dikia* as *Unfug* or dis-juncture. Although I cannot go into the detail of Heidegger's text here, [37] what interests Derrida is Heidegger's attempt, firstly, to suspend all traditional conceptions of law as calculative, metaphysical and deconstructable, and to seek to think justice in relation to the donation of time, namely the presencing of the present (*das Anwesende des Anwesen*), and to think something like Being non-metaphysically in relation to this presencing.

However, and in a way that will be familiar to Derrida-watchers, he poses the following critical question to Heidegger. Namely,

> Once one has recognized the force and the necessity of thinking justice on the basis of the gift, that, beyond right, calculation and commerce... is there not a risk of inscribing this whole movement of justice under the sign of presence, albeit the presence to meaning of the *Anwesen*, of the event as coming into presence, of Being as presence joined to itself, of the proper of the other as presence? (SdM 55/27)

Thus, if Heidegger thinks justice in relation to the presencing of the present, that is, in terms of a jointure that gathers and harmonizes, Derrida's question is to whether justice, understood with Levinas as a disjunctive relation to the other, "supposes on the contrary the irreducible excess of a disjunction or an anachrony, some *Un-Fuge*, some 'out of joint'..."(SdM 55/27). In the interrogative mode (but does a question, or a series of questions, constitute an argument? Is it enough? Is one persuaded? A vast question), Derrida engages in a reversal of Heidegger where he hypothesizes that justice as disjuncture — "the de-totalizing condition of justice" (SdM 56/28) — is the condition for the presencing of the present. It is in this way (and Derrida recognizes the hastiness and provisionality of his formulations at this point) that the relation of deconstruction to the possibility of justice can be thought, where justice — "that which must (without debt and without duty) render itself to the singularity of the other" (SdM 56/28) — is the undeconstructable condition of possibility for deconstruction.

Although the way in which Derrida links his argumentation to Heidegger and Shakespeare is novel, the above conclusion — deconstruction is justice — will hardly be surprising to readers of "Force of Law." However, what *is* novel are two subsidiary claims that Derrida tags on to the above argumentation: firstly, this account of justice is called a "desert-like messianism" by Derrida, "the messianic: the coming of the other, the absolute and unpredictable singularity of the *arrivant as justice*"(SdM 56/28). Secondly, this notion of the messianic is interpreted as "an *ineffaceable* mark... of the heritage of Marx" (SdM 56/28). Thus, combining the two claims, the heritage of Marx that Derrida wants to endorse is that of a messianic appeal for justice.

The theme of the messianic, allied to the name of Marx, recurs at crucial points in SdM. After stating that he endorses the kind of critical analysis (of ideology and capital) that we have inherited from Marxism, Derrida links this to the *"schwache* messianische Kraft" of Benjamin's "Theses on the Philosophy of History, "what he calls, emphasizing the adjectival rather than substantive usage, a "messianique sans messianisme"(SdM 96/181, cf.103/59, 112/65). (A further parenthetical worry begins to take shape here: namely, if this messianic appeal for justice is the way in which the heritage of Marxism is to be assumed, then, Derrida goes on,

> Failing which (*Faute de quoi*) one would reduce the event-ness (*l'événementalité*) of the event, the singularity and the alterity of the other.
> Failing which (*Faute de quoi*) justice risks being reduced once again to juridico-moral rules, norms of representations, within an inevitable totalizing moment... (SdM 56-57/28).

My question would be: is the passage from the messianic appeal for justice to laws, norms and rules always a fault (*une faute*), always in default? If so, why is it a fault and what sort of fault is it? Clearly for Derrida, to refer the messianic appeal for justice to moral and legal conditions is a transgression of the apparent priority, or indeed *apriori* antecedence of the messianic — what Derrida elsewhere calls "the universal dimension of experience"[38] — but is this transgression not also a necessity? Is it not the most necessary of necessities, namely the moral-legal-social *instantiation* of justice, the *aposteriori* and particular instance of the *apriori* status of the messianic? To employ the language of the above quote, is not totalization inevitable? Isn't the question not *whether* to totalize, but *how* to totalize, that is, *how* to link the *apriori* and the *aposteriori,* the universal and the particular, the transcendental and the empirical? As we will see below, the notion of the New International recognizes the necessity of instantiation, totalization, the *aposteriori,* the particular and the empirical, but I have two further telegraphic thoughts in this regard:

(i) Is not this faulty move from justice to law precisely that which is thought by Levinas in terms of the move from the other (*autrui*) to the third party (l*e tiers*), from ethics to politics? It might also be noted that, in "Ideologie et idéalisme," Levinas also defines Marxism as an ethical "prophetic cry...the revolt of Marx and of Marxists beyond Marxist science,"[39] but that, for Levinas, politics would be the *measure* brought to the ethical relation to the other, without which the latter would risk being "angelic," "the spirituality of angels"(if not specters) that is the source of his critique of Buber's I-Thou relation. How is one to combine (is one to combine?)

the thought of justice with the thought of measure, which, of course, also entails the question of judgement?

(ii) In a recent debate with Axel Honneth, I have, with some significant and important reservations, attempted to support and amplify his attempt to show the possible compatibility or mutual supplementarity of Derrida's recent reflections on ethico-political issues with the Habermasian programme of discourse ethics, in order to show how the messianic appeal for justice conceived as a relation to the irreducible singularity of the other might be combined with a broadly Kantian and procedural theory of justice, capable of testing the validity of moral-political norms. The question here is: if it can be shown that the reciprocity and symmetry axiomatic to Habermasian discourse ethics stand in need of supplementation by a non-reciprocal, asymmetrical appeal to justice or the messianic, then is not the same true *vice versa*?)[40]

However, on the question of Marxism and messianism, are we not evading a rather basic and crude question? Marx had many swinging and unkind things to say about the Young Hegelians, but what he endorsed in their approach was their critique of religion, writing famously that, "Religion is the sigh of the oppressed creature, the feeling of a heartless world and the soul of soulless circumstances. It is the opium of the people."[41] As the *Theses on Feuerbach* make clear, the problem with the Young Hegelians is that their concept of alienation is restricted to the critique of religion, a critique which is "essentially complete."[42] So, against Marx, Derrida would seem to want to maintain the irreducibility of the religious in its "desert-like" form. Is this plausible? At least four features can be noted here:

1. The irreducibility of the spectral is linked to the irreducibility of the religious for Derrida, where Marx's critique of religiosity would be part and parcel of his ontological approach. *Hantologie* is premised upon the irreducibility of forms of non-identity and alterity, where the religious is a privileged form of such alterity.

2. More specifically, in Derrida, the irreducibility of the religious is the desire to maintain the *sublimity* of the religious, which is expressed in Benjamin's messianism and elsewhere (in Levinas, in negative theology). Derrida opposes, and this is a theme one can find dealt with at great length in *Glas*, any notion of religiosity rooted in what I called above a phenomenology of *incarnation* (which one might also call a phenomenology of the beautiful), the incarnation of the living presence of the divine in the form of the person of Christ and, ultimately, in the spiritual form of the community in Hegel and the material form of communism in Marx.

3. In opposing this logic of *incarnation* in religion, Derrida works to undermine (i) the historical teleology of religion in Hegel which leads irresistably to Christianity, the *revealed* religion; (ii) the *Aufhebung* of religion in philosophy found at the end of the *Phenomenology of Spirit* and *one* condition (only one, the

other being the becoming-spirit of the subject) for the possibility of Absolute Knowing; and (iii) the *Aufhebung* of the Young Hegelian critique of religion into the critique of political economy in Marx. All of these gestures would be ontological for Derrida.

4. Is one led to conclude from the above that the irreducibility of religious sublimity in Derrida's notion of the messianic allows one to identify his position with that accorded by Hegel to Judaism, as an abstract and formalistic religion of duty, where justice is placed above love? Is *hantological* Marxism a continuation of what we might call "philosophical Judaism" by other means? And is this justifiable?

Derrida goes some way to addressing this question in his most revealing discussion of the messianic which comes close to the end of SdM (SdM 266-67/167-69). Derrida asks: what is the relation between Marxist messianism, as "a universal structure"(SdM 266/167), and that other desert-like Abrahamic messianism of Judaism? Having set up the question nicely, Derrida doesn't really give a satisfying response, asking himself whether Abrahamic messianism would be a prefiguration or (to use Levinas's word, which is how he refers to the divine as the trace of illeity[43]) *"prénom"* of Marxist messianism. Why not, perhaps. Nonetheless, and always in the interrogative mood, Derrida asks, "Can one conceive an atheological heritage of the messianic?"(SdM 266/168) and suggests a few lines later that "One may always take the *quasi-atheist* [my emphasis] dryness of the messianic to be the condition of the religions of the Book..."(267). Derrida goes on to qualify the messianic in terms which recall my discussion of *différance* and *la démocratie à venir* in terms of "imminence" and "urgency," and calls it "a 'messianism' that despairs"(SdM 268/169). A religion of despair, then? Perhaps.

However, taking as a cue Derrida's qualification of the messianic as "quasi-atheist" (although what exactly does the coy 'quasi' mean here?), another avenue can be briefly pursued. In his reading of *The German Ideology,* Derrida comes across Marx's citation of Stirner's words "*Ja,* es spukt in der ganzen Welt," poorly rendered into French as, "*Oui,* le monde entier est peuplé de fantômes"(SdM 216/136). What holds Derrida's attention is the phrase *es spukt, het spookt, ça spectre, it spooks.* Derrida comes back to this phrase right at the end of SdM (SdM 272/172); what interests him is the way in which the logic of spectrality is expressed *verbally* (*es spukt* from *spuken*), that is, as a movement, what Derrida calls the "passive movement of an apprehension." This passive movement is the very movement of haunting, of the ghost, of the ghosting of the ghost, *la revenance du revenant.* Derrida makes an interesting parallel between the spookiness of haunting and the experience of *Unheimlichkeit* in Freud and Heidegger (SdM 273-77/173-75). However, specifically in relation to the question of religion, I would like to associate the *es spukt* with the uncanniness of the *il y a* as this is figured in the work of Levinas and Blanchot. Although I cannot go into detail here, [44] the *il y a* should not be confused with the

Heideggerian *es gibt* (might one link the *es spukt* with the *es gibt: es spukt Sein, es spukt Zeit?*), for it is both Levinas's word for Being and his attempt to ruin the *Seinsfrage*. With the *il y a,* Levinas asks us to undertake a thought experiment, "Let us imagine all beings, things and persons, reverting to nothingness?" But what would remain after this annihiliation of all *Seienden*? Nothing? Levinas claims that this very nothingness of all existents would itself be experienced as a kind of presence, not the presence of the *lebendige Gegenwart,* but what he calls elsewhere "An atmospheric density, a plenitude of the void, or the murmur of silence."[45] To compress to the point of incomprehensibility, the experience of the *il y a,* is what Blanchot would call *le neutre* which is opened in the experience of writing and literature. I have claimed that the *il y a* is the secret of Blanchot's work, its primal scene, which is an experience of dis-aster, of the night without stars. [46] What interests me here is the way in which the experience of the *es spukt,* that is, the impossible experience of spectrality (i.e. the ghost is there, but does not exist; it is neither present nor absent) shares certain features with the *il y a.* The latter is an experience of the night, the night of imsomnia for Levinas or what Blanchot calls the other or essential night towards which the desire of the writer tends. It is also, crucially, an experience of haunting, it is the night of ghosts, which Levinas illustrates with the example of Banquo's ghost which returns after death to haunt Macbeth. [47] In the night of the *il y a,* which is also the space of many of Blanchot's *récits,* the frontier between the living and the dead is criss-crossed: the living are unable to either live or die and the dead refuse to lie down. The *il y a* is an experience of the impossibility of death — horror of horrors — which Derrida has himself explored in his recent *Aporias.*[48] Death is the impossibility of my possibility which outstrips my powers, it is that of which I am ultimately unable (*je ne peux plus pouvoir*). With this in mind, we might explore some of the specters in Levinas's text, particularly his discussion of the return of *le revenant* of scepticism after its refutation, which, it has been claimed, is the specter of Derrida in Levinas's *Autrement qu'être.*[49] However, the thought that I would like to pursue here is the following: might not the "quasi-atheist" messianism of SdM be linked with the *es spukt* and the *il y a,* not as a religious messianism, but precisely as an experience of atheistic transcendence? Does the impossible experience of the *es spukt,* the spectrality of the messianic, look upwards to a divinity, divine justice, or even the starry heaven that frames the Moral Law, or rather does it not look into the radically atheist transcendence of the *il y a,* the absence, dis-aster and pure energy of the night that is beyond law?

The Political

I suggested above that what is perhaps most impressive and most urgent about SdM is its call for a re-politicization of deconstruction in terms of a Marxist *hantologie.* I also indicated two of the political consequences of a pre-deconstructive Marxist *ontologie*, and suggested that the logic of spectrality in Derrida could be linked to the neo-Gramscian logic of hegemony in the work of Ernesto Laclau. It is time to try and make good on these suggestions.

In what we might justifiably refer to as his deconstruction of Marxism — that is, a reading that identifies a double gesture within Marx's texts — Laclau radicalizes Gramsci's critique of the economistic stagism and historical determinism of traditional Marxism.[50] Roughly and readily, Laclau opposes the almost mechanistic vision of historical materialism advocated in the Second International and in certain Marxist texts (the example given is the Preface to the *Contribution to the Critique of Political Economy*), with an account of history based on the irreducibility of class struggle and antagonism, a tendency that one can also find within Marx's texts, for example at the beginning of the *Communist Manifesto*. Thus, although Laclau would endorse the traditional Marxist account of capitalism in terms of its often pernicious dislocatory effects, he does not think that these dislocations can simply be referred to the alleged economic and historical objectivity of contradictions between the forces and relations of production, the effects of the infrastructure on the superstructure, but are rather the consequence of continual "hegemonic articulations" (for me, the key concept in Laclau's work), of incursions of the political and the ideological into the socio-economic-historical realm, where infrastructure and superstructure form what Gramsci would call a "historical bloc." Such hegemonic articulations temporarily fix or stabilize the meaning of social relations in a transient equilibrium. Such a "hegemonic equilibrium" of the social is not to be transcended in a communist society free from power, contingency, antagonism and politics itself — the millenarian vision of communist society that sometimes gets the better of Marx and which, with the privilege of hindsight, it is all too easy to confuse with the totalitarian myth of social transparency. In contradistinction to the traditional Marxist theodicy that would claim that the dislocations of capitalism lead inexorably to the simplification of the class structure, and the emergence of the proletariat as the revolutionary class and privileged agent of history, Laclau argues that the very dislocatory effects of late capitalism — what we might think of as the phenomenon of combined and uneven development — lead instead to a progressive fragmentation of the social and a proliferation of social actors (for example, the decline in the organizing power of the state and in the credibility of traditional political parties and the increasing prominence of ethnic, national, sexual or ecological protest movements). Perhaps Laclau's most challenging and controversial thesis is that these phenomena of dislocation and fragmentation lead not only to a proliferation of political possibilities, but are also the conditions under which something like freedom is possible; that freedom is a consequence of dislocation. The democratic transformation of society — what I still want to call socialism — is *one* of these political possibilities (and only one, there are others, particularly on the radical right, which have been significantly more successful at hegemonizing in recent decades), but there is no economic or historical inevitability to such an outcome. Socialism will only be the consequence or, better, the permanent activity of intense hegemonic articulation and political effort. It is, to say the least, unclear whether the traditional notion of the political party, confined within the nation state is adequate to such a task.

An expanded notion of hegemony becomes a way of arguing for the primacy of politics over socio-economic relations, although the former can in no way proceed without continual reference to the latter and the former is done for the sake of the latter. As such, the concept of hegemony points in two different temporal directions at once: first, with regard to history, hegemony is a way of explaining how certain social relations became fixed, and shows that such fixing is not the consequence of the "objective" contradiction of forces and relations of production, but rather is the product of contingency, antagonism and power, that is to say, it is the consequence of a *decision* (i.e. the transformation of history into genealogy). Second, the concept of hegemony leaves the future radically open and indeterminate, which means that nothing is guaranteed, but neither is anything lost, at least not yet. On this view, rather than standing at the end of history, it might be said that we stand at some sort of beginning, at the point when we can recognize the radical contingency and limitedness of our finitude. Such a situation need not lead to the pessimism of an Adorno or the passivity or the resignation of a later Heidegger, but can also be the condition for a "new militancy and new optimism."[51]

If deconstruction is the attempt to show the constitutive undecidability, radical incompletion or untotalizability of textual, institutional, cultural, social and economic structures, then hegemony is a theory of decisions taken in the undecidable terrain opened up by deconstruction, and which, in my view, is precisely the way in which we might begin to think about the politics of deconstruction.[52] The burning question here is whether and how we can combine the logic of deconstruction with the logic of hegemony: does undecidability paralyze the possibility of the decision or does it, on the contrary, enable it?

With regard to SdM, the fate of the question of deconstruction and hegemony, to my mind, turns on how we interpret the following thought: in relation to the generalized dislocation of the contemporary world, Derrida claims, the messianic hesitates, it trembles; he writes:

> This messianic hesitation does not paralyze any decision, any affirmation, any responsibility. On the contrary, it grants them their elementary condition. It is their very experience. (SdM 269/169)

Is messianic hesitation the experience of the decision? That is the question, as Hamlet might soliloquize. If our response is positive, then we might be able to solder the logics of deconstruction and hegemony at this point.

In SdM, Derrida indeed speaks of hegemony, using the word — which is, to my knowledge, relatively new to his vocabulary [53] — on at least eight occasions (SdM 69[x2], 73[x2], 90, 91, 96-7, 149/37[x2], 40[x2], 51, 52, 55, 90), mostly during the discussion of Fukuyama and the so-called death of Marxism. The first time he uses the word, he even refers to Laclau's work, making the interesting and valid point that "Haunting belongs to the structure of every hegemony"(SdM 69/37). However, rather than viewing hegemony as a theory of the decision and the positive possibility of politicization, Derrida (mis)understands hegemony negatively in its traditional sense as domination. He writes, for example, that, "...a dogmatics is attempting to install its worldwide hegemony in paradoxical and suspect conditions. There is today in the world a *dominant* discourse..."(SdM 90/51) This is unfortunate. However, if the concept of hegemony is (mis)understood traditionally in SdM, there is nonetheless, I believe, a *logic* of hegemony at work in the text. This logic turns around a phrase that forms part of the book's subtitle, and which, in Georges Sorel's terminology, we might describe as the mobilizing "myth" of SdM: *The New International*.[54] In many ways, this is the key to SdM, but my worry is whether the key fits the lock of the present political situation.

Derrida lists what he calls the ten afflictions of the 'New World Order' in a kind of *tableau noir* (SdM 134-39/81-84). After listing unemployment, homelessness and other woes, the final item on his list, which is privileged above the other terms (*"surtout, surtout"*, he writes, SdM 138/83) is the present state of international law, which he rightly sees as being dominated by the interests of certain "hegemonic" nation states. In contradistinction to this, Derrida suggests that we require a New International that, "is being sought through these crises of international law, it already denounces the limits of a discourse on human rights that will remain inadequate, sometimes hypocritical, and in any case formalistic..."(SdM 141/85). This reference to the formalism of human rights, echoing the Hegelian-Marxist critique of their abstraction and one-sidedness, is illuminating and is followed by some qualifications of the New International. He writes of the bond around which something like solidarity might form, "It is a link of affinity, suffering and hope, a still discreet, almost secret link, like that around 1848, but more and more visible — we have more than a sign of it"(SdM 141/85). Thus, the New International would be focussed around a common bond or link, that — at this point in history at least — is almost secret. Derrida goes on to claim that this bond would be, "without party, without country, without national community (International before, across, and beyond any national determination), without co-citizenship, without common belonging to a class"(SdM 142/85). A strange bond, then: without reference to the figures of community, class, party, nation or the other traditional means of collective identification or hegemonization. Yet, Derrida insists, this bond of the New International is inspired by at least one of the spirits of Marxism. Which one? Clearly not the ontological Marxism of *the* proletariat, *the* party and *the* revolution characterized above as ontological. Derrida continues in a luminous passage, which I quote at length:

> Now if there is a spirit of Marxism which I will never be ready to renounce, it is not only the critical idea or the questioning stance [which Derrida qualifies on the previous page as the spirit of the Enlightenment]...It is rather a certain emancipatory and *messianic* affirmation, a certain experience of the promise that one can try to liberate from any dogmatics and even from any metaphysico-religious determination, from any *messianism.* And a promise must promise to be kept, that is, not to remain "spiritual" or "abstract," but to produce events, new forms of action, of practice, of organization, etc. To break with the "party form" or with such and such form of the State or the International does not mean to renounce every form of practical or effective organization. It is exactly the contrary that matters to us here.(SdM 146-47/89)

I couldn't agree more. The New International must be in the spirit of the Marxist idea of critique (critique of ideology and of capital) and the quasi-atheist notion of messianic affirmation or promise that we discussed above and which proceeds in the name of justice and emancipation. Furthermore, such critical and messianic promises must be made with the intention of being kept, and thus the promise of the New International must in its turn give rise to new forms of organization, activism and political aggregation. In relation to what I said above about the *injunctions* of *différance* and *la démocratie à venir,* the urgency of the New International cannot be deferred or postponed indefinitely; it must be approached in messianic terms as *l'ici maintenant sans présence.* The New International is happening now, at this very moment; Derrida writes:

> And there are signs. It is like a new International, but without a party, or organization, or membership. It is searching and suffering, it believes that something is wrong, it does not accept the 'new world order'...[55]

To my mind, Derrida would here seem to be trying to sketch the preconditions for a new socialist hegemonic articulation, a political decision taken in the name of justice and in the face of the world's afflictions.

The only question I have here is the following: *how is the New International to be hegemonized?* What forms and means should it employ? Around what figures should it agitate? Should it agitate around figures? Who does it include? Who does it oppose? *Does* it oppose? *Does* it exclude?

I do not have convincing answers to these questions and I am not really in the habit of delivering prophecies to the masses, but, in closing, let me hazard three critical thoughts.

1. I find Derrida's suggestions on the subject of the New International a little vague, suggesting that, "the new International belongs only to anonymity"(SdM

148/90). He goes on, in the same paragraph, to suggest that within the academic and intellectual world, the New International includes those who have resisted the anti-Marxist dogma of recent years and remained hyper-critical in the Enlightenment spirit, without renouncing the ideals of democracy and emancipation. Who does Derrida have in mind here? Jürgen Habermas?

2. Also, the limits of the New International begin to look a little vague when Derrida writes that, "Whether they wish it or know it or not, all men and women, all over the earth, are today to a certain extent the heirs of Marx and Marxism"(SdM 149/91). Perhaps this is right. But so what? Couldn't the same be said — perhaps with even greater justification — about Adam Smith or John Locke? Are we not all heirs to their marketing strategies? Thus, there is the risk of a rather empty universalism on Derrida's part at this point.

3. Finally, on the question of organization, although Derrida is rightly dubious of the idea of a communist party as the privileged and sole means for revolutionary transformation, he tends to link this to a rather questionable historical positivism which claims that, "What tends perhaps to disappear in the political world that is announcing itself, and perhaps in a new epoch of democracy, is the domination of this form of organization called the party..."(SdM 167/102). Again, on the next page, he says of this hypothesis "...that this mutation has already begun; it is irreversible"(SdM 168/103). Derrida tags two claims onto this hypothesis: (i) that the correlate of the party, i.e. the state, is also exhausted; and (ii) that the notion of the party cannot adapt to the exigencies of the contemporary public space with its domination by the media and tele-technology. In relation to this second point, I have two words to offer: *Forza Italia.* If Derrida is right, how does one explain the brief but stunning electoral success of this alliance which would seem (entirely cynically, to my mind) to combine a fairly classical party structure with the exigencies of the televisual media forms? An analysis of the 1994 elections in South Africa, although with a more progressive outcome, might also consider this question of the relation between the party form (in this case, the ANC), the media and the democratic process. However, to return to the first point, my question is the following: if the political party is not an adequate vehicle for promoting something like a New International, which might be justified although I have my (doubtless nostalgic) doubts about this, then how does one hegemonize something like the New International outside of traditional party structures? What means of identification, figuration and hegemonization are available? Furthermore, how does one work outside traditional party structures without collapsing into a "divide and rule" designer politics of individualism or confining oneself to the always modest socio-economic changes of single issue politics, or, worst of all worlds, devoting oneself to an intra-academic politics of vacuous radicalism and reaction?

The Economic

The concept of economy has played a continual, discrete, but perhaps organizing rôle in Derrida's work since the 1960's. One immediately thinks of the discussion of restricted and general economy in Bataille and of psychic economy in Freud in *Writing and Difference.*[56] Indeed, what Derrida calls "the point of greatest obscurity" in his work, "the very enigma of *différance,*" can be redescribed in economic terms as a relation between two impossibilities. That is, thinking in particular of Derrida's reading of Bataille, two claims are made: (i) that the calculable expenditure, exchange and restitution that governs a restricted economy cannot but be interrupted by the force of a general economy, by an incalculable expenditure without reserve; (ii) that there can be no pure giving or expenditure without reserve that does not fall back into the restricted economy it attempts to leave behind. Derrida's major insight might be thought of as the necessity of thinking together of two impossibilities, that of a purely restricted and a purely general economy. One might claim that *différance* is the name for this necessary and impossible thinking together, this relation between the economic and an-economic.[57]

Of course, as Gido Berns has shown, this distinction between the economic and the an-economic is classical and finds its philosophical origin in Aristotle's *Politics.*[58] As is well known, for the Greeks, economy was primarily concerned with establishing the rules or *nomoi* of the household or *oikos.* The *oikos,* what Derrida would call "la clôture économique"(SdM 53/26), is the enclosed sphere of the home and the hearth, wherein Aristotle thought it possible to have a virtuous relation to economic goods insofar as one practices "equalizing justice," that is, insofar as economic exchange between *oikoi* takes place on the basis of service and mutual use, repaying good with good. Over against the sphere of economy — the sphere of the proper — stands what Aristotle calls *chrematistics,* money making. Berns has shown how, for Aristotle, the art of money making (*chrematistike techne* — and I note the association of chrematistics, capital accumulation and technics at this point, which is not peripheral to our concerns here) is essentially *improper* to ethical life and should not be part of the proper conduct of human nature. Chrematistics only arises when the use value of an object has been exceeded by exchange value, that is to say, when the de(con)structive infiniteness of accumulation and desire has been introduced into the finite circle of the *oikos.* In this sense, and I will return to this below, we might say, adapting one of Wallace Stevens's *Adages,* that *money is a kind of deconstruction.*[59] In this Aristotelian sense — counter-intuitively, insofar as we would associate chrematistics with modern capitalist economy — money is an-economic.

Aristotle's model of economy, tied as it is to ethical and political reflection, betrays, according to Berns, a nostalgia for small, quasi-agrarian communities.

Such nostalgia has a long and powerful heritage and modern analogues can be found firstly in the Young Hegel's longing for *verlorene Sittlichkeit*, and perhaps even in the mature Hegel's concept of the State where the latter's rational and ethical *telos* would attempt to contain or circumscribe the boundlessness of chrematistic desire; and secondly, in Marx's effective reproduction of the distinction of economy and chrematistics, where socialism would be identified with the former and capitalism with the latter. Economy is chrematistic under conditions of capitalist relations of production, and in a communist society, "there will be no money-capital at all"[60] Of course, it should be noted that there is another, liberal and capitalist, tradition of economic reflection, beginning in Locke and definitively expressed by Adam Smith, which, whilst still articulating itself in relation to a moral vision (Adam Smith is the author of *The Theory of Moral Sentiments*, as well as *The Wealth of Nations*), analyzes the chrematistic nature of economy as an essentially autonomous, value-free domain. For Adam Smith, money is a consequence of the division of labour, a division rooted in that most advantageous feature of human nature, the propensity to truck and barter.

Before returning to SdM and trying to focus some critical questions, I would like to follow Berns one step further and look at a passage he discusses from Derrida's *Given Time*, where the distinction between economy and chrematistics is discussed in the context of Baudelaire's "La fausse monnaie."[61] Derrida summarises Aristotle's distinction between economy and chrematistics, noting that

> for Aristotle, it is a matter of an ideal and desirable limit, a limit between the limit and the unlimited, between the true and finite good [the economic] and the illusory and indefinite good [the chrematistic].(158)

Economy is the thought of a limit, it is the attempt to master that limit and control the thought of the unlimited, the *apeiron* that would overstep the *peras*. As such, the opposition between the economic and the chrematistic is that between "the supposed finiteness of need and the presumed infinity of desire"(158). Now, the infinity of desire will always transcend the finitude of need (and the fact that Derrida's language at this point recalls that of Levinas is perhaps not accidental, as Levinas is one of the rare thinkers who reserves a privileged place for money in his work)[62] once *money* has appeared on the scene. Derrida continues, in a gesture that will be familiar to readers of his work, "As soon as there is monetary sign — and first of all sign — that is, *différance* and credit, the *oikos* is opened and cannot operate its limit"(158). Thus, money is a kind of deconstruction, it opens the closure of the *oikos* to the unrestricted "economy" of desire where money circulates and where wealth is accmuluated or squandered, the nomadic and quasi-automatic flows of capital.

But — and this is what interests me — this ruination of the ethicality of economy, this transgression of its limits, which are the limits of the family, hearth and home, is also "the chance for any kind of hospitality...the chance for the gift itself. The chance for the event"(158). Derrida is suggesting here, and we cannot go into the detail of his reading of Baudelaire at this point, that money is the possibility of a form of an-economic giving, for a donation without return, for an *event*. As a long footnote makes clear (159), the word "event" is clearly to be understood in its Heideggerian sense as *Ereignis*, and where Derrida associates money (*to khrema*) with *der Brauch* or usage (*to khreon*), which, according to Heidegger, names Being as the presencing of the present in "that oldest fragment of Western thinking."[63] Thus, the possibility of money, that is to say, the possibility of "*différance* and credit"(p.158), breaking the restricted economy of the proper, is also the possibility of the gift, of the "ethicality" of the gift. We are, doubtless all too allusively, on the brink here of a new thought of the event, of *Ereignis* as the injunction, or what I called above the *disjuncture* of *différance* as the possibility of justice: *es gibt Sein, es gibt Geld*.

What is the bearing of this argumentation to SdM? How are we to link the injunction or disjuncture of *différance*, thought in relation to money making and capital, to the spirit of Marxism we spoke of above? For a book that deals with Marx and Marxism for 279 pages, Derrida is strangely reticent about economics. However, I have already discussed at length Derrida's suspicions of an ontological Marxism, which, at the level of economy, could be linked to the economistic stagism of traditional Marxism criticized by Gramsci and Laclau, and which leads to the assertion of the primacy of politics (i.e. *hantologie* and hegemony) over economics. In SdM itself, the economic is mentioned on a couple of occasions (SdM 48, 53/23, 27), and is taken up in the discussion of the specter of exchange value in chapter 5. Most interestingly, Derrida defines justice as the incalculability of the gift and "l'ex-position an-économique à autrui"(SdM 48/23), where the relation to the other might be associated with a certain thought of ethical chrematistics.

However, the central economic question with regard to Derrida, in SdM and elsewhere, as I see it, is the following: *what is the relation between capital and deconstruction?* Doesn't the entire argument of SdM for the irreducibility of a logic of spectrality necessarily entail that capitalism cannot and should not be overcome, for it is only under the conditions of capitalist economy, with its unlimited chrematistic desire, that the radical donation of justice is possible? Is not capitalism the possibility of justice? Is this not the entire thrust of the discussion of the irreducible spectrality of exchange value and commodity fetishism in chapter 5 of SdM? If Derrida is trying to establish the spectral origin of Capital and the specters of Marx that must continue to haunt capitalism, as he would seem to be doing, then is he not also implying a certain dependence of the deconstructive logic of spectrality upon capitalism? Don't Derrida's suspicions of the ontology underpinning Marx's work at least imply the exorcizing of some *Spectres de Marx*, namely the spectre of the revolution and the transcendence of the bourgeois order in a communist society? Furthermore, if, as I have suggested, money is a kind of deconstruction, then is the reverse not also true, namely that deconstruction is a kind of money, perhaps even an art of money-making? For what is money, if not a specter or a sign, as Derrida himself suggests (SdM 80/45), the spectrality of *différance* that haunts the "real" value of the notes and coins in our pockets? Might not deconstruction be redescribed as a *chrema-tologie*, a logic of money-making?

These questions seem critical, but they needn't be. I mentioned above how Laclau claims that the possibility of radical democracy is directly linked to the structural dislocations of late capitalism, and that the increasing disorganization of these dislocations enables the possibility of new hegemonic articulations, some of which might lead to the democratic transformation of society. Should we not simply conclude that the only way to assume the heritage of Marxism at the present time is by presupposing capitalism as the unstable but staggeringly resiliant economic form of the contemporary world? Capitalism, as Marx himself perspicuously foresaw, has become a global economic system that has pushed beyond the state boundaries of national economies and which exists in a neurotic state of permanent revolution, "tearing down all obstacles that impeded the development of productive forces, the expansion of needs, the diversity of production and the exploitation and exchange of natural and intellectual forces."[64] Contemporary capitalism, particularly the activity of the financial markets, would indeed seem to be a total chrematistics that is increasingly free from the regulatory control of any particular economy, whether national or quasi-federal like the EU. At once extraordinarily creative and wasteful, able to recuperate any opposition and every *avant garde* by repackaging it as a commodity, contemporary capitalism is a near-chaotic order (or a near-orderly chaos) whose endless mobility and movement — its sheer velocity, and strange love of chance — is its best protection against subversion.

How does one respond to contemporary capitalism? Two possible responses offer themselves:

1. the first, offered by Berns, with which I have some sympathy, is what I would call the *defensive* or *reactive* response, which would concentrate on the need, in Derrida's words, "To calculate with the incalculable."[65] That is to say — picking up on the definition of *différance* given above as the necessary and impossible thinking together of the economic and the an-economic — particular economies, such as states or federations of states, must attempt to negotiate with the radical chrematistics of late capitalism, for example by trying to control the value of a given currency against the speculative flows of the financial markets. As numerous recent

examples show, this is an infinite and possibly futile task, but it is perhaps the only possibility available for ensuring the integrity of the state or super-state territory and guaranteeing effective economic management, political government and adequate social provision for citizens of a given territory.

2. However, if the first response to late capitalism is the defense of economy against chrematistics, which would attempt to negotiate them into a new relation — in many ways, this is the friendly old specter of European social democracy — then the second possible response is a good deal more radical, and I derive it loosely from the notion of *creation* as developed by Deleuze and Guattari. Why calculate with the incalculable? Why not rather *incalculate* with the incalculable? What is so troubling about capitalism to many on the Left is its extraordinary hybridizing energy, its ability to assume new forms, to hegemonize itself, to recuperate what was originally intended as opposition and to sell it as a commodity (situationist graffiti crops up on record sleeves and t-shirts). What is more disturbing is capitalism's ability to renew and propagate itself not out of any reactive gestures but rather out of a cheerfully superficial affirmativeness. The problem with the "bad Nietzscheanism" of contemporary capitalism is that it refuses to place in question the very social, economic and political premises of its own system and the gross iniquities, inequalities and wastefulness that it creates. In Adornian terms, intriguingly invoked by Deleuze and Guattari, contemporary capitalism lacks a *critical* and *utopian* moment.[66] But why oppose this extraordinary chrematistic energy with a defensive, reactive strategy? Perhaps what is required is some kind of exacerbation of the enormous creative energy of late capitalism, some sort of *active* affirmation where those energies are transformed into revolution, where rather than trying to oppose capitalism with a reterritorialization on the level of the economy, the state and law — or even a utopian reterritorialization — one would try to accelerate the deterritorializing effects of late capitalism. As Deleuze and Guattari write, "Philosophy takes to the absolute the relative deterritorialization of capital."[67] Absolute deterritorialization, then. Is this a spirit of Marxism? Is there a secret path that leads from chrematistics to revolution? Perhaps.

The Technological

As is well known, Marx had some remarkably prescient things to say about technology, showing how the capitalist drive for efficiency and the mastery of time results in the increasing mechanization of the production process, the creation of a reserve army of the unemployed and an opposition between, on the one hand, technologized capital and, on the other hand, living labour. However, Marx's views could not be said to be anti-technological, unlike the agrarian utopia of Fourier, and a communist society would resolve the contradiction between technology and labour by allowing the former to become the property of the latter, of free associated labour.

Derrida recognizes Marx as a thinker of technics (SdM 92/53), and the question of technics, whilst not a dominant theme in SdM, is powerfully linked to the logic of spectrality. In relation to the modern media or tele-technologies, Derrida insists that the media still require a Marxist analysis. Of course, Derrida is thinking of Marxism here in the sense of *hantologie*, and the claim would seem to be that only such an approach is capable of grasping the truly spectral nature of the media, of the ways in which the contemporary public space is constituted through tele-technology, a technology that is neither living nor dead, neither present nor absent, but which haunts our most intimate private spaces with its imagery of power. In a footnote, Derrida reminds the reader that the portion of the heritage of Marx that he wants to preserve concerns the irreducibility of the spectral, which he then links to the *virtual* and the increasing virtualization of politics and the public space (SdM 225-6/190). It would here be a question of an affirmative thinking together of tele-technology or the media with what Derrida says of the public space of democracy. The link between the increasing virtualization and media-tization of the public space and the process of democratization becomes clearer in a second passage, which directly precedes the statement of the hypothesis with which we began this lecture. He writes:

> But also at stake, indissociably, is the differantial of *techne*, of techno-science or tele-technology. It obliges us more than ever to think the virtualization of space and time, the possibility of virtual events whose movement and speed prohibit us more than ever...from opposing presence to its representation, "real time" to "deferred time," effectivity to its simulacrum, the living to the non-living, in short, the living to the living-dead of its ghosts. It obliges us to think, from there, another space for democracy. For *la démocratie à venir* and thus for justice. (SdM 268/169)

However, it should first be asked: what is technology, or better, technics? As Bernard Stiegler recalls at the beginning of *La technique et le temps*, a text footnoted in the above passage, Western philosophy arguably begins with the distinction of *techne* and *episteme*, where Socrates distinguishes himself from the Sophists by showing how the pursuit of knowledge in critical dialogue is superior to and independent of sophistic rhetoric and mnemotechnics.[68] As the *Phaedrus* shows, philosophy has no need of writing and rhetoric, technologies of the self which lead not to genuine knowledge, but only to the loss of memory, or what Husserl called the forgetfulness of origins. In its ancient and modern forms, and in its major tradition, philosophy has sought to constitute the realm proper to it, the realm of the proper — whether this is the transformed space of the polis, the intersubjective space of dialogue and uncoerced communication, or the solitary realm of contemplation, reflection and the soul's dialogue with itself — by making any form of technicity secondary. In its drive for authenticity philosophy has, as Stiegler puts it, repressed the question of technics, a repression that sees technics and technicization as a perversion, a corruption and a constant threat of contamination.[69] Stiegler shows how this tradition of repression is continued in more recent philosophy, for example in Heidegger, where, despite his subtle remarks about the Janus face of *Gestell* and *Ereignis*, that is, where a meditation on the essence of technics would be a prelude to the appropriative event of time and Being, Heidegger's entire analysis proceeds upon the metaphysical distinction of actual technics, thought as pure calculation or reckoning, and the essence of technics. But equally in Habermas, technics is thought under the categories of Weberian rationalisation or as an instance of *Zweckrationalität* leading to technocracy, that is, as a perversion of the space of communicative action and a contamination of the *Lebenswelt*.

In contradistinction to this tradition where philosophy would coincide with the repression of the question of technics — a tradition which risks being rendered quite irrelevant by the sheer speed of the contemporary world, a speed which is that of technical acceleration — Stiegler hypothesizes a thought of *originary technicity*.[70] Technics would here be thought not as an inauthentic perversion secondary to properly philosophical activity, but rather as the very condition of possibility for the constitution of something like human life. Technics is that process of exteriorization, the use of means, of media and mediation whereby the human takes shape. As Stiegler puts it, technics is the "poursuite de la vie par d'autres moyens que la vie."[71]

What of Derrida, then?[72] Although, to say the very least, this is not how he has been read, might not Derrida best be approached as a thinker of originary technicity? In this respect, it is worth reconsidering a number of examples of "classical" deconstruction: if one thinks of Derrida's insistence on the rôle of writing given by Husserl in the constitution of ideality in "The Origin of Geometry," or the irreducibility of the indicative sign in *Voice and Phenomenon*, or the place of writing in the constitution of *logos* and *phone* in "Plato's Pharmacy," or the logic of iterability in "Signature, Event, Context," then each of these discrete arguments might plausibly be viewed as claims for the irreducibility of technics, where the grammatological would be equiprimordial with the technological.[73] That is, there is a *necessity* for a detour through technics in the constitution of philosophical *episteme*, whether this is a realm of dialogue, of the soul conversing with itself, or the pure ideality of speech and meaning. Yet the necessity of the detour through technics is also the ruination or rendering *impossible* of the very project that it was intended to make possible. One way of following Derrida's work would be to see it as a claim for the irreducibility of technics in the constitution of the philosophical *episteme* and, more generally, in any attempt to constitute what is proper, authentic or appropriate to the human. Authenticity or appropriation are always impurely traced and contaminated by the inauthentic and the inappropriate. Indeed, the former are inconceivable without the latter. We might say that the human, or the event of the human, only comes to itself by virtue of technical mediation, by virtue of what Derrida calls above, the "differantial deployment of *techne*." There is no event of the human without technical *différance*, without the technological differentiation of the human from itself in relation to the non-human.

In this connection, some more examples might be illuminating. Think of the whole chain of technical figures that haunt Derrida's texts: the mystic writing pad in "Freud and the Scene of Writing;" the machines that haunt his readings of Hegel, notably the *machine à draguer* that is the key to *Glas*; the persistent ringing of the telephone in *La carte postale*; the gramophone in the essay on Joyce; the photograph in the essay on Barthes; the ubiquitous Mackintosh in *Circonfession* (this list could be continued).[74] It should not therefore be surprising that Derrida should choose the question of technics, and specifically the *metaphysical* character of the distinction of the essence of technics from actual technics, as one of his four *fils conducteurs* in his reading of Heidegger in *De l'esprit*.[75] For me, a privileged example of technicity in Derrida to be explored is the brief discussion of Leibniz's plan for a "General Characteristic" (a kind of 17th Century mechanical artificial intelligence programme) in *De la grammatologie*, where it might be possible to conceive of grammatology as a general grammar of technics and technicity as a condition of (im)possibility for logocentrism.[76] Thus, it would be a question here of wresting grammatology from its "literary" and "philosophical" receptions and even from the direction taken by some of Derrida's later work and reclaiming it as a general theory of technics.

The thesis of originary technicity, as the claim that the human only comes to itself as such through a movement of technical *différance*, opens the possibility of thinking the relation of the human to the non-human, of the *justice* of a relation to the non-human other, whether animal, vegetable, mineral or machine. This perhaps illuminates Derrida's persistent attempts to interrogate and deconstruct the limit that divides the human from the animal and to widen the notion of *le vivant* outside the realm of carnal sacrifice, and also, as we have seen in SdM, to employ the figure of the spectre or ghost to deconstruct the limit between the living and the non-living.[77] As Stiegler reminds us, *différance* is defined by Derrida as a process of *life* of which the human would only be a particular instance and it would here be a question of linking technicity to biologization, of thinking through the implications of the new biological technologies — of eugenics — and perhaps reactivating all the biological metaphors of Derrida's work: the pro-gramme, dehiscence, khora, invagination, etc.[78]

In this sense, I do not think that it would be at all implausible to recast the entire argument for a logic of spectrality in SdM in terms of a claim for the irreducibility of technicity in the constitution of the human, social and political space of the contemporary world. Technicity is not a perversion but a fatality, a fatality that we should not approach reactively, but *amorously*, that is, affirmatively, perhaps even erotically. Learn to love your ignorance of the future!

The task barely broached here consists in trying to think together and productively the following three elements:

(i) originary technicity as both a media-ted and a biological process,

(ii) capitalization conceived in a relation of originary supplementarity with technics, and

(iii) the movement of democratization and the possibility of justice.

But this task overflows not only the bounds of this essay, but also the limits of my competence and your patience.

NOTES

1. The following is the text of a lecture delivered in October 1994 to the meeting of the Society for Phenomenology and Existential Philosophy in Seattle. I would like to thank John D. Caputo for giving me the occasion to prepare this lecture. It was subsequently presented, in various guises, to a conference on "Deconstruction and Politics" at the University of Essex (October 1994), to the Cambridge Graduate Seminar in Literary Theory at King's College (November 1994), to the Amsterdam School of Cultural Analysis (February 1995) and to the "Spectres of Derrida" conference at Birkbeck College, London (May 1995). An abriged version of the present text appeared as "On Derrida's *Specters of Marx*," in *Philosophy and Social Criticism*, 21, 3 (1995), 1-30.

2. References to SdM will be given to the pagination of the French Text (Galilée, Paris, 1993) followed by a reference to the extremely accurate English translation (trans. P. Kamuf, Routledge, London and New York, 1994).

3. Derrida momentarily ventures this hypothesis in *Mémoires for Paul de Man* (Columbia University Press, New York, 1986, p.18) before quickly dismissing it. As Stanley Cavell points out, America is, "*the* anti-Marxist country" (*Must We Mean What We Say*, Cambridge University Press, Cambridge, 1969, p.345-46). But if America were deconstruction, then what spirit of Marxism would haunt it? I am referring to work in preparation on Cavell and in particular to his extraordinary discussion of the Marx Brothers in 'Nothing Goes Without Saying' (*London Review of Books*, January 6, 1994, 3-5), where, in the final paragraph, and in a clear allusion to Derrida, Cavell suggests that, better even than Emerson or Thoreau, access to "that tangle of American culture" might best be had by "a few days immersion in half a dozen Marx Brother's films". What is the specter of Marx for America? Is it Karl-o or Groucho?

4. On the influence of Tran Duc Thao's *Phénoménologie et matérialisme dialectique* (Editions Minh-Tan, Paris, 1951), see Derrida's remarks in an interview with *Le Monde* in 1982 (*Entretiens avec 'Le Monde'* [Editions la découverte, Paris, 1984], 79); and remarks in the "Avertissement" to *Le problème de la genèse dans la philosophie de Husserl* (Presses Universitaires de France, Paris, 1990), vii. On economy, see "From Restricted to General Economy: A Hegelianism Without Reserve", in *Writing*

and Difference, trans. A Bass (Routledge, London and New York, 1978), 251-77. On politics, see *Les fins de l'homme. A partir du travail de Jacques Derrida* (Galilée, Paris, 1981), 526-27.
5. See *The Ethics of Deconstruction: Derrida and Levinas* (Blackwell, Oxford, 1992), 20-31, 88-97.
6. On *hantologie*, see SdM 31, 89 & 255/10, 51, 161.
7. Cf. 'Of an Apocalyptic Tone Recently Adopted in Philosophy', trans. J.P. Leavey, *Oxford Literary Review*, 6, 2 (1984), 3-37.
8. Cf. 'Preface to a *Contribution to the Critique of Political Economy*', *Marx/Engels Selected Works* (Lawrence and Wishart, London, 1968), 182.
9. *The German Ideology* (Lawrence and Wishart, London, 1970), 42.
10. (Cambridge University Press, Cambridge, 1994), xv.
11. A permanent risk of SdM, I feel, is its tendency to attempt to reinvent the wheel with respect to Marxism by ignoring the attempts, within the Marxist philosophical tradition itself, to refine and revise Marx's work and to save it from its theoretical and practical distortions, whether we think here of Lukacs, Gramsci, or Adorno and Horkheimer. Might we not ascribe this tendency to what one might call an Althusserian "tic" in SdM (Althusser is clearly a specter thoughout this text, SdM 147/89), that is, that one can bracket out the previous history of Marxist philosophy insofar as that has somehow been contaminated by "la grande dérive soviétique" and return to Marx's text, and, literally, *lire le Capital.* The only real exception to this rule is Benjamin, who is a decisive specter in SdM. But why is Benjamin accorded this unique state of exception? For the most part, Derrida's scholarly sources on Marx (excluding references to external classical sources, like Freud and Heidegger) are exclusively French — Etienne Balibar is treated very well, Michel Henry less so, and Blanchot's piece "Les trois paroles de Mar"' is the intellectual framework for Chapter 1. Indeed, SdM could be seen as a contemporary rewriting of Blanchot's essay, particularly if we take seriously Derrida's extremely astute remarks on the analogies between the 1950s "end of ideology" thesis and the 1989 "end of history" thesis.
12. Laclau has responded to the reading of *Specters of Marx* attempted here in his review essay "The Time is Out of Joint," to appear in *Diacritics,* which offers some important critical clarification of Derrida's arguments, particularly on the question of necessity for discourses of incarnation and the irreducible teleology of the classical discourse of emancipation that Derrida supposedly wants to endorse. However, Laclau is unconvinced of the necessity for the move from a notion of messianic promise to an ethico-political injunction in the way I develop it in the present essay and in my other work. For Laclau, no ethical injunction of a Levinasian kind flows from undecidability and democratic politics does not need to be anchored in such an injunction. He concludes by focussing what he sees as an ambiguity in Derrida's work, between undecidability as the terrain of radicalization of the decision and undecidability as the source of an ethical injunction. If this is indeed an ambiguity in Derrida (and I am not wholly convinced of this), then Laclau and I stand at opposing poles of this ambiguity. However, my ambition in the discussion of the political given below is to show how these two poles can enter into some form of productive tension.
13. On incarnation, see Laclau "The Time is Out of Joint."
14. Which still leaves open the question of whether there can be a phenomenology *of* spectrality, a phenomenology of the inapparent, to take up Heidegger's phrase from the Zähringen seminar in 1973. As the title of the final chapter of SdM suggests, "L'apparition de l'inapparent: l'escomatage' phénoménologique," Derrida is here alluding to debates about the status of French phenomenology and its alleged theological turn. On this debate, see Dominique Janicaud, *Le tournant théologique de la phénoménologie française* (L'éclat, Combas, 1991) and Jean-Luc Marion, *Réduction et donation. Recherches sur Husserl, Heidegger et la phénoménologie* (Presses Universitaires de France, Paris, 1989).
15. On Husserl, see the intriguing and slightly hurried note (SdM 215-16/189), where Derrida, pondering the question of the specter in Husserlian phenomenology, focuses on the notion of the *noema,* as that "intentional but *non-real* component of phenomenological lived experience", which

would be "the condition of any experience..."
16. A view perversely parallelled in the Mormon doctrines of baptism for the dead and spirits for the unborn as described by Harold Bloom in *The American Religion* (Simon & Schuster, New York, 1992), 112-28.
17. "Force of Law: The Mystical Foundation of Authority," in D.Cornell et all (ed.), *Deconstruction and the Possibility of Justice* (Routledge, London and New York, 1992).
18. I discuss this in more detail in "Deconstruction and Pragmatism — Is Derrida a Private Ironist or a Public Liberal?," *European Journal of Philosophy*, 2, 1 (April 1994), 1-21, see esp. 14-16.
19. Cf. *Marx*, 2 Vols.: 1. *Une philosophie de la réalité*. 2. *Une philosophie de l'économie*, (Gallimard, Paris, 1976). For an abridged introduction to Henry's reading of Marx, see his essay "Marx," to appear in *Blackwell's Companion to Continental Philosophy*, ed. S. Critchley (Blackwell, Oxford, forthcoming).
20. See, in particular, 'Sur-vivre' in *Parages* (Galilée, Paris, 1986), 117-218.
21. In Henry, "Marx."
22. Derrida, "The Deconstruction of Actuality," *Radical Philosophy*, 68 (Autumn 1994), 32.
23. Mention of the restlessness and lightness of Derrida's prose in SdM can be related to a common complaint one often hears in circles otherwise highly sympathetic to Derrida's work. It is claimed that Derrida's early work, in particular *La voix et le phénomène*, is philosophically decisive in the deployment of deconstruction and that it possesses a rigour sadly lacking in his later work, which too often seems to have been written in undue haste. Perhaps there is some truth to such a claim. However, what such a complaint consistently overlooks is precisely the question of the *urgency*, or the *injunction* that drives Derrida's later work, and its relation to what one might call the *performativity* or *event-character* of deconstruction. *Specters of Marx* is clearly not *La voix et le phénomène*. It is a text that was written with enormous urgency to address a specific context at a specific historical moment, to make an intervention at once theoretical, cultural and political. As such, I think that *Specters of Marx* should be viewed as a certain *enactment* of the injunction that the book seeks to describe or prescribe. Might we not view *Specters of Marx* in terms of what it says about the event (SdM 125-26/74-75), namely the event of the injunction of *différance* happening here and now without presence? *Specters of Marx* is an event, a performance, a staging which, as Samuel Weber has shown (I refer to an unpublished paper, "Piece-Work," given at the University of Essex in October 1994), is utterly pervaded by its own *theatricality*, most obviously in Derrida's deployment of *Hamlet* as a frame for his reading. A serious question arises for me at this point, however: if we take on board Derrida's remarks on the need for a non-negative, non-reactive thinking of tele-technology and the media, might one not have doubts about whether the book — however staged, however theatrical, however performatively conceived — is the most felicitous medium for the enactment of such a singular event? How about the use of other media: theatre, television, compact disc, internet?
24. cf. "The Question of the Question: An Ethico-Political Response to a Note in *Of Spirit*," in *The Ethics of Deconstruction*, op.cit. 190-200.
25. I owe the last two sentences to a conversation with Samuel Weber. On the hand in Heidegger, see "Geschlecht II: Heidegger's Hand," in *Deconstruction and Philosophy*, ed. J.Sallis (Chicago University Press, Chicago, 1987), 161-96.
26. In some improvised remarks on deconstruction and pragmatism, Derrida distinguishes the thought of the messianic, as the here and now of justice, from the conventional meaning of utopia (which does not exclude the possibility of other meanings for utopia). See *Deconstruction and Pragmatism*, ed. C. Mouffe (Routledge, London and New York, forthcoming). I quote: "The messianic experience of which I spoke takes place here and now; that is, the fact of promising and speaking is an event that takes place here and now and is not utopian. This happens in the singular event of engagement, and when I speak of *la démocratie à venir* this does not mean that tomorrow democracy will be realised, and it does not refer to a future democracy, rather it means that there is

an engagement with regard to democracy which consists in recognizing the irreducibility of the promise when, in the messianic moment, it can come *(ça peut venir)*. There is the future *(il y a de l'avenir)*. There is something to come *(il y a à venir)*. That can happen...that can happen, and I promise in opening the future or in leaving the future open. This is not utopian, it is what takes place here and now, in a here and now that I regularly try to dissociate from the present."

27. See *The Ethics of Deconstruction*, 241.

28. In *Illuminations*, trans. H. Zohn (Fontana/Collins, London, 1973), 255-66.

29. *Totality and Infinity*, trans. A. Lingis (Duquesne University Press, Pittburgh, 1969), 22-24.

30. *Totality and Infinity*, 52.

31. Ibid, 52.

32. *The Ethics of Deconstruction*, op.cit. p.30.

33. *Totality and Infinity*, op.cit. p.24. Incidentally, if this view of Levinas's conception of history is right, then it makes little sense to claim that Levinas is an anti-historical thinker, as Derrida appears to do in "Violence and Metaphysics" (in *Writing and Difference*, 94).

34. *Otherwise than Being or Beyond Essence*, trans. A. Lingis (Kluwer, Dordrecht, 1981), 10.

35. *Time and the Other*, trans. R. Cohen (Duquesne University Press, Pittsburgh, 1987), 80.

36. In this regard, see Levinas's "Vérité du dévoilement et verité du témoignage," *Archivio di Filosofia* (1972), 101-10.

37. "The Anaximander Fragment," in *Early Greek Thinking*, trans. D. Krell & F. Capuzzi (Harper and Row, New York, 1975), 13-58.

38. See, "The Deconstruction of Actuality," op.cit,36. On the *apriori*, see ibid, 32.

39. In *De dieu qui vient à l'idée* (Vrin, Paris, 1986), 19.

40. Cf. 'Habermas und Derrida werden verheiratet: Antwort auf Axel Honneth," *Deutsche Zeitschrift für Philosophie*, 42, 6 (1994), 981-92.

41. Cf. David McLellan, *The Thought of Karl Marx* (Macmillan, London, 1971), 23.

42. Ibid, 22.

43. *Otherwise than Being or Beyond Essence*, 185.

44. For a much fuller discussion of the *il y a*, see "A Dying Stronger than Death (Blanchot with Levinas)," *The Oxford Literary Review*, 15 (1993), 81-131.

45. Cf. *Existence and Existents*, trans. A. Lingis (Kluwer, Dordrecht, 1978), .57-64.

46. "A Dying Stronger than Death," 119-20.

47. *Existence and Existents*, 62. It might be recalled that it is Levinas who writes in *Time and the Other* (72) that "it sometimes seems to me that the whole of philosophy is only a meditation on Shakespeare."

48. Trans. D. Dutoit (Stanford University Press, Stanford, 1993).

49. Robert Bernasconi, "Skepticism in the Face of Philosophy," in *Re-reading Levinas* (Indiana University Press, Bloomington, 1991), 149-61.

50. My brief presentation of Laclau's work is based on the eponymous opening essay from *New Reflections on the Revolution of our Time* (Verso, London, 1990, 3-85), rather than Laclau and Mouffe's *Hegemony and Socialist Strategy* (Verso, London, 1985), which presents the same deconstruction of Marxism from within a genealogy of the concept of hegemony.

51. *New Reflections on the Revolution of our Time*, 82.

52. In this regard, see Laclau's short article "Discourse," in *The Blackwell Companion to Contemporary Political Philosophy*, eds. R. Goodin & P. Pettit (Blackwell, Oxford, 1994), 431-37.

53. Although Derrida speaks of "l'hégémonie centralisatrice" and "l'hégémonie nationale" in *L'autre cap* (Minuit, Paris, 1991), 45, 48.

54. This notion is first introduced in chapter 1 (SdM 58/29), but receives a fuller discussion as the centrepiece of chapter 3.

55. "The Deconstruction of Actuality," 39.

* These provisional remarks on the question of the economic in Derrida are entirely indebted to the work of Gido Berns, and particular to a course given at Essex University in June 1994 on "Economy and Difference." See his "Politique et justice dans un style déconstructif," in *Filozovski Vestnik* (Slovenian Academy of Sciences, forthcoming).
56. "From Restricted to General Economy: A Hegelianism without Reserve" & "Freud and the Scene of Writing" in *Writing and Difference* (Routledge, London & New York, 1978).
57. "Différance," in *Margins of Philosophy* (Harvester Press: Brighton 1982), 19.
58. Cf. Aristotle, *Politics*, I, 3, 1256a-1258b.
59. Stevens's adage reads 'Money is a kind of poetry'. In *Opus Posthumous* (Faber, London, 1957), 165.
60. Marx, *Capital*, Vol.II (Moscow, 1954), 318.
61. *Given Time* (University of Chicago Press, Chicago, 1992), 158-59. It might be noted that these pages also offer a reading of Heidegger's "Der Spruch der Anaximander," which we could connect to the discussion given above.
62. Although there are many references to money scattered throughout Levinas's major works, see in particular 'Socialité et argent', *Emmanuel Levinas. Cahier de l'Herne* (Editions de l'Herne, Paris, 1991), 134-38.
63. "The Anaximander Fragment," .52 et passim.
64. *Karl Marx. Selected Writings*, ed. D. McLellan (Oxford University Press, Oxford, 1977), 364.
65. "Force of Law: The Mystical Foundation of Authority," in D. Cornell *et al* (ed.), *Deconstruction and the Possibility of Justice* (Routledge, London and New York, 1992), 16.
66. See Deleuze and Guattari, *What is Philosophy?* (Verso, London, 1994), 99.
67. *What is Philosophy?*, 99.
68. *La technique et le temps*, Vol.1 *La faute d'Epiméthée* (Galilée, Paris, 1994).
69. Ibid., 11.
70. Ibid., 30
71. Ibid., 31
72. The following remarks are indebted to conversations with Richard Beardsworth.
73. *Edmund Husserl's "Origin of Geometry": An Introduction*, trans. J.P. Leavey (University of Nebraska Press, Lincoln, 1989); *Speech and Phenomena*, trans. D. Allison (Northwestern University Press, Evanston, 1973); "Plato's Pharmacy" in *Dissemination*, trans. B. Johnson (University of Chicago Press, Chicago, 1981); "Signature, Event, Context," in *Margins of Philosophy* (University of Chicago Press, Chicago, 1982).
74. See, respectively, *Writing and Difference*, op.cit. pp.196-231; *Glas*, trans. J.P. Leavey & R. Rand (University of Nebraska Press, Lincoln and London, 1986); *The Post Card: from Socrates to Freud and Beyond*, trans. A. Bass (University of Chicago Press, Chicago, 1987); "Ulysses Gramophone: Hear Say Yes in Joyce" in *Acts of Literature*, ed. D. Attridge (Routledge, London & New York, 1991), 253-309; 'Les morts de Roland Barthes', trans. P.A. Brault & M. Naas, in *Continental Philosophy 1: Philosophy and Non-Philosophy since Merleau-Ponty*, ed. H.J. Silverman (Routledge, London and New York, 1988), 259-97; *Jacques Derrida*, trans. G. Bennington (University of Chicago Press, Chicago, 1993).
75. *Of Spirit*, trans. G. Bennington and R. Bowlby (University of Chicago Press, Chicago, 1989).
76. *Of Grammatology*, trans. G.C. Spivak (Johns Hopkins University Press, Baltimore and London, 1976), 75-81.
77. "'Eating Well,' or the Calculation of the Subject: An Interview with Jacques Derrida," in *Who Comes After the Subject*, eds. E. Cadava *et al* (Routledge, New York and London, 1991), 96-119.
78. Cf. *La technique et le temps*, 147.

ASCA AWARD 1995

Every year ASCA organizes an interpretation contest. The best interpretation is awarded the so-called ASCA Award, which is sponsored by Van Gorcum Publishers. In 1995 participants were invited to give an interpretation of Angela Carter's "Impressions. The Wrightsman Magdalene." The following text won the ASCA Award for the best interpretation.

Mary Magdalene in a Time/Person Continuum

Sasha Vojkovic

The Interdependence of Marys

> See. She carries it already. She carries where, if she were a Virgin mother and not a sacred whore, she would rest her baby, not a living child but a *memento mori*, a skull. (Carter, 146)

As much as I was determined to start from the very beginning of Angela Carter's short story "Impressions: The Wrightsman Magdalene"[1] and return to the above lines in a later phase, I soon ended up just where I started, at the very end. I was hoping to find the key, or a hidden meaning that would miraculously release Mary Magdalene from her paradoxical existence, and thought that if I carefully exchanged one Mary for another, I would learn the ultimate secret about Mary Magdalene. Mary Magdalene and Virgin Mary are described early in the text as twin paradoxes: one is not what the other is, that is, one is a virgin and a mother and the other is a non-virgin and childless. Yet the corollary of the three sentences quoted above yields the same result: a Virgin mother is not a sacred whore, thus, she rests her baby, which is not a living child, but a *memento mori*, a skull. Conversely, because Mary Magdalene is a sacred whore and not a Virgin mother, she will not rest her baby, her living child. Unlike and like the Virgin mother who would rest her baby, she will rest a *memento mori*, a skull.

On the one hand, the attempt to "exchange" one woman for another proves illusory because knowledge about Mary Magdalene remains perpetually postponed in this exchange, while on the other hand, the impossibility of knowing one Mary without constantly shifting to the other indicates that it is precisely this impossibility, manifested in the interdependance of Marys, which makes the production of knowledge possible. There is an additional element that plays a crucial role in this exchange, however, condensed in the first sentence of the cited text: "See." Here, the second person is addressed: both my "I" and my eye are solicited. But my eye only allows me to see that there is no vision of Mary Magdalene unless my "I" is engaged in an intersubjective discourse.

Hence, the crucial issue in Carter's text is how to exchange the object of representation for a subject of representation, or how to enter "the blue absent space," the imaginary space of the discourse where George de La Tour's *Wrightsman Magdalene* can become "something other than herself," where she can become "I" and where "she" can become "you."

The Exchange of Temporal Continuums

The exchange of Marys mirrors the exchange of temporal continuums; in the beginning of the story we learn about the end of Mary Magdalene's journey to repentance and by the end of the story we realize that the events she is about to undertake in the near future are those which had already taken place in the past. The time loop, which lends a structure to Carter's text, locks Mary Magdalene in this perpetual journey through the past, the present and the future.

The story commences with the supposed facts about Mary Magdalene's life: her journey to France in a boat with Mary, the mother of Jesus, Mary, the mother of St John and the servant named Fatima, her separation from her companions, and finally, her arrival at the cave where she will spend thirty-three years of her life. The journey with the two other Marys that ends in Mary Magdalene's isolation functions as both the point of departure to and the point of arrival at her repentance.

The Exchange of Persons

The "second person" is invited into the discourse in the very first sentence of Carter's short story: "For a woman to be a virgin and a mother, you need a miracle..."(140). Although the events that follow occured in the past, this addressing of the second person shifts the discourse into the "now" of the reader, that is, into the present. In addition, the imperative mode with which second persons are sollicited, as in "don't run away with the idea" or "don't forget Fatima," insinuates that it is not only the "I" telling the story who is the experiencer of the given events, but also that the "you" should constantly revise and recapitulate these "experienced" facts. Another person-function is then introduced, however, through the collective narrator, the first person plural: "But there the two stern mothers and Fatima — don't forget Fatima — set up a chapel, at the place we now call Saintes-Maries-de-la-Mer" (140). Here, the "you" and the "I" temporarily merge into a collective experiencer, the one who produces and preserves the seemingly indisputable collective knowledge. Nevertheless, our collective knowledge is challenged when confronted with de La Tour's *Wrightsman Magdalene.* It is challenged by the "you" who put the scarlet dress on:

> George de La Tour's picture does not show a woman in sackcloth, but her chemise is coarse and simple enough to be a penitential garment, or at least, the kind of garment that shows you were not thinking of personal adornment when you put it on. (141)

The "you" who could theoretically put that kind of garment on are all of us, the "you" who painted it is de La Tour, but the only one who is actually wearing the dress is Mary Magdalene. She is implicitly addressed here, as if she donned that dress of her own accord. The subtle confusion of the second person with the actual object of the discourse has a double effect: it not only underscores the status of the object of the second person, but also points to the potential "I" of Mary Magdalene.

What is also challenged here is the chronology of the already established facts. The image of Mary Magdalene in de La Tour's painting does not correspond visually to the woman who is "gaunty as famine and hairy as a dog," but more importantly, the image does not correspond to the woman chronologically. Mary Magdalene's "now," established through the "first person" looking at de La Tour's Mary Magdalene in a scarlet dress, is clearly not the present nor the future of Mary Magdalene, who has been living the life of a hermit. George de La Tour's Mary Magdalene could only be the past image of a woman who has become a saint and the "false" present therefore needs to be placed where it belongs, that is, into the past.

The "time travel" is radicalized through the intercourse with the candle flame which opens up the gate to the "blue absence," an imaginary space where "persons", temporal continuums and Marys can be exchanged.

First Person, Second Person, Same Person

Mieke Bal explains that the concept of second personhood has a triple allegiance:
1. It indicates the derivative status of personhood; the fundamental impossibility to be, both psychologically and socially, a person without the traces of the person's grafted being.
2. As presented by Benveniste and subsequent theorists in his vein, it indicates the reversible relationship of complementarity between first- and second-person pronouns whose use produces subjectivity and constitutes the essence of language precisely because the pronouns do not refer to fixed positions.
3. It indicates those persons, subjects or discourses formerly referred to as the "object" but now engaged in the dialogue of the performance. Considering that the first and the second- person positions are by definition reversible, Bal explains that one of the ways to measure the engagement of the second person in the production of knowledge is precisely to examine the actual reversibility.[2]

In Carter's story, the reversibility of the first — and second — person positions can best be examined at the moment when the exchange of "I" and "you" allows the "she," Mary Magdalene, to become someone else, or more precisely, when it allows the whore and the saint to become the "same person." This new knowledge about Mary Magdalene is generated through an intersubjective process which accounts for the position of the second person, thus ultimately, for the position of Mary Magdalene. The process of exchanging places with de la Tour's *Wrightsman Magdalene* is traceable in the discursive units that follow; Mary Magdalene as a "she," gradually becomes inextricable from "I" and "you."

In the first instance she is referred to as the "third person": "Now she is gazing at the candle flame, which doubles itself in the mirror" (143). Although Mary Magdalene is referred to as a "she," her act of gazing is occuring now, at this very moment, alluding immediately to the narrator's presence at the scene. The coevalness implied in this sentence is seemingly disturbed in the following paragraph where the narrator's "I" evokes her experience from the past: "When I was in labour, I thought of a candle flame" (143). The narrator's recourse to the experience of giving birth creates a temporary distance but it also provides a bridge between a "she" and the "I" in the subsequent unit:

> Look at the candle flame as if it is the only thing in the world. How white and steady it is. At the core of the white flame is a cone of blue, transparent air; that is the thing to look at, that is the thing to concentrate on. (145)

The reader's "I" is solicited, but there are two "I"s who may be initiating this discourse, explicitly the narrator's "I," and implicitly, Mary Magdalene's "I." As the reader and the implied "second person", I am addressed here and invited to exchange places with the implied "I." This process of exchanging the "first person" with the "second person," secures eventually a position of the subject for Mary Magdalene; the former "third person" and a "she," becomes the same as "I" and "you."

The "second person" discourse will abruptly shift in the next sentence into the "first person" discourse, but only to confirm that sameness is interdependent with difference:

> When the pains came thick and fast, I fixed all my attention on the blue absence at the heart of the flame, as though it were the secret of the flame and, if I concentrated enough upon it, it would become my secret, too. (145)

This is clearly the narrator's "I" speaking from the past, but the sentence contains a clause where the "first person" possessive pronoun is conditioned. The "I" momentarily becomes ambiguous because the narrator's past experience of her labour told in "first person," is merging with the "I's" quest for the secret of the candle flame. This ambiguous "I" could also be me, looking through Mary Magdalene's eyes, or it could be Mary Magdalene looking through my eyes, or the narrator's.

The "she," the "you" and the "I" become the "same person" involved in the "intercourse" with the candle flame. Via the flame, all "persons" enter the imaginary space, and the blue absence of the "I"s past converges into the blue absence of the "I"s present. The birth of that new "same person" secures Mary Magdalene's future, perpetual journey to repentance.

The Exchange of Secrets

Considering that The Wrightsman Magdalene is an actual painting, it would seem more than reasonable to rely primarily on the eye. But as it turns out, I see the skull in her lap, but my eye cannot see the memento mori. I cannot see it, because it is impossible to decide whether it is a memory of a past or of a future death. Additionally, if by looking at the painting, I see that "she carries it already,"[3] I actually both see it and do not see it because I do not share the space of Mary Magdalene's womb. The space of Mary Magdalene's "living child"/"*memento mori*" remains hidden to my eye. The paradoxical existence of Mary Magdalene is then also interconnected with the paradox of looking, for looking itself cannot tell, unless that imaginary space of the discourse is established: "the blue absence" where "I" and "you" can exchange places.

In the blue absence at the heart of the flame, persons and temporal continuums exchange places, and so do secrets. If I concentrated enough upon it, my secret would become Mary Magdalene's secret, and reversely, her secret would become mine. It is in this imaginary space that the secret of a paradoxical existence is hidden, and the secret can be sought only in the perpetual exchange of persons. Through this intersubjective journey through the past, the present and the future we might see the secret of becoming someone else; we might see that Mary Magdalene's living child and her *memento mori* are in fact the "same person."

NOTES

1. Angela Carter, "Impressions: The Wrightsman Magdalene", *American Ghosts and Old World Wonderers* (London: Vintage 1994) 140-146.
2. Mieke Bal, "First Person, Second Person, Same Person: Narrative as Epistemology," *New Literary History* 24 (1993) 293-320. In this study Bal examines three works: Lorraine Code's, *What Can She Know*, Johannes Fabian's, *Power and Performance*, and Hubert Damosch's, *L'Origine de la Perspective* and explains that the specificity of these works lies in their concern with investing the object of knowledge with subjectivity by placing the subject in the position of the object. When she points to the triple allegiance of the concept of second personhood, Bal asserts that narrative as a discursive posture and structural form allows us to study the intertwinements of these allegiances.
3. "That which she already carries" is much more evident in Georges de la Tour's *Terff Magdalene.*

WORK IN PROGRESS

Prefaces - Philosophy goes on

Hester IJsseling

In philosophy, when asked what one's dissertation is on, one can often mention one or two names of philosophers and leave it at that with some justification. Unfortunately, when asked what my dissertation is about, I always feel hesitant to begin, because it seems impossible to indicate the subject adequately with a catchword or two. Even if two philosophers, Hegel and Nietzsche, play an important part in the script, it wouldn't be right to say the dissertation is about them.

I read their prefaces. I read their prefaces to show how they make use of this type of text, and to consider what they implicitly and explicitly say about the textual phenomenon of the preface. And why does this interest me? Because the fact that philosophy is written and the practice of philosophical writing interest me. And philosophical writing has become particularly interesting since the time when the concept of truth lost its authority. This development has called for many revisions and refashionings on both the theoretical and the material level of philosophy. Not only are the things that are written about (truth, consciousness, subjectivity, etc.) called into question, but also the way in which the writing is done - the genres, the styles of philosophical discourse. All sorts of traditional writing practices have lost their self-evidence.

The problem of leaving the desire for truth behind interests me, and particularly the difficulty of doing this. I look at the places where this difficulty shows, in writing. For example, it shows in the desire for the definition of a proper textual genre for philosophy; in the desire for our texts to be read and understood;

in the desire for coherence and linearity in our argumentations; and in the desire for the fulfilment of a promise that philosophy seems to hold.

These four themes are considered in the four chapters I have planned for my dissertation. The first chapter is called "Proper and Improper" and is about the desire for a proper genre for philosophy, and more specifically for a proper beginning. The point of entrance for the elaboration of this theme is Hegel's contention that the preface is an improper genre for philosophy. Interestingly enough, he says this in a sixty page preface to the *Phenomenology of Spirit.* In the first chapter of my dissertation, I look into the friction this causes.

The second chapter is called "Inside and Outside" and is about the book as a space, the preface as a signboard. Its function is to lure the readers into the book: "Come inside, and read all these wonderful ideas I have!" Nietzsche will help us here to see that it is questionable whether writing, even publishing, a book necessarily means that one wants the reader to come inside, that is to say, that one wants to be read and understood. Again, there is a friction.

The third chapter is called "Before and After" and is about the desire for coherence and line. Although Nietzsche problematized the demand for coherence as a simplifying gesture of minds too weak to deal with contradictory perspectives, he seems not to be able to get away from a similar desire himself. At some point he starts looking back on his own life and writing, and then he seems to give in to the desire to show the "necessary development" in his work, to draw a line and show the coherence of his thinking. This becomes particularly clear in the prefaces of 1885, retrospective prefaces he wrote for the second edition of some of his books.

The fourth chapter is called "Promise and Fulfilment", and will be about the promise of philosophy. Any philosophical text seems to hold a promise of some sort. A promise (a preface) of the truth? But what if the concept of truth is left behind? Then the promise still seems to remain. Still, philosophy seems to be going somewhere. Does going somewhere imply a goal? What could be the nature of this implied goal, this promise, if the belief in its attainment, its fulfilment, is gone. Philosophy goes on. What drives it?

In short, these chapters are about the desire to understand and to be understood, the desire for a true beginning and a true end, and the desire to leave these metaphysically oriented desires behind. All of these themes are chosen to show the friction between the desire for truth and the desire to leave the very concept of the truth behind. The dissertation is about the changes philosophy attempts to bring about in itself, and the difficulties it encounters in this attempt. Philosophical writing, particularly the preface, and more particularly the prefaces of Hegel and Nietzsche, serve as points of entry into this problematic.

Looking Back At Livingstone: Presentation of a Dissertation

Isabel Hoving

Postcolonial literary theory is a highly contested practice. When I began to prepare my dissertation about Anglophone African and Caribbean migrant women's writing, I did not know this. As a matter of fact, I did not even know that there was such a thing as postcolonial theory. When I finally discovered this wide and hardly definable field, I was elated. For it seemed to offer me a valuable framework for the analysis of the recurring themes, issues and textual strategies in the corpus I was studying. Three issues presented themselves during my analysis of many novels, poems and essays: place, voice, and silence. The issues are so crucial that I structured my dissertation around them: each issue forms the main concern of one of the three parts of my dissertation. Happily, I found that place (or space, or location) and voice (or language, silence) are also two crucial issues within the post-colonial theory as presented in the influential and disputed handbook by Ashcroft et al.,[1] as well as in the work by renowned scholars such as Homi Bhabha and Gayatri Chakravorty Spivak. *The Castration of Livingstone* continuously relates to their reflection.

Now that my dissertation is completed, I find that my study does not so much appropriate postcolonial theory as a framework, as that it stages a sometimes vehement confrontation with postcolonial theory. These confrontations are organized around the question about the *framing* of this writing. Questions are raised such as: Is it productive to read these texts as post-colonial texts? Or should I become more specific and read them as (for example) *British* literature? Could one argue too that these texts are part of a worldwide feminist literary practice, or, more modestly, of the feminist/womanist writing within the African Diaspora? Or should one concentrate instead on the continuity of these Caribbean migrant texts with the rest of Caribbean literature? There is no easy answer to these questions. None of these positions in itself offers a satisfying understanding of the texts. Instead, *The Castration of Livingstone* stages a debate about the ways in which multiple texts such as these can be read. This study shows which insights are produced by different post-colonial, postmodern and feminist readings of a text, and which blind spots are produced alongside them. Finally, the book shows how these reading positions relate to each other.

Let me consider in detail one important aspect of the book's discussion of reading positions: my emphasis on the need for situated readings. The possibility of situating these highly multiple texts within post-colonial writing is very appealing indeed for a scholar trained within Western-European institutions. For one thing, postcolonial theory offers a general comparative approach to the recurring literary strategies in a whole range of texts, whether they are written in Asia, Australia, Africa, or elsewhere. This approach allows one to situate several striking textual phenomena within the context of an abstract, general body of postcolonial texts, without having to make a profound study of the specific cultural and literary context within which a specific text was written.

One could say, sarcastically, that this approach saves a lot of work. However, my dissertation hopes to show that the work skipped here is very urgent, and in fact indispensable. If one prefers to leave it aside, one risks missing the specificity of the literary practices which are developing today. In different chapters, I present an argument to sustain this statement. I will give two examples. Chapter three (in part I, "Place") discusses a novel by a British-Guyanese author, Beryl Gilroy's *Frangipani House* (1986). I propose to read this novel as a critique of dominant discourses of time and space. However, I argue too that this does not mean that the novel aligns itself to postmodern deconstructions of concepts of time. The chapter offers several arguments to motivate this view. I'll name only one. The chapter shows that the novel does not stop at deconstruction. It also offers an alternative perspective on time, which is based on African-Caribbean concepts of time. In fact, this African-Caribbean concept of time can be seen as the starting point for both its critique of dominant Western and Caribbean discourses, and its feminist/humanist message. Instead of being part of the Western project of cultural self-critique, the novel offers its own constructions of time, its own ethics. Without taking into account African-Caribbean concepts of time, it is hard to assess the *situatedness* of the novel's presentation of time, motherhood, family life and migration. In fact, one would fail to see the very project undertaken by this novel.

A second example of the fruitfulness of studying the cultural context of a literary text can be found in chapter eight (in part III, "Silence"). This chapter discusses the work of Tobago-born, Canada-bound writer Marlene Nourbese Philip. I propose to read her playful texts as post-colonial, gender-specific theories of language and silence. Silence can be understood as an authentic maternal language, which could complement the all-encompassing, alienating paternal language (the colonial tongue). Both languages are indispensable for expressing an irrecoverable hybrid postcolonial subjectivity. One of the recurring images in Philip's poetics is that of the womb: the site of a protecting, maternal silence. Instead of understanding this trope within a Western context, and associating it with Kristeva's *chora*, I propose to begin by relating the trope to a concept which is central to Caribbean women's writing, the *kumbla*. The concept refers to a (also) feminine language strategy of adapting to the white colonial order. By reading Philip's womb through the image of the *kumbla*, it becomes possible to see that Philip reinforces and reshapes the Caribbean women's project of creating a new, non-colonial, non-sexist literary language. At the same time, her texts can be read as an intimate critique of both Lacanian psychoanalysis and Kristeva's work. Philip's insistence on the inter-relation of language and desire seems to be inspired by psychoanalysis. This perspective leads to a fruitful broadening of the concept of the *kumbla*.

After these two arguments, it will be clear that one of the main points of my dissertation is that these novels should not be read within the context of a general post-colonial literature all too easily. Rather, these are texts which inscribe themselves within a specific Caribbean literary practice, and they help in shaping a feminist or womanist tradition in Caribbean writing. Before assessing the importance of these novels, one should study aspects of Caribbean literature and culture, and Caribbean scholarship on these issues. However, even if I defend heatedly this situated way of reading, this is not my final answer to the question about the literary context within which these texts might best be read. If I stress this reading position, it is because I see a polemic need for defending situated readings. Moreover, I wish to argue that these texts' irreducible multiplicity is in itself a feature of Caribbean culture and literature. On the other hand, I often show that the novels also address African-American (women's) writing and they echo and subvert British literary traditions. They inscribe themselves within African written and oral traditions too. Indeed, these texts call for a multiple, nuanced, well-informed approach, which is sensitive to the many different literatures and audiences each texts addresses. At the same time, this approach should consider the specificity of this multiple address.

The Castration of Livingstone is not primarily written as a critical contribution to post-colonial criticism. Looking back, I prefer to describe my dissertation as a case of cultural analysis through post-colonialism. The study's focus on post-colonial "hot issues" is questioned by its firm stand within the practice of cultural analysis. Indeed, scholars inspired by cultural analysis will inevitably scrutinize the theories they are addressing as critically as the literary texts they are looking into. Perhaps more importantly, this study also joins the project of cultural analysis by insisting on reading the literary texts as if they were theory (too). *The Castration of Livingstone* is based on a large amount of detailed close-readings. This attention to the texts made it impossible to accept the tendencies towards universalizaton in post-colonial criticism. In addition, the texts never allowed me to forget that they sprang from oral practices, from political commitment, and from a tradition of survival. As a result, *The Castration of Livingstone* often explicitly resists the Western emphasis on textuality. Instead, it ponders the possibilities of seeing a continuity between writing and (for example) giving birth, walking, speaking, acting, fighting, without reducing the latter practices to mere textual practices. In this way, *The Castration of Livingstone* even hopes to bring into Western literary debates the alternative approach to literature suggested in some of these wonderful texts.

Looking back on *The Castration of Livingstone*, I can see that its close-readings are the main source from which its crucial insights spring. The dissertation is only beginning its critique of post-colonial criticism, and its exploration of the interrelation between post-colonial, black theory and cultural analysis. A lot remains to be done, in reading and writing. On the other hand: writing is not the only way in which one may contribute to the multiculturalization of this part of the world. And the academy is not the only place where writing or other critical action is possible. My colleagues within cultural analysis will be the first to acknowledge the dubious boundaries by which the academy is closed off from the rest of society. Would it not be wonderful if ASCA were to initiate a project not only to criticize but to transgress these boundaries? I would be most eagerly among those who would support such a project.

NOTE

1. Ashcroft, Bill, Gareth Griffiths, and Helen Tiffin. *The Empire Writes Back: Theory and Practice in Post-colonial Literatures.* London: Routledge 1989

Melanchton and Meaning

Rob Pauls

The history of concepts often tends to coincide with the history of books. Take Curtius's famous *Europäische Literatur und Lateinisches Mittelalter* which, being immensely influential, has contributed to a definition of topos from a merely literary-critical point of view. Admittedly, Curtius's book has produced an entire *Toposforschung*, in particular in Germany. There is reason, however, to doubt its effectiveness as far as philosophy and the history of ideas are concerned. Identification and classification seem to be all there is to it. Efforts to relate the *Toposforschung* to a more historically oriented philosophy (often inspired by Heidegger's later thought about being), have been hardly productive thus far. The limits of *Toposforschung* seem to be identical with the limits of philosophy itself. This is also the case for the attempts to discover, in the topical philosophy of both the Renaissance and the humanistic movement, a hidden layer of *historical* thought in order next to distinguish this historical element from both medieval scholasticism and modern philosophy. A possible reason for this failure may be the factual nature of 'topics' which prevents this distinction from being useful. However that may be, the present *research* into topics is so matter-of-fact-like as to be unable to make such distinctions meaningful.

Perhaps it makes sense to restore the original meaning of the concept of *topos*, applying it to texts that are important in the history of ideas. Admittedly, Curtius was partly right in founding the literary turn he lent to the concept of *topos* in the historical developments of rhetoric and literature in the Roman Empire. However, in the Middle Ages the concept of *topos* (which, ever since Cicero, was translated in Latin as *locus*) clearly survived within the bounds of those *artes* in which it had originated: rhetoric and dialectics. As for the changes in western thought which were brought about by the emergence of humanism, they are to be appreciated within the framework and setting used by the humanists themselves: the rhetorical and dialectical loci. For this reason it is necessary to know the medieval roots of the concept of *loci* before being able to understand the emergence of the modern period from a *historical* point of view.

This also applies to the Reformation theology of Melanchton. Ironically, protestant tradition has been quite unable to appreciate sufficiently the humanistic nature of Melanchton's theology. In my view this was because it failed to understand the key concepts of this theology, in particular the way those concepts operated both on a formal and a material level. For instance, the protestant interpreters of Melanchton tended to use *loci* and *loci communes* indiscriminately. Agricola, in his *De Inventone Dialectica*, had radically abandoned late-medieval formalistic logic under whose spell the concept of *locus*, having become part of the (formalistic) doctrine of *consequentiae*, had also fallen. Agricola, on his part, restored *locus* to its original function within the *inventio*. Consequently, it became once more a point of view which enabled one (i.e. the user of language) to collect material that might contribute to the construction of a discourse or that might be helpful in understanding a text. It was Melanchton who gave a didactic turn to dialectics. For him, dialectics was a means, a method first to organize and next to transmit knowledge. The theological subject-matter that was thus "discovered" with the help of a dialectical *locus* — which, of course, was not really waiting to be discovered because, belonging to the *corpus* of set items, it was already there — was presented in a didactic manner. Thus theology was subdivided, and disintegrated, into spatial *loci* in which the theological content — the *loci communes* — was both assembled and stored. As a result, theology in its entirety turned into one big *locus*, the different parts of which, i.e. the different *loci* all with their own particular content, could be opened like drawers in a cupboard in order to take out the theological material required at a particular moment and for a particular purpose. This method could be used, for instance, to refute possible opponents, or to convert people to the right religion, or — that being Melanchton's chief purpose — to present the faithful with the right doctrine and to strengthen them in their faith by convincing them in an argumentative manner of the correctness of that faith.

Melanchton's dialectical approach appears to be doctrinal. It is by implication to be called propositional since it is only in a propositional fashion that something can be both discovered and stored away dialectically. However, the opposite is the case. His is a very practical theology. As mentioned before, Melanchton was preoccupied with practical, didactic issues. Not only does he present a *corpus* of theological propositions which man must know in order to be saved, he also teaches those propositions at the same time. He wants to convince his readers/listeners of their correctness. He relentlessly drives faith in those propositions into the reader's head. Or, to phrase it in the rhetorical terminology, proceeding in such a didactic manner, he applies the *ars inculcandi*, not only in a spatial sense but also, as with Aristotle, in the shape of a *habitus*. For Melanchton dialectics is an "event," theology means "action." In the same way that in Reformation thought *doctrina* means "to teach," Melanchton's theology comes into being by performing itself. It *is* the act of the *inculcare*, the driving the point home, i.e. the endless repetition of the doctrine which is to be taught. In this sense Melanchton's theology cannot be called doctrinal. Rather the "teaching"/*docere* is the way in which this theology lives and moves as a discourse.

What then is being taught? Here we may run into trouble. For if it is impossible to say what is being taught, then this theology is wrongly described as didactic. In that case, there may well be a kind of movement in Melanchton's theology, albeit an empty one. Consequently, its discourse is present in the shape of its own absence. It cannot be denied that this is precisely what is happening in Melanchton's theology. One of the reasons why *loci* and *loci communes* are often used indiscriminately with regard to Melanchton, is the fact that for him the dialectical method of *loci* automatically results into his *loci communes.* However, in rhetoric the latter can be described as common places in the shape of *sententiae.* This is quite unlike the *loci* proper which are of a conceptual nature. The dialectical method, for its part, requires propositions (rather than just concepts), and, additionally, it manifests itself in an endless repetition of those propositions. Within the well protected walls of his *loci* all Melanchton can do is spin around. Through repetition, the propositions of his theology turn into common places, *loci communes,* with a life of their own. Inside Melanchton's theology, they start running after each other. Ultimately, this very running after each other *is* Melanchton's theology. If there is any movement in it, it is of a rather macabre nature. The theological propositions are being hammered into the head of the reader so relentlessly and uninterruptedly as to become independent in the process. They are being "inculcated," but to what purpose? They are being used as arguments, as an art of persuasion in the service of faith. Which faith, so one might ask? Exactly what is being argued? All one sees is arguments without one being instructed as to the subject of that argumentation. Melanchton's theology breaking down into dialectical divisions and subdivisions results into its *loci communes* remaining unconnected. Each of them is hermetically closed off like a room without a view. They neither give nor receive light to and from each other. Both propositions and concepts within the *loci communes* are closed off. They do contain their own proper meaning preventing the latter from breaking out into a wider discourse. Gospel, justification by faith, Christian liberty, all of these are *loci communes.* But the latter originate, in turn, in a series of smaller, ever recurring loci communes. They run after one another like the tautologies they are. Just as, according to Roland Barthes, in Stalinistic ideology, where name (*dénomination*) and value (*jugement*) coincided, resulting in one value explaining another one, such is the case in Melanchton's theology, where one concept or proposition is supposed to explain another one. However, since those concepts and propositions coincide with their meaning which is stored away and imprisoned in their very own selves, this procedure is bound to be tautological. This method of practicing theology banishes any content whatsoever. This presentation presents but itself. Beneath the surface there is nothing to be found. Once more it is Roland Barthes who provides us with the perfect characterization of Melanchton's theology: *La clôture du langage est parfaite.*

Impossible Archeology

Michael Punt

For even those with only a passing interest in cinema, it must be almost impossible not to have notice that 1995 generated some special interest as cinema's centenary was celebrated. Generally this occasion was being used as an opportunity to mount exhibitions of any number of aspects of the cinema, and to run programs of films not specifically chosen from the early period. The historical breadth of these projects may have been unclear as well, since a close examination of exactly what was being celebrated raises fundamental questions of film history which have not been satisfactorily answered. What happened in 1895, on December 28 to be exact, was that the Lumière brothers hired a space, for 35 Francs a week, at the Grand Café and demonstrated their *cinématographe* to a paying public. They did not think that they were presenting anything portentous, merely a technological spectacle which might attract an audience for a few months. This event is conveniently cited by

European scholars as the beginning of the cinema. Notwithstanding that the apparatus had been patented eleven months earlier and demonstrated to professional groups since March 1895, that in all but the vaguest sense the films shown at these seances bear only a slender relationship to the cinema as the institutional entertainment that followed — let alone cinema as we now know it. To further complicate the issue some priority to the invention of the basic cinematic apparatus is often awarded to Thomas Edison, who, in 1894, offered his kinetoscope to enterprising Americans to install them in parlours, much as they had done with the phonograph, charging a flat rate per individual viewing. However, even more complications arise once the net is cast wider over the rest of Europe and Scandinavia, other versions of the same basic machine are found to have been invented earlier, as for example by Louis Bouly, who took out patents in 1892 and 1883, or with Max Skladanowsky who projected moving pictures to audiences in Berlin in October 1895. In addition, historical research into forms of entertainment has identified what might legitimately be claimed as prehistoric versions of the cinema in the elaborate magic lantern shows and phantasmagoria which were prevalent in Europe from the sixteenth century. Cinema it seems did not start in 1895, but rather, around that year, it began to be formed in a particular way which, with a bit of creative effort, we recognize as an ancestor of the cinema we know today.

The complexity of cinema's origins has stimulated a fascinating archeological project in film studies which has taught us much about the social organization of mass culture in the nineteenth century, and how the cinema as an institution was formed by a mesh of determinants rather than a simple technological teleology. However, in all but the more esoteric debates, the actual origins of the apparatus and how it came to be "invented" has been a minor issue. Most attention has focused on the respective priority of Edison, Lumière, and other more shadowy contenders to the title of the "inventor of cinema." This research has concentrated on the question of legal ownership and patent litigation rather than on the idea that the circumstances of the invention might have had any profound bearing on the cinema's development as an institution. It is assumed that since cinema technology has remained virtually unchanged since the end of the nineteenth century, the formation of the institution called cinema was the consequence of social and economic pressures on the production, distribution and exhibition of the "software" of the industry — the films themselves. This assumption has proved to be a satisfactory working hypothesis for effectively defining the parameters of film studies, providing the useful periodization of prehistory, invention, early period, classical, and finally post classical. Most important, it has provided a framework for a somewhat haphazard collection of film material to be organized into coherent archives in time to prevent the complete loss of valuable cultural objects.

However the assumption that Edison and the Lumières were concerned with the same project, and both racing for the patent office to claim cinema as their own is beginning to present some problems for film studies in general and film history in particular. In general, it is beginning to be apparent that some aspects of the development of what are called "new technologies" — video games and computer interfaces for example — can be seen as a recirculation of cinema's early history. This raises fundamental questions about history and historical method, and at the same time, it provides a social resonance for film studies as well as a future corpus for research which acknowledges the intermediality of cinema. As for film history in particular, it begins to expose a significant deficit in early cinema history. True, substantial explanations for the development of film styles, and the changing nature of the product — from apparently crude single-reel stories shown in ad hoc store front theatres to high class multi-reel movies exhibited in purposely built cinemas — have been convincingly argued. But the lack of any account of why the kinetoscope and the cinematographe ever became predominantly entertainment machines, rather than a scientific apparatus, and why its exhibition form was public and theatrical rather than domestic, is being increasingly felt as more historical evidence comes to light. This particular gap in film history has a contemporary resonance which suggests its resolution may have a general application to the popular interpretation of other technologies of entertainment. For example, how is it that the highest of high-tech entertainment media, the interactive CD Rom, which it was feared would be the death of fiction and even the printed word, is beginning public life as a "pulp" product — a free gift with magazines or more often simply included in junk mail?

My work in ASCA is a part of an ongoing research project concerning the representation of the body in the Department of Film and Television Studies. I am attempting to meet the particular deficit in film history outlined above as an end in itself, but it is also envisaged as a contribution to a wider debate concerning the current interpretation of technology and the role of film studies within that project. Its starting point is to situate the cinematic devices patented by Edison and the Lumières within a broad interpretive framework of entertainment and science. This includes the perception of technology in popular culture in the nineteenth century and the body as an apparatus for the inscription of knowledge during the same period. My assumptions are: (i) that culture is not determined by technology; (ii) that Edison and the Lumières did not share a set of common goals nor did either of them interpret their inventions in the way that mass culture eventually did; and (iii) that the meaning and use of a technology is the consequence of a mesh of interpretations of unequal weight which temporarily stabilize. One implication that follows from these assumptions is that what was being celebrated in last year's centennial events was the power of an active social body to have some influence in determining the meaning and use of science and technology.

Obituary
Wil van Gerwen (June19, 1953- July 22, 1995)

Helga Geyer-Ryan

On Saturday July 22, 1995, Wil van Gerwen died suddenly and unexpectedly. He was in his fourth year as a PhD candidate at the Institute of Comparative Literature at the University of Amsterdam, completing a doctoral thesis on "Walter Benjamin auf Ibiza." His death came at a moment when his professional plans and personal aspirations had, for the first time, crystallized into a pattern that promised to reward his efforts with a productive and satisfying future.

His bewildering demise left not only his wife and two young sons, but also his countless friends and colleagues, desolate. There is probably no one amongst the many who knew him who did not witness at one time or another his optimism, his enthusiasm and his constant readiness to provide help and support wherever it was needed. His presence was so strong that his death will leave all who loved and valued him hard pressed to believe that he is gone forever.

He will be missed not only by those who were close to him, but also by the academic community upon which he had already left an indelible mark. For Wil van Gerwen was unquestionably a very fine and dedicated scholar. When he delivered his first paper at the International Walter Benjamin conference at the University of Osnabrück in 1992, his fierce commitment and unconventional approach, combined with the originality of his findings made an unforgettable impact on the audience. His recent presentation of a paper at the invitation of the Philosophical Institute of the University of Frankfurt, in the series "Frankfurter Benjaminvorträge," was sadly fated to be his last.

Without Wil van Gerwen, both the keen reception of Walter Benjamin in the Netherlands today and the flourishing of international organizations devoted to the study of Benjamin's life, work and influence would be inconceivable. Wil was the inspiration behind the formation in 1992 of the *International Walter Benjamin Foundation* (The Netherlands), and served as its secretary. He was an influential member of the editorial board of the *Benjamin Journaal*, likewise launched in 1992, and published by the Historische Uitgeverij in Groningen; he also initiated and co-founded the *International Walter Benjamin Association* in 1995, and he was the chief organizer of the International Walter Benjamin Conference which will take place in Amsterdam in 1997. Wil's negotiations with the publisher Rodopi led to the latter's agreement to publish the Association's yearbook *Benjamin Studies*, of which he would have been one of the editors. At the time of his death, his favourite project, a Walter Benjamin Documentation Centre to be run in collaboration with ASCA, had begun to look as though it might at last become a financially viable concern. Last but not least, he translated into Dutch several texts by Walter Benjamin, including the famous *Städtebilder* and the essay on surrealism.

Wil van Gerwen's deep affection for the personality and ideas of Walter Benjamin had much to do with his own character and circumstances. He displayed an endless curiosity about everything that happened in the world, an uncompromising intellectual rigour and an uncorruptible personal integrity. His formidable capacity for sustained hard work was matched only by the intensity of the pleasure he took in being alive. He loved the literature of all times and cultures. As a member of our society, he felt a deep solidarity with the suffering of other people, regardless of social distinctions. In addition he had an acute and critical awareness of our global political plight.

The first time I met Wil van Gerwen, in a course on modernist literature organized by the *Studium Generale* of the Catholic University in Tilburg, I could not help being deeply impressed by this remarkable man. That impression never changed through all the years I knew him. We will all — his family, his friends and his colleagues —miss him deeply. But although he has gone, he will, in a truly Benjaminian sense, live on in our memory. We will never forget him, for he was one of those rare beings of whom we can truthfully say that the world is the worse for losing him.

CONFERENCES

Report on ASCA's Second International Conference: The Practice of Cultural Analysis June 27-30, 1995

Laura Quinn

The second ASCA International Conference was held on June 27-30 in the Felix Meritis Foundation building. In many ways, the building itself could serve as a metaphor for this staging of interdisciplinary analysis. The structure's role as a theater, both before and after serving as the Dutch Communist Party headquarters, generated a doubling effect — a production within a production. Its saturated spaces gave at first the appearance of bulk and mass, only to disappear around an unexpected corner that might or might not lead to an apparent destination. The towering bookcases of the second floor's Zuilenzaal room stood empty while their functioning doors supported no glass panes. This metaphor is not to imply, most certainly, that the gathered practitioners of cultural analysis were functioning as part of a mere facade in such a stage (the stage and its supporting structures themselves being virtually indistinguishable). Rather, by focusing on the how-to of the practice of cultural analysis in the arena of academia, these very performative (even theatrical) aspects were made visible in and by the perspectives that were generated.

The theatrical aspect of the building was further underscored by a work of art, commissioned for this conference, that hung — and moved with the air — in the spacious stairwell. Artist Edwin Janssen had proposed his view of interdisciplinary interpretation by means of large transparent panels with blown-up details of Brueghel's *Parable of the Blind.* Two evening shows complemented this work. Janssen engaged a visual dialogue with photographer Janneke Lam, shown in alternating slides. Filmmaker Tom Verheul presented a preview of his documentary on Dutch veterans of the "dirty war" in Indonesia, as a cultural therapy to overcome trauma.

With the goal of acting out comparative and interdisciplinary perspectives on cultural phenomena, an invocation that the world is, indeed, a stage, can be read more provocatively than the cliché might suggest. Indeed, it was not necessary that the various intellectuals appearing on the stage agreed on what play they were jointly performing. *The Practice of Cultural Analysis: A Workshop on Interdisciplinarity* was certainly not a populist summer stock production playing to an unchallenging audience's desire for a familiar and cohesive narrative. On the contrary, the very words cohesive, desire, audience and play (in Gadamers sense, as well as its more common usage) could be said to have been challenged by both the speakers and the audience at various moments throughout the four-day production. Certainly, the exceptional efforts of the ASCA conference organizers, as well as the unique facilities of the Felix Meritis Foundation, were greatly responsible not only for the highly successful formulation of open lectures followed by smaller workshop components, but also for providing an atmosphere in which conference participants could comfortably engage in the collegial disputes and discussions that overflowed the conference's more formal discursive sites.

The theme of the conference, *The Practice of Cultural Analysis: A Workshop on Interdisciplinarity* provided two basic working assumptions on the function of cultural analysis. First, cultural analysis represents a mode of addressing forms of cultural production as specific sites which can be excavated for their interpretive meaning(s). This practice is one which attempts to make obvious the means of its own process. In this sense, the practical work of cultural analysis was represented by the practices of a broad spectrum of intellectuals who addressed both its theoretical and applied possibilities. The second assumption concerns the way in which the very questions of interdisciplinarity served to motivate the more specific analyses presented. Indeed, if the title of the conference had been "A Workshop *in* Interdisciplinarity," this would have assumed far too much. The wide range of papers presented did not erase disciplinary boundaries, but rather stressed the need for interrogating what questions are at stake in their maintenance or reinterpretation.

Throughout much of the conference, my own interest in visual theory focused on the various formulations of the objects of analysis, which experienced a number of inversions and positionings that belie a simple approach to their reality. Theo de Boer's graph of the formulations of desire, distantiation and insight applied to phenomenology, psychoanalysis and literary analysis, for instance, was far from a categorizing impulse. He made visible that it is not the graph itself that forces the boundaries embedded in the science of analysis, but rather that the need to perceive fixity is what cultural analysis can productively challenge. Yet if, as De Boer quoted, "human kind cannot bear very much reality" (Eliot), then Stephen

Bann's formulation of the object of analysis bore witness to a desire to reposition this burden through a retrieval of historical investigation. Bann's approach, considered in reference to Eco's and Barthes's structuralist semiotics, raised a number of questions as to how history might function in relationship to the analysis of cultural artifacts. Yet it was revealing to note that, even within the constructed context of interdisciplinarity, his art-historical impulse left virtually unproblematized the complex distinctions between iconographic analysis, the construction of historical facts, and semiotic meaning in contemporary visual analysis.

The subject matter of the workshop I attended, "Canons in Dispute," ranged from revisionist Biblical studies to questioning gay canon formation to Hegel as consummate deconstructionist. Because of the variety of subject matter, what linkages that were plausible focused particularly on the subject's ability to be constructed within and/or by unifying versus fragmented experiential concepts. And again, it was frequently the case that discussions became polarized by challenges to the framework, rather than the specific content, of the arguments. Indeed, it was this contested territory and attempts to negotiate and/or define boundaries which allowed for productive sites of exchange among a diverse and often seemingly unconnected group of texts and practitioners, making the workshops a particularly successful (if occasionally contortionistic) element of the conference. The workshops likewise provided a significant contribution to the larger plenary lectures by allowing for at least a partial perspective on who constituted the audience. By establishing a cumulative, albeit limited, knowledge of the interests of workshop participants, questions and specific references made during the larger sessions provided a more specific context that informed later workshop discussions.

In the midst of disputing the content of analytical perspectives, it would seem that a reconsideration, as well, of the forms in which cultural analysis is presented and/or performed is in need of further evaluation. In this regard, while the various creative events, presented mainly in the evening program, did not have a profound influence on the academic format, and even though traditional academic approaches were criticized and disputed, the process of argumentation did have a distinctive ring of more traditional, academic discourse premised upon logical, scholarly argumentation. This seems to me to be an issue that has implications yet to be fully considered, if, indeed, cultural analysis is more than merely posing alternative questions to traditional disciplinary assumptions. If cultural analysis is to continue its dynamic practice, then it may be most productive to consider the practice as a space rather than a thing. A space not necessarily for agreement, but for dispute. From this perspective, the conference was a vivid and extremely satisfying performance of the instability of interdisciplinary practice and its productive interrogation by those who have chosen to practice cultural analysis.

Announcements

June 27-28, 1996 ASCA Colloquium: Film, Love and History

Film, Love and History is the title of an ASCA colloquium with Kaja Silverman and Harun Farocki. Silverman will give a lecture entitled"The Active Gift of Love," and a seminar based on several sections of her work. Farocki will show the film *Images of the World and the Inscription of War*, and answer questions afterwards. Farocki will also give a seminar on a second film, *The Workers Leaving the Factory*. For further information: tel: 31 20 5253874, fax: 31 20 5253052, e-mail: asca@let.uva.nl.

August 5-9, 1996 Culture-Sign-Space

The Conference Culture-Sign-Space is organized by the Dutch and German Associations of Semiotics, in cooperation with the Goethe Institute and ASCA. Keynote speakers are R. Posner, president of the International Association for Semiotic Studies (Berlin), M. Bal (Director of ASCA), G. Wienold (Dokkyo University, Tokyo), P. Bouissac (Victoria University, Toronto), Y. Tobin (Be'er Sheva University), P. Pennartz (University of Wageningen), T.A. Sebeok (Indiana University). Papers will be read concerning topics such as: Natural Space - Cultural Space; Space and Ritual; Semiotic Machines; Queer Space - Subcultural Territories; New Spaces of Music and Culture; Space and Law; Space and Design; Space and Theatre; Cultural Conflict and Semiotics of Space; Language, Space and Culture; Pictural Space; Space and Sculpture; and Space and Dance. For further information: Dr Jürgen Müller, tel: 31 20 5252995, fax: 31 20 5252938/ Dr Aart van Zoest tel/fax: 31 72 5641721

ASCA Workshop on Territorialism and Desire

One section of the Conference on Culture-Sign-Space is organized by ASCA: a Workshop on Territorialism and Desire. Humans and animals can be terribly territorial. One level at which territorialism surfaces is in individualism, and the politics of individual identity, whether around gender, local allegience, ethnicity, sexuality, in brief: all the axes of identity we have grown accustomed to finding important, and to both defending and respecting in others. Another level is nationalism. And still another one, less commonly included in reflections on the topic, is "human chauvinism", which is involved in the increasing domination and exploitation of nature. Territorialism is an inward movement, a folding back of subjects onto themselves and the likes of them, which needs the casting out of "others" as "different" in order to be able to cherish the "self" at ease. Territorialism is an attitude toward space which puts the self at its center. And, although acting it out implies the unfolding of time, territorialism pursues stasis, stability, permanency: it gives conservatism a literal meaning.

But human beings are also subject to desire. Synonyms for desire are longing, craving, yearning, hunger, and lust. Desire implies a movement outward, putting the self at risk of merging with the other. It also implies time. Desire happens, which makes it so apt for representation in the narrative media. In order to be lived through, to happen at all, reaching fulfilment or frustration as its outcome, desire requires development over time, thus giving "progression" a literal meaning.

The two movements, inward and conservative on the one hand, and outward and progressive on the other, constitute the basic axes of human cultures. It seems, therefore, an appropriate focus for a workshop whose mission it is to present the program of cultural analysis within a conference devoted to the semiotics of space. Three areas emerge immediately from this topic:

- territorialism itself, as a subject of reflection concerning a specific way of "being" in space, connecting the subject to space in a particular manner;
- desire as such, insofar as thinking about it and representing it implies spatial notions and metaphors;
- and the tension between territorialism and desire, which may be terribly oppressive when the former thwarts the latter, or which is utopian in its redeeming, liberating aspects, that is, when desire subverts and undermines the very possibility to maintain one's territorial tendencies.

The idea is to make the workshop flexible, including 20 minute papers and shorter statements for discussion. Depending on the number of good quality proposals for papers, the workshop will be held in one or more sessions (also depending on availability of time slots). All proposals, whether interdisciplinary or not, will be seriously considered. One page outlines should be sent to the ASCA office or by e-mail to "Mieke.Bal@let.uva.nl" by May 1st. For further information: Dr Eloe Kingma tel: +31 20 5253874, fax: +31 20 5253052, e-mail: asca@let.uva.nl.

July 24-26, 1997 International Walter Benjamin Conference

The International Walter Benjamin Association will hold its Conference on July 24-26, 1997 in cooperation with Felix Meritis, the Goethe Institute, and ASCA. The theme of the conference is "Perception and Experience in Modernity" and its structure will comprise plenary double lectures followed by a series of workshops. The subsections of the workshops are: Vision and Multimediality; Politics of Image and Space; Figures of Experience 1, Presence, Power, Performance; and Figures of Experience 2, Allegory, Memory, History. Participants include: George Steiner, Werner Hamacher, Martin Jay, Samuel Weber and many others. Abstracts of up to 300 words should be sent to the International Walter Benjamin Association University of Amsterdam, Spuistraat 210, 1012 VT Amsterdam, fax: +31 20 6206863 or 525 3052, e-mail: Benjamin@let.uva.nl, tel. +31 20 6226762.

Contributors

Mieke Bal is Professor of the Theory of Literature at the University of Amsterdam and Director of ASCA

Simon Critchley is Senior Lecturer in Philosophy at the University of Essex

Jonathan Culler is Professor of English and Chair of the Department of Comparative Literature at Cornell University, Ithaca

Thomas Elsaesser is Professor of Film and Television Studies at the University of Amsterdam and a Member of the Board of ASCA

Helga Geyer-Ryan is Associate Professor of Comparative Literature at the University of Amsterdam

Werner Hamacher is Professor of German and Humanities at The Johns Hopkins University, Baltimore

Isabel Hoving is a Lecturer in Comparative Literature at the University of Amsterdam

Hester IJsseling is a Doctoral Candidate at ASCA in the field of Philosophy

Martin Jay is Professor of History at the University of California, Berkeley

Rob Pauls is a Doctoral Candidate at ASCA in the field of Religion

Michael Punt is a Doctoral Candidate at ASCA in the field of Philosophy

Laura Quinn is a Doctoral Candidate in the Program in Visual and Cultural Studies at the University of Rochester

Sasha Vojkovic is a Doctoral Candidate at ASCA in the fields of Film and Television Studies and Comparative Literature

Hent de Vries is Professor of Philosophy at the University of Amsterdam and Chair of the Board of ASCA

Slavoj Žižek is Senior Researcher at the Institute of Sociology and Philosophy at the University of Ljubljana

Edit Zsadányi is a Lecturer in Comparative Literature at the University of Budapest; a Guest Researcher at ASCA and at the University of California, Berkeley.